Gateless Gate

Kōun Yamada

Gateless Gate

Translated with Commentary by Zen Master
Kōun Yamada

SECOND EDITION

The University of Arizona Press   Tucson

The University of Arizona Press

First edition copyright © 1979; second edition copyright © 1990 by the Estate of
Kōun Yamada Roshi
All rights reserved

"Mumonkan" calligraphy by Kōun Yamada.
This book was set in 10 on 13 Sabon.
Manufactured in the United States of America
ⓧ This book is printed on acid-free, archival-quality paper.
94 93 92 91 90   5 4 3 2 1

Library of Congress Cataloging-in-Publication Data

Yamada, Kōun, 1907–
    Gateless gate / translated with commentary by Zen master Kōun
Yamada. — 2nd ed.
        p.   cm.
    Includes translation of Hui-k'ai's Wu-men kuan.
    ISBN 0-8165-1209-4
        1. Hui-k'ai, 1183–1260. Wu-men kuan.   2. Koan.   I. Hui-k'ai,
1183–1260. Wu-men kuan. English. 1990.   II. Title.
    BQ9289.H843Y34   1990
    294.3'4—dc20   90-39577
                                                         CIP

British Library Cataloguing in Publication data are available.

Contents

Preface to the Second Edition

Yamada Kōun Roshi was not only my father but also my Zen master for over thirty years. The fact that his *Gateless Gate* has been appreciated by many Zen practitioners abroad is a source of great joy for me, and also, as it seems, a very significant matter in various ways.

Yamada Kōun Roshi was a person of such thorough Zen enlightenment that he seems almost without parallel in the modern history of Zen. This is unquestionable to me, who happened to be with him at the moment of his kensho experience. The depth of his great enlightenment was probably equal to that of the patriarchs, called "old buddhas," in the history of Zen.

Each Case of the *Mumonkan* presents to the readers the world of satori in a straightforward way. It is extremely meaningful that this work is explained by Yamada Roshi, who possessed the deepest experience of enlightenment.

It is often the case that an English explanation is clearer and more direct than a Japanese one. Non-Japanese practitioners who read the present book will have the opportunity to meet a *Mumonkan teishō* that may be more distinct and straightforward than a *teishō* in Japanese. Thus the present book is a valuable work indeed in an era when Zen is becoming more and more international. I believe that the second edition of the *Gateless Gate* will continue to contribute a great deal to spreading the true Buddhist Dharma.

Lastly, let me express my gratitude to Dr. Migaku Sato for taking pains to revise the former edition and to Dr. Julian Gresser for arranging for the publication of this new edition.

Ryōun-ken
Masamichi Yamada
November 1989

Editorial Note on the Second Edition

There are a number of differences between the second edition and the original edition of 1979. First, errors in spelling and punctuation and minor errors in the translation of the original Chinese texts and in historical facts have been corrected. Second, stylistic and formal improvements in the Roshi's commentary have been made. Third, under the direction or consent of the Roshi, some corrections in the content of the commentary have been incorporated. The notes derive not from Yamada Roshi himself but either from the editor of the first edition or from the translators of the German edition (*Die torlose Schranke,* trans. L. Fabian and P. Lengsfeld [Munich: Koesel Verlag, 1989]) in collaboration with me.

Migaku Sato

Foreword

In order to appreciate the unique character of Yamada Roshi's translation of the *Gateless Gate* and his *teishō*, we need to understand two basic instructional tools used in traditional Zen training.

The first of these is the koan, which is much more than a paradoxical riddle designed to prod the mind into intuitive insight. The koan is quite literally a touchstone of reality. It records an instance in which a key issue of practice and realization is presented and examined by experience rather than by discursive or linear logic. It serves as a kind of precedent, like a classic legal decision. Just as a legal precedent is cited to guide one in clarifying the law, so the koan (literally, "public case") establishes a baseline of insight to help us penetrate more deeply into the significance of life and death in order to diagnose our blindspots and remove obstructions to our vision. To the student of Zen, the koan offers an opportunity to measure one's understanding against that of the ancient master whose understanding of a given point is embodied in the case.

By entering into the spirit of a given koan, which is usually a dialogue or saying from Zen history or from the sutras, the Zen student is obliged to shed his limited perspectives and to see through the eyes of the Buddhas and patriarchs. Doing this systematically year after year under the close guidance of a qualified successor to those very patriarchs, one can move far beyond the opinions and conditionings of his own worldview and gain the precision, clarity, depth, and breadth of enlightenment.

A second instructional device of Zen is the *teishō* (literally, "to take in hand and speak out"). Unlike a sermon or lecture, the *teishō* does more than exhort or inform. Its basic aim is to present the Dharma directly. *Teishō* is enlightenment or Buddha nature revealed directly, a living experience of the point in question. The *teishō* thrusts its meaning in the face of the listener, challenging him to grasp it and make it his own. Usually based upon a koan, the *teishō* may raise many more questions than it seems to answer and leaves its audience with renewed determination to answer those questions themselves from their own living experience.

The *teishō* is characteristically pithy and penetrating. It presents a formidable challenge to the Zen student. The skillful Zen teacher can detect where the understanding of his audience is unclear or stuck and can use the *teishō* to confront students with the need for greater clarity of vision. The *teishō* is aimed almost exclusively at an audience already involved to some degree in the personal practice of Zen. This is not to say that *teishō* are necessarily incomprehensible to the non-Zen student. They may actually provide a gateway to practice. Once through the gate, the discovery is made that "the gate" is actually not a barrier or opening through which to pass but is simply reality presenting itself.

This book is not only Yamada Roshi's translation of the *Mumonkan*, or *Gateless Gate*, the most basic koan collection in the literature of Zen; it is also a collection of *teishō* delivered by him to Western Zen practitioners under his guidance at San'un Zendo in Kamakura and during sesshin which he held in Germany, Hawaii, and the Philippines. They demonstrate lessons that are beyond boundaries of culture, race, and history, though they emerge from a particular cultural and historical context.

The function of the book is properly twofold: for Zen students already working with a teacher, the cases are offered as useful tools and encouragement; for general readers, it is hoped that their reading will inspire them to seek out guidance and to embark on the journey of Zen practice.

The reader will note that Yamada Roshi repeatedly stresses the necessity of personal experience of enlightenment, or kensho (literally, "seeing one's true nature"). This emphasis clearly refutes the mistaken notion that one need not experience kensho or that some vague faith in the enlightenment of others will suffice for oneself.

Mumon was the fifteenth successor of Master Rinzai and was also the eighth successor in the Yōgi school of Zen. Although he had no direct connection with the Japanese Sōtō school, Mumon's influence is important and pronounced. Despite the current emphasis on seeming differences between the Rinzai and Sōtō schools, there have always been great masters and patriarchs in both whose vision has freely crossed such artificial boundaries.

Master Mumon's Japanese successor was the priest Shinji Kakushin

(1207–1298), who was first ordained at age twenty-nine under Vinaya Master Chugaku of Tōdaiji Temple. Shinji Kakushin later went on to receive the Bodhisattva Precepts from the founder of Sōtō Zen in Japan, Dōgen Zenji (1200–1253). Although Priest Kakushin and Dōgen Zenji never actually studied together, the very fact of receiving the Bodhisattva Precepts from a teacher indicates the existence of a special kinship. In 1249, seven years after his meeting with Dōgen Zenji, Kakushin journeyed to Sung-dynasty China. He visited various monasteries and finally received Dharma Transmission in 1252.

When Shinji Kakushin (also known as National Teacher Hōtō) was about eighty years old, he was visited by Keizan Zenji (1267–1325), who was then in his late teens and had just received permission from his teacher to go on pilgrimage to other teachers as part of his training. Keizan Zenji went on to become a co-founder of Japanese Sōtō Zen and the founder of Sōjiji Monastery. Thus one of the two founders of Japanese Sōtō Zen, at a most impressionable age, studied with Shinji Kakushin when the Rinzai National Teacher was at the peak of his accomplishment. The influence of this encounter on Master Keizan can be traced quite clearly throughout his later work. Significant as this encounter was, a still more important link exists between the great teaching lineages of the Sōtō and Rinzai sects.

A successor of Shinji Kakushin named Kohō Kakumyō received the Bodhisattva Precepts from Master Keizan soon after the latter opened Yōkōji Monastery in Ishikawa Prefecture in 1312. Ten years later, having gained the confidence of the Emperor Godaigo, Priest Kakumyō conveyed ten questions about the Dharma from the emperor to Keizan Zenji, then residing at Sōjiji. The emperor was so impressed with Master Keizan's reply that on August 8, 1322, he formally made Sōjiji chief monastery of the Sōtō sect. I feel there was a rapport and profound mutual respect that bridged the gap between the two seemingly different traditions of Sōtō and Rinzai Zen. Later when Keizan Zenji resigned as head of Daijōji Monastery to move into Jōjūji Temple, he asked another successor of Shinji Kakushin, named Kyōō Unryō, to succeed him as third abbot of Daijōji.

In these days of sectarian rivalry, we can be deeply grateful for Keizan Zenji's profound sense of appreciation for and benevolence towards the Dharma, which went far beyond mere personal friendship.

Master Mumon's teaching lineage was not allowed to die out. His great successor Shinji Kakushin had two major successors of his own: Bassui

Tokushō (1327–1387) and Ji'un Myōi (1274–1345). The former established Kōgakuji Monastery in Yamanashi Prefecture, and the latter, Kokutaiji Monastery in Toyama Prefecture. In both these monasteries Master Mumon's lineage is maintained to this day.

A continuity with the great traditions of both Dōgen Zenji and Keizan Zenji has been established in the United States through the twentieth-century teachers Daiun Sogaku Harada Roshi and his successor Haku'un Yasutani Roshi, the latter one of my own teachers. Both Harada Roshi and Yasutani Roshi exhibited the clarity and openness of vision which characterizes the legacy of Masters Keizan and Dōgen. Their deep devotion and realization led them far beyond sectarian concerns.

Yamada Roshi was born in 1907 in the town of Nihonmatsu in Fukushima Prefecture in northeastern Japan. His early life was profoundly influenced by his grandparents. His grandfather was a former samurai who became a pioneer in Japan's silk industry by introducing mechanized techniques from America. His grandmother was a reflective lady steeped in Chinese classics.

He attended the prestigious Dai-Ichi (the First) High School in Tokyo, where his roommate was the future Rinzai Master, Nakagawa Sōen Roshi. The two friends attended university together, where Yamada specialized in law. Still later, they traveled to Manchuria, Yamada as a young married businessman, Nakagawa as a young monk and attendant to Yamamoto Gempō Roshi.

In Manchuria at age thirty-eight Yamada began zazen training. Three years later he returned to Japan and settled in Kamakura with his wife and three children.

Once set on his course in Zen, Yamada pursued his goal relentlessly. Although he was managing director of a large Tokyo firm, he went twice a day to dokusan with Asahina Sōgen Roshi. After his first kensho was approved, he engaged in koan study for three years and then continued his studies under Hanamoto Kanzui Roshi.

In 1953, Yamada invited Yasutani Haku'un Roshi to Kamakura, and together they organized the Kamakura Haku'un-kai. In November 1954, Yamada experienced the unusually deep satori recorded in *Three Pillars of Zen* under the initials K.Y.

In 1960, Yamada completed his study of 600 to 700 required koans and received his new name in the Dharma. To his great surprise and joy, it was Kōun, his grandfather's name, which Yasutani Roshi had unknowingly chosen.

In the early 1960's, Nakagawa Sōen Roshi was directly responsible for bringing Yasutani Roshi to the United States. The leading representative of the Harada lineage in our time, Yasutani Roshi was a seminal influence in establishing a strong American Zen practice which draws freely from both Rinzai and Sōtō roots.

In 1961, Yamada Kōun became Yasutani Roshi's authentic Dharma successor, and in 1970 he became president of the Sambō Kyōdan, which Yasutani Roshi founded.

Yamada Roshi lives with his wife in Kamakura. They commute daily to Tokyo where he is administrator and she chief of staff of the large Kembikyōin Public Health Foundation. They have built a small zendo, called San'un Zendo, on the grounds of their home which is open every day to disciples who wish to sit. Zazenkai (meditation meetings) are held there bimonthly, and sesshin are held five [from 1987: four] times a year.

My elder Dharma brother, Yamada Roshi, progressively continues to ripen his understanding and accomplishment although past his seventieth year. Despite an extremely busy schedule, he guides the practice of numerous students, including many Roman Catholic priests, monks, nuns, and laypersons from the West. He also makes periodic teaching visits to Hawaii, the Philippines, and Germany.

Yamada Roshi's *teishō* on the *Gateless Gate* are the embodiment of his compassion, arising from his crystal-clear understanding. May they lead us not only towards and through the gateless gate but onto the open road which extends endlessly beyond.

Taizan Maezumi
Zen Center of Los Angeles
Autumn, 1979

Preface

Since the time of Marco Polo, Europeans of every generation have become intrigued with the Far East. Many of them, despite the danger and difficulties of the trip, have ventured to go there. It is only recently, however, that Westerners have traveled to the East to seek solutions to their religious problems. Christians, too, have been part of this group. Their pilgrimage has had as its purpose the learning of ways of Oriental meditation such as Yoga and Zen and the integration of this in their spiritual life.

Every religion has as its general direction some kind of "ultimate" or "last reality." This goal is sometimes called "God" or "Absolute" or even "Nothing" or "Without Name." In the words of Teilhard de Chardin, "All things that rise must converge." Christians have found and are continuing to find that they can attempt Yoga and Zen without jeopardizing their own religion.

While it is true that some people find "it" without a search, these are the exception. For most people the supreme goal requires a lifelong search. And, sad to say, many get to the point of life where they are facing death and realize that everything they have sought in life cannot fill their heart and free them from anxiety. This is a very critical time for such people, and they may become frightened and desperate. Others try to find a substitute in secondary things. But those with courage admit they are not satisfied with whatever is offered them by way of earthly happiness and say, "Not that! Not that!"

Happy the man who comes to this point and can find an experienced guide who can show a way to reach the final goal quickly and safely. I use that last word advisedly. There are many sidepaths existing today which look attractive but in reality turn out to be delusive.

It is true that most religions have developed a way of their own to reach that supreme goal. A cursory glance at these ways may reveal apparent differences, but a deeper study shows they have a common element. In Zen, one of the entrances to that common element is expressed in the word "Mumonkan," which means "a barrier without a gate." This "gateless gate" is known not only by Zen masters but also by Christian mystics.

Even a superficial knowledge of the writings of the mystics reveals the fact that they frequently express their experience as "not-knowing." One of the Christian authors of the fourteenth century called it "the cloud of unknowing" and wrote a little book with that title. Once very popular, this book fell into disuse for many centuries, but it has recently been "found again" and has become very popular with Christian Zen disciples in the West. Many of the actual expressions appearing in the book could have been used by Zen masters. This fact should not be surprising, since the end, whether called "God" or "Absolute," is after all ONE.

What does the above-mentioned barrier mean? Each koan of the forty-eight cases compiled in this book is a barrier. Ordinary people cannot enter it (the koan) because it has no gate. But anyone whose Eye is opened to this True Self can easily enter, because for him there is no gate at all.

Now, coming to Zen, we can truly say that it has found a very effective way to pass through the barrier, or more accurately, to make the barrier disappear. This is at the level of consciousness where we can meet the ONENESS. The *Gateless Gate* is a goad to drive us past our attachments and aversions to this Oneness, where we are face-to-face with ourselves. Here we rub eyebrows with the Buddhas and patriarchs and know in "not-knowing" God.

Zen practice has nothing to do with Buddhist philosophy. One glance through the collection of koans which follow in the book will verify this. There are other collections of koans which excel in other ways. But as far as the barrier point is concerned, the *Gateless Gate* is the most effective and straightforward. Zen masters know this from long experience, and the great majority prefer to confront the new student with the *Gateless Gate (Mumonkan)* first.

This translation of the *Gateless Gate* with commentary has been compiled with foreign readers in mind. The author, Kōun Roshi, is always conscious of the fact that his non-Japanese disciples have been brought up in a culture different from his own and that they belong to different religious traditions, including a good number of priests and sisters. Kōun Roshi never loses sight of these particulars when he speaks to his disciples or directs them to *dokusan* (private interview). It may be added that by means of these intimate contacts with his disciples for so many years, he has deepened his understanding of Western culture and religion. All of this, added to his own deep experience and profound knowledge of Zen, has made him a most suitable guide not only for Buddhists and Japanese but also for Westerners.

In conclusion, it may be said that this book is very much to be recommended to all those who are on the Way of Zen. But I believe that also those who take an interest in Zen though not practicing it will read this book with pleasure and profit.

H. M. Enomiya-Lassalle, S.J.

Author's Preface to the First Edition

It has been several years since I first began presenting English *teishō* on the second and fourth Saturdays of each month to the non-Japanese members of the San'un Zendo. So far, I have delivered two series of *teishō* on the *Gateless Gate* and presently am giving a series on the *Blue Cliff Record*. This book is the second series of *Gateless Gate teishō* with a number of additions and changes. I am very happy to have this chance to publish the book through the efforts of Maezumi Roshi and his staff and would like here to offer them my heartfelt thanks.

The entrance into Zen is the grasping of one's essential nature. It is absolutely impossible, however, to come to a clear understanding of our essential nature by any intellectual or philosophical method. It is accomplished only by the experience of self-realization through zazen. And the koans used in Zen can be seen through only when looked at from the essential point of view. Therefore to the person whose enlightened eye has not been opened, Zen koans seem impractical, illogical, and against common sense. Once this eye has opened, however, all koans express natural matters and relate the most obvious of realities.

The individual cases of the *Gateless Gate* are each famous in their own right and are immediately comprehendible to persons who have had a true enlightenment. I think such persons will be able to read this book with great interest. For those lacking this experience, however, the koan will probably seem like gibberish. Nonetheless, even a person with no Zen realization who reads on with patience will experience an upwelling of desire to see the Zen world with his or her own eyes. This is greatly to be welcomed; indeed, an important function of these *teishō* lies in promoting this urge.

It is no exaggeration to say that Zen is on the verge of completely dying out here in Japan. Some people may think I am stretching the point, but, sad to say, this is the actual state of affairs. How have things come to such a state? I believe we can offer two main reasons for this. First, there is the fact that teachers have sometimes confirmed as kensho the obviously incomplete experience of their students. The responsibility for this lies not with the student but with the teacher. The task of determining whether or not a certain experience is a true Zen realization is a grave responsibility and rests solely in the hands of the person assuming guidance. Should the Zen realization of the teacher not be clear and that person use his or her own incomplete experience as the basis for determining the realization of another, the result is the confirmation of an incomplete experience as kensho. We have here a case of the blind leading the blind.

The second stems from the Zen teacher not truly realizing that the Zen path is endless and that, no matter how far one progresses along it, there is always a "limitless beyond." Although in a state of incomplete enlightenment, these teachers are satisfied with having completed koan study "in the room," and they lose the brave and determined spirit necessary for the continued striving toward a pure and stainless state of Buddhahood.

I have inherited the teachings and Dharma line of Harada Daiun Roshi. This line extends from Harada Daiun (Great Cloud) Roshi through Yasutani Haku'un (White Cloud) Roshi on down to myself, Yamada Kōun (Plowing Cloud). The three "un" in these names are the three clouds from which we derive the name of our *dōjō* (training hall), the San'un (Three Clouds) Zendo.

Both Harada Roshi and Yasutani Roshi stressed the extreme importance of the kensho experience. I feel this to have been both an alarm sounded against the decline in the significance accorded to kensho in the modern current of Zen and a manifestation of the great compassion of the bodhisattvas to save all sentient creatures. I earnestly pray that the present work will in no way harm the true Zen Buddhism transmitted to me by these two great masters. As the same time, I pray that it will provide some inspiration for a number of its readers earnestly to seek the way of Zen.

In closing, I would like to thank Ms. Brigitte D'Ortschy and Sister Elaine MacInnes, who provided so much valuable advice and assistance toward making my imperfect English a more complete product, and Ms.

Joan Rieck and Mr. Paul Shepherd, who took time from busy schedules to type and make corrections and suggestions in the manuscript and proofs.

Yamada Kōun
San'un Zendo
Kamakura, July 1979

Note on Chinese and Japanese Terms by the Editor of the First Edition

For ease of reference and pronunciation, proper and place names have been given in Japanese instead of Chinese throughout the text of the *Gateless Gate*, e.g., "Zen" rather than "Ch'an." The historical Introduction and the vertical lineage charts give both Japanese and Chinese readings, the latter in parentheses, e.g., "Mumon Ekai (Wu-men Hui-k'ai)." The glossaries at the end of the book give complete correlations, Japanese to Chinese and Chinese to Japanese. Because of their increasing familiarity and frequency of use and their specific meaning, the following terms have been regarded as English words and, accordingly, have been left untranslated and unitalicized: koan, mondo, roshi, zazen, kensho, and satori. For the reader new to Zen parlance, the sense of these terms is explained in the Foreword, Author's Preface, Preface by Father Enomiya-Lassalle, and the Introduction by Thomas Cleary.

In the title of this book the word "commentary" is used. This is an English translation of the word *teishō*, which is a technical Buddhist term in Japanese for a direct expression of the Buddha mind. In its strictest sense, *teishō* are nondualistic and are thus distinguished from Dharma talks, which are ordinary lectures on Buddhist topics. It is not explanatory or analytical in intent but a presentation of the awakened state itself. The word "commentary" does not do justice to the powerful *teishō* of Yamada Roshi transcribed and printed here as the *Gateless Gate*.

Shūan's Preface

If it is called "gateless," everybody on the great earth will be able to enter within. If it is said that "there is no gate," our dear master should not have chosen this title. He dared besides to add several footnotes, which is like putting one hat on top of another. He also urged old Shū to praise it. This would mean to press the sap out of dried-up bamboo and spread it on a children's book such as this one. Throw it away without waiting for me to throw it away myself. Don't let even a drop of it fall on the world. Even Usui who gallops a thousand miles would never be able to pursue it.

Written by Shūan Chin Ken at the end of July,
the first year of Jōtei (1228 A.D.).

TEISHŌ ON SHŪAN'S PREFACE

Shūan Chin Ken is thought to have been born in 1197 A.D., during the reign of Emperor Neisō of the Southern Sung dynasty, and to have died at the age of forty-five in 1241 A.D., during the reign of Emperor Risō.

His family name is Chin, his personal name is Ken, and his courtesy name is Chūwa. Shūan is his Zen name.

It is said that he was precociously bright and passed the government civil service examination at around twenty years of age. He was later appointed to such high government positions as member of the editorial staff for national history in the privy council and as local governor. Shūan is reputed to have been a man of high culture and refined taste, having a special fondness for landscape gardening.

We cannot find any trace of his Zen study in ancient Zen literature, but from this preface we can assume that he must have been a very close acquaintance of Mumon and have had a deep understanding of Zen.

Now let us come back to his preface.

"If it is called 'gateless,' everybody on the great earth will be able to enter within. If it is said that 'there is no gate,' our dear master should not have chosen this title."

What Shūan means is the following:

"Dear Master, you titled the book *Gateless Gate*. On the one hand you say 'gateless.' If there is no gate, everybody will be able to enter within freely. Why is it necessary to preach anything more? That would be nonsense. On the other hand, you say there is a gate. If there is a gate, why do you say, 'gateless'? Isn't that unreasonable? Your first words—in other words, the title of the book—must, therefore, be self-contradictory from the beginning."

All koans, including the forty-eight cases in this book, are barriers set up by the Buddhas and the patriarchs of the past. It is impossible for the ordinary person to pass through them. If you want to pass through these barriers, you must realize your own self-nature. This is called self-realization or enlightenment, satori or kensho in Japanese. When you once attain true self-realization, these barriers disappear in an instant as though they were nothing but mirages, and you will find that from the very beginning you have always been in a world where there is neither inside nor outside. That is what "gateless" means. Therefore, all koans are impassable barriers for those who are unenlightened, but for the enlightened there is no gate at all. They can come in and go out quite freely.

Mumon himself says in his commentary on the first case of this book:

"For the practice of Zen, you must pass the barrier set up by the ancient patriarchs of Zen. To attain to marvelous enlightenment, you must completely extinguish all thoughts of the ordinary mind."

What I said earlier is speaking from the point of view of the process by which we progress upwards through the practice of zazen, but when I speak from the point of view of the essential world, all beings are within it from the beginning.

It is related that the bodhisattva Manjusri was once standing at the gate, and seeing him, Shakyamuni Buddha called to him, "Manju, Manju, why don't you come inside the gate?" Manjusri replied, "I don't see anything outside the gate."

Let us return to the preface, which says:

"He dared besides to add several footnotes, which is like putting one hat on top of another."

"Footnotes" means the commentaries and verses which Mumon added to every case. The first hat means the book itself, and the second means the whole of the commentaries and verses added to it. The first hat is itself useless. Far more useless is a second hat placed on top of the first.

Shūan is speaking from the essential point of view. His form of expression is extremely paradoxical. He seems to speak ill of Mumon but only on the surface. In his heart, he deeply appreciates Mumon's work. Paradoxical and ironic expressions of this kind appear often in Zen writings and should not be taken literally or superficially.

Shūan goes on to say:

"He also urged old Shū to praise it. This would mean to press the sap out of dried-up bamboo and spread it on a children's book such as this one. Throw it away without waiting for me to throw it away myself. Don't let even a drop of it fall on the world. Even Usui who gallops a thousand miles would never be able to pursue it."

He means that Mumon urged him to write the preface to praise the book, but that is totally foolish and useless, for it would mean to squeeze the sap out of dried-up bamboo—a metaphor for something totally absurd—and spread it on a silly children's book such as this. Throw the book away, otherwise I will do it myself. Don't allow even one copy of the book to appear in the world. Once you commit the fault of letting a copy fall into the world, even an excellent steed such as Usui who gallops a thousand miles would never be able to pursue it.

Usui is the name of a fine horse owned by the famous Chinese hero-general Kōu. Shūan means that once the fault is committed of allowing even one copy of the book to appear in the world, that fault can never be rectified.

Dedication to the Throne

On the 5th of January, in the 2nd year of Jōtei (1229),[1] I reverently celebrated the sacred anniversary of your Majesty. I, your subject, monk
Ekai,[2] on the 5th of November of last year, published commentaries on the
forty-eight koans given by the Buddhas and patriarchs. I dedicate this book
to the throne, praying for your Majesty's eternal health and prosperity.

I respectfully express my wish that your Majesty's sacred wisdom may
be as bright as the sun and the moon, your royal life as long as that of the
universe. May all the people of the eight directions sing the praises of the
highly virtuous emperor, and the four seas enjoy your supremely blessed
reign.

Respectfully written by
Your subject, monk Ekai,
The Dharma transmitter,
Former abbot of Kudoku-Hōin'yūji Zen temple
Dedicated to Empress Jii[3]

NOTES

1. Five years after the enthronement of Emperor Risō of the Southern Sung.
Two years earlier, Dōgen Zenji had returned to Japan from China.

2. Mumon Ekai was the compiler of the *Mumonkan*. Mumon was his Zen
name, Ekai his personal name as a monk. He was born in 1183 A.D. during the
reign of Emperor Kōsō of the Southern Sung dynasty and died in 1260 at the age
of seventy-eight.

Mumon lived in the period of decline of the power of the Southern Sung dynasty due to increasing pressure from two neighboring states, Kin and Gen.

He was ordained as a monk by Master Tenryū. He later studied under Master Gatsurin Shikan and was given the koan, "Dog, Buddha nature" which appears in the *Gateless Gate* as the first case. He worked persistently on this koan for six years. It is said that when he felt sleepy or in low spirits, he would bump his head against a pillar. One day, standing near the Dharma hall, he heard the sound of the drum signaling lunchtime and was suddenly enlightened. He wrote the following poem about that experience:

> *A peal of thunder under the bright blue sky!*
> *The multitude of living beings on earth have opened their eyes.*
> *All things in the world bow alike.*
> *Mount Sumeru jumps up and dances Sandai.*

(Sandai is a kind of dancing, extremely lively in its movements.) The next day, Mumon presented his understanding of the koan to Master Gatsurin, who confirmed his enlightenment. Mumon eventually succeeded to the Dharma of his master.

When Mumon was sixty-four he founded Gokoku-ninnō Zen temple by order of the emperor. Though he desired to spend his last years in quiet retirement near West Lake, his seclusion was regularly disturbed by visitors eager for instruction.

Mumon's biographer describes him as follows: "The master looked thin but of clear spirit. His words were artless but profound. His hair was dark, his beard long and rough. He wore a shabby and dirty robe." In his monastery, Mumon was referred to as the "Founder of the Way."

3. Twelve years after the death of Empress Jii (wife of the third emperor Kōsō of the Southern Sung dynasty and mother of the fourth emperor, Neisō), a temple was erected for the repose of her soul. Master Gatsurin was invited to be its first abbot. This temple was called Hōin'yūji Zen Temple.

Mumon's Preface

THE GATELESS GATE OF THE ZEN SECT

Zen makes the words and the mind of Buddha its foundation. It makes no-gate the gate of Dharma. It is no-gate from the start. How can we pass through it? Haven't you ever heard the old saying, "Things that come in through the gate are not family treasures"? What is gained by causation is continuously going on, forming and disintegrating.

Such remarks are just like raising heavy waves when there is no wind or gouging a wound into fine skin. How much more ridiculous to adhere to words and phrases or try to understand by means of the intellect. It is exactly like trying to strike the moon with a stick or to scratch an itchy spot on the foot through the surface of the shoe. What concern do they have with reality?

In the summer of the first year of Jōtei (1228), I, Ekai, was at Ryūshō in Tōka[1] as head monk. At that time, the monks asked me to instruct them. I finally took up the koans[2] of the ancient masters and used them as brickbats to knock at the gate, inducing the students according to their capability and aspiration. I recorded those koans, and they have un-willingly formed a collection.

From the start, I did not arrange them in any order. They amount to forty-eight cases in all. I call them as a whole, *Mumonkan* (the *Gateless Gate*). If a man is a fellow of valor, he will rush straight into the barrier like a dagger. Even Nada,[3] the eight-armed demon, will not be able to hold him back. Even the Four Sevens of the West and the Two Threes of the East[4] will beg for their lives on seeing his face from afar.

If he hesitates, however, he is like a man who watches a horse pass by outside a window. If he blinks his eyes, it is already gone.

THE VERSE

The great Way has no gate;
There are a thousand different roads.
If you pass through this barrier once,
You will walk independently in the universe.

TEISHŌ ON MUMON'S PREFACE

"The Gateless Gate of the Zen Sect"

Since ancient times there have been two different interpretations of these opening words of the *Mumonkan*. One view takes these words to be the title of the book, and the other view takes them to be the beginning of the book. If we take the latter view, the opening of the book becomes: "The gateless gate of the Zen sect makes the words and mind of Buddha its foundation." That is quite understandable. I shall, however, take the traditional and commonly accepted view that these words are the title of the book.

"Zen makes the words and the mind of Buddha its foundation."

The foundation of Zen is the words and mind of Buddha. The words and mind of Buddha, however, become reduced simply to the mind of Buddha because the words arose from the mind as the explanation of its experience. But we must recognize that from the essential point of view there is no difference between the mind of Buddha and that of us ordinary people. So Hakuin Zenji says in his *Song of Zazen:* "All living beings are intrinsically Buddha."

"It makes no-gate the gate of Dharma."

For unenlightened people, every koan is a barrier. For the enlightened person, however, there is no gate, no barrier at all. This is because the essential world is totally void. We cannot see anything there. There is neither gate nor barrier, and so-called enlightened people are those who have realized this fact.

"Things that come in through the gate are not family treasures. What is gained by causation is continuously going on, forming and disintegrating."

The "family treasure" is the treasure endowed within us which is no other than our essential nature. "Things that come in through the gate" means experiential knowledge gained through the intellect.

Things that come in through the gate and that which is gained by causation are both appearances in the phenomenal world and are constantly changing. There is another world, on the other hand, called the essential world, which is totally empty. When we look at the world from the essential point of view, there is nothing to be seen at all. That empty world is no other than our essential nature.

"Such remarks are just like raising heavy waves when there is no wind or gouging a wound into fine skin."

Even making such a statement is like raising waves on the tranquil sea or making a wound in fine skin. It is not only superfluous but also rather harmful.

"How much more ridiculous to adhere to words and phrases or try to understand by means of the intellect. It is exactly like trying to strike the moon with a stick or to scratch an itchy spot on the foot through the surface of the shoe. What concern do they have with reality?"

The essential world cannot be grasped by intellectual contemplation or by reasoning or philosophical conceptualization. There is no way other than to realize it in our own living experience. It is, therefore, quite foolish to try to understand it by following the meaning of words. It can never be attained that way. It is just like trying to strike the moon with a stick or scratch an itchy spot on the foot through the surface of the shoe—we cannot touch the spot at all.

At the end, Mumon says:

"If a man is a fellow of valor, he will rush straight into the barrier like a dagger. Even Nada, the eight-armed demon, will not be able to hold him back. Even the Four Sevens of the West and the Two Threes of the East will beg for their lives on seeing his face from afar."

Someone who wants to attain enlightenment must be brave. He must rush into the crowd of enemies with a dagger. In the practice of Zen, enemies are our delusive thoughts and passions. The brave practitioners working on the koan Mu plunge into their delusive thoughts and passions with the sharp sword of Mu. When you devote yourself to the practice of Mu with your whole heart, all delusive thoughts and passions will be cut off and disappear. From ancient times, it is said, therefore, that Mu is Jōshū's sharpest sword. (See the first Case of this book.) Nobody can hinder him. Even the strongest demon or patriarchs of the highest virtue, when they see such a brave person in the distance, will beg for their lives in wonder.

"If he hesitates, however, he is like a man who watches a horse pass by outside a window. If he blinks his eyes, it is already gone."

To blink one's eyes means to move the brain with doubt for even an instant. What Mumon means here is: "If one tries to understand it intellectually for even a moment, the real truth of our essential nature will be lost in that instant."

ON THE VERSE

"The great Way has no gate."

"The great Way" means the essential world. The essential world is no other than our essential nature. There is no gate in our essential nature.

"There are a thousand different roads."

"Roads" refer to koans. Every koan is a road which leads everybody to the essential world, namely to great enlightenment.

"If you pass through this barrier once,

You will walk independently in the universe."

When one realizes the essential world through great enlightenment, one is for the first time a man of true freedom. He or she can walk independently through the universe whenever and wherever.

NOTES

1. The Zen temple Ryūshō was one of the most famous in China, located at Mt. Kōshin in Sekkō province. Tōka refers to eastern China.

2. Koan (Kung-an): "Ko" means public or official or governmental. "An" means a document pertaining to examinations. Literally, a koan is an official document possessing an authority upon which everyone can rely. In Zen, it is the highest truth expressed by the Buddhas and patriarchs. Concretely, koans are words or phrases intended to guide or instruct, questions and answers (mondo) or remarks made by Buddha and the patriarchs. Koans have the power to cut off the student's delusive thinking, opening his eyes to true reality. See also pp. ooo, oooooo.

3. Eight-armed Nada is a demon in Indian mythology, son of Vaisravana, a guardian of the true Dharma. Nada has four faces, eight arms, and possesses great strength.

4. The twenty-eight Indian and six Chinese patriarchs.

Jōshū's Dog

1

A monk asked Jōshū in all earnestness, "Does a dog have Buddha nature or not?"

Jōshū said, "Mu!"

MUMON'S COMMENTARY

For the practice of Zen, you must pass the barrier set up by the ancient patriarchs of Zen. To attain to marvelous enlightenment, you must completely extinguish all thoughts of the ordinary mind. If you have not passed the barrier and have not extinguished all thoughts, you are a phantom haunting the weeds and trees. Now, just tell me, what is the barrier set up by the patriarchs? Merely this Mu—the one barrier of our sect. So it has come to be called "The Gateless Barrier of the Zen Sect."

Those who have passed the barrier are able not only to see Jōshū face to face but also to walk hand in hand with the whole descending line of patriarchs and be eyebrow to eyebrow with them. You will see with the same eye that they see with, hear with the same ear that they hear with. Wouldn't it be a wonderful joy? Isn't there anyone who wants to pass this barrier? Then concentrate your whole self into this Mu, making your whole body with its 360 bones and joints and 84,000 pores into a solid lump of doubt. Day and night, without ceasing, keep digging into it, but don't take it as "nothingness" or as "being" or "non-being." It must be like a red-hot iron ball which you have gulped down and which you try to vomit up but cannot. You must extinguish all delusive thoughts and beliefs which you have cherished up to the present. After a certain period of such efforts, Mu will come to fruition, and inside and out will become one naturally. You will then be like a dumb man who has had a dream. You will know yourself and for yourself only.

Then all of a sudden, Mu will break open. It will astonish the heavens and shake the earth. It will be just as if you had snatched the great sword of General Kan: If you meet a Buddha, you will kill him. If you meet a patriarch, you will kill him. Though you may stand on the brink of life and death, you will enjoy the great freedom. In the six realms and the four modes of birth, you will live in the samadhi of innocent play.

Now, how should you concentrate on Mu? Exhaust every ounce of energy you have in doing it. And if you do not give up on the way, you will be enlightened the way a candle in front of the altar is lighted by one touch of fire.

THE VERSE

Dog—Buddha nature!
The perfect manifestation, the absolute command.
A little "has" or "has not,"
And body is lost! Life is lost!

TEISHŌ ON THE CASE

Jōshū Jūshin was one of the greatest and most famous Zen masters in ancient China. Actually, Jōshū is the name of the place where his monastery was located. He was born in 778 A.D., in the reign of Emperor Daisō of the T'ang dynasty, and died in 897 at the age of 120. When only eighteen years of age, he attained a great kensho and for the next forty years continued to practice Zen under the eminent master Nansen (famous for killing a cat; see Case 14). Nansen died when Jōshū was about sixty years old. Jōshū then started traveling around the country, searching for good Zen masters in order to deepen his Zen experience through Dharma combats with them. When he was about eighty years of age, he settled down for the first time in a small monastery, where he stayed for about forty years, devoting this remaining period of his life to instructing Zen practitioners.

Jōshū's Zen had a unique characteristic that came to be called "lips-and-mouth Zen." When instructing his disciples, he did not beat them with a stick as Tokusan did nor did he shout "kwatz!" as other Zen masters such as Rinzai used to do. He would give his instructions in such a low voice that it was sometimes almost a whisper. His words, though simple and quietly spoken, had power like the sharpest of swords to cut through his disciples' delusions. It is said that as he spoke, a sparkling light came from his lips and mouth.

Dōgen Zenji, who criticized other Zen masters severely, paid the highest respect to Jōshū, calling him "Jōshū, an old Buddha!"

The story is as you read it: Once a monk asked Jōshū, "Does a dog have Buddha nature?" Jōshū answered, "Mu!" The Chinese character means "nothing," or "nonbeing," or "to have nothing." Therefore, if we take this answer literally, it means, "No, a dog does not have Buddha nature."

But that is not right. Why not? Because Shakyamuni Buddha declared that all living beings have Buddha nature. According to the sutras, when Shakyamuni Buddha attained his great enlightenment, he was astonished by the magnificence of the essential universe and, quite beside himself, exclaimed, "All living beings have Buddha nature! But owing to their delusions, they cannot recognize this."

The monk in the story could not believe these words. To him Buddha nature was the most venerable, most highly developed personality, and a Buddha was one who had achieved this perfect personality. How then could a dog have Buddha nature? How could a dog be as perfect as Buddha? He could not believe that such a thing was possible, so he asked Jōshū sincerely, "Does a dog have Buddha nature?" And Jōshū answered, "Mu!"

Jōshū, great as he was, could not deny Shakyamuni's affirmation. Therefore his answer does not mean that a dog lacks Buddha nature.

Then what does Mu mean?

This is the point of the koan. If you try to find any special meaning in Mu, you miss Jōshū and you'll never meet him. You'll never be able to pass through the barrier of Mu. So what should be done? That is the question! Zen practitioners must try to find the answer by themselves and present it to the roshi. In almost all Japanese zendo, the explanation of Mu will stop at this point. However, I'll tell you this: Mu has no meaning whatsoever. If you want to solve the problem of Mu, you must become one with it! You must forget yourself in working on it. Your consciousness must be completely absorbed in your practice of Mu.

ON MUMON'S COMMENTARY

Mumon teaches us very forcefully but very kindly how to practice Mu. He himself attained great enlightenment after practicing Mu heart and soul for six years. This commentary is his *teishō* on the koan Mu and is a vivid account of his own experience. Read it many times and you will learn the true way to practice Mu.

Mumon says, "For the practice of Zen, you must pass the barrier set up by the patriarchs of Zen."

The barriers set up by Zen patriarchs are called koans. Among them, the koan Mu is exemplary. It may, indeed, be one of the best, for it is very simple and leaves almost no room for concepts to enter. That is the most desirable requisite for a koan.

Mumon continues: "To attain to marvelous enlightenment, you must completely extinguish all thoughts of the ordinary mind. If you have not passed the barrier and have not extinguished all thoughts, you are a phantom haunting the weeds and trees."

"A phantom haunting the weeds and trees" means a person who has no firmly established view of life and the world. In China, as well as in Japan, phantoms or ghosts are thought to have no legs. They are unable to stand by themselves and are always floating about among the undergrowth or among trees such as willows.

Since the time of Jōshū, innumerable Zen students, in both China and Japan, have come to enlightenment by practicing Mu. In Japanese, practicing Mu is called *tantei* or *nentei,* which means, "solely taking hold of." Do it totally to the very end. And what is the end? It is, of course, nothing other than enlightenment itself. You must persevere until you attain it. Concentrate your whole energy on Mu. By "energy" I do not mean physical energy but the spiritual energy necessary to keep from letting go of Mu. While you are practicing the *nentei* of Mu you must be constantly and clearly conscious of Mu. Identify yourself with it. Become truly one with Mu. Melt yourself into Mu. To do this, you must forget everything, even yourself, in Mu.

Referring to this stage, Mumon says, "Concentrate your whole self into this Mu, making your whole body with its 360 bones and joints and 84,000 pores into a solid lump of doubt." In old Chinese physiology, the human body was thought to have 360 bones and 84,000 pores, but in the present day the numbers are simply taken to mean the whole human body. Being absorbed in Mu, you should extinguish the awareness of "I". All concepts and dualistic ideas, such as subject and object, you and I, inside and out, good and bad, the Buddha and living beings—all these must completely disappear from your consciousness. When absorption in Mu has become pure and complete, your body and soul will become like one solid iron ball of Mu. Referring to this state, Mumon says, "It [Mu] must be like a red-hot iron ball which you have gulped down and which you try to vomit up but cannot."

When this happens, don't stop! Don't be concerned! Press on! Then suddenly the ball of Mu will break open and your true self will spring forth instantly, in a flash!

Mumon says, "It will astonish the heavens and shake the earth."

You will feel as though the whole universe has totally collapsed. Strange as it may seem, this experience has the power to free you from the agonies of the world. It emancipates you from anxiety over all worldly suffering. You feel as though the heavy burdens you have been carrying in mind and body have suddenly fallen away. It is a great surprise. The joy and happiness at that time are beyond all words, and there are no philosophies or theories attached to it. This is the enlightenment, the satori of Zen. Once you have attained this experience, you will become perfectly free.

Mumon says, "It will be just as if you had snatched the great sword of General Kan: If you meet a Buddha, you will kill him. If you meet a patriarch, you will kill him. Though you may stand on the brink of life and death, you will enjoy the great freedom. In the six realms and the four modes of birth, you will live in the samadhi of innocent play."

General Kan was a celebrated warrior under Emperor Ryūhō, founder of the Han dynasty. He brandished a great sword, cutting down numerous enemies. He is still worshipped as a deity of war in China. The wonderfully free state of mind of someone who attains deep realization through practicing Mu is here compared to the mind of one who deprives General Kan of his sword.

It is hardly necessary to add that when Mumon says, "If you meet a Buddha, you will kill him. If you meet a patriarch, you will kill him," he is not talking about killing Buddhas and patriarchs bodily. His words refer to eradicating all concepts about Buddhas and patriarchs.

The six realms mentioned by Mumon are the six different stages of existence according to ancient Buddhist philosophy. These are: hell, the world of hungry ghosts, the world of beasts, the world of fighting spirits, the world of human beings, and the world of gods and devas. As for the four modes of birth, it was once thought in Indian physiology that the modes of birth of all living beings could be classified into four types: viviparous, oviparous, from moisture, and metamorphic. So the phrase "In the six realms and four modes of birth" means all the circumstances of one's life, whatever they may be.

ON THE VERSE

Dog—Buddha nature!
The perfect manifestation, the absolute command.
A little "has" or "has not,"
And body is lost! Life is lost!

"Dog—Buddha nature!" The main case is condensed into one phrase. It is nothing other than Mu. Dog, Buddha nature, and Mu are totally one. It is the perfect manifestation, the absolute command. By this, our true self is perfectly manifested with absolute authority to cut off all delusions. If you think that Jōshū's answer means the dog does not have Buddha nature, you are quite wrong. For when Jōshū answered "Mu!" he was far removed from the world of dualistic concepts. Therefore the verse says, "A little 'has' or 'has not', and body is lost! Life is lost!" If you have the slightest thought about the dog having or not having Buddha nature, your essential life will be killed by that thought. Now, just show me: Dog—Buddha nature!

Hyakujō and the Fox

THE CASE

Whenever Master Hyakujō delivered a sermon, an old man was always there listening with the monks. When they left, he left too. One day, however, he remained behind. The master asked him, "What man are you, standing in front of me?" The old man replied, "Indeed, I am not a man. In the past, in the time of Kashyapa Buddha,[1] I lived on this mountain (as a Zen priest). On one occasion a monk asked me, 'Does a perfectly enlightened person fall under the law of cause and effect or not?' I answered, 'He does not.' Because of this answer, I fell into the state of a fox for 500 lives. Now, I beg you, Master, please say a turning word[2] on my behalf and release me from the body of a fox." Then he asked, "Does a perfectly enlightened person fall under the law of cause and effect or not?" The master answered, "The law of cause and effect cannot be obscured." Upon hearing this, the old man immediately became deeply enlightened. Making his bows, he said, "I have now been released from the body of the fox and will be behind the mountain. I dare to make a request of the Master. Please perform my funeral as you would for a deceased priest."

The master had the Ino[3] strike the anvil[4] with a gavel and announce to the monks that after the meal there would be a funeral service for a deceased priest. The monks wondered, saying, "All are healthy. No one is sick in the infirmary. What's this all about?" After the meal, the master led the monks to the foot of a rock behind the mountain and with his staff poked out the dead body of a fox. He then performed the ceremony of cremation.

That evening the master ascended the rostrum in the hall and told the monks the whole story. Ōbaku thereupon asked, "The man of old missed the turning word and fell to the state of a fox for 500 lives. Suppose every time he answered he made no mistakes, what would happen then?" The master said, "Just come nearer and I'll tell you." Ōbaku then went up to the master and slapped him. The master clapped his hands and, laughing aloud, said, "I thought the barbarian's beard was red, but here is a barbarian with a red beard!"

MUMON'S COMMENTARY

Not falling under the law of cause and effect—for what reason had he fallen into the state of a fox? The law of cause and effect cannot be obscured—for what reason has he been released from a fox's body? If in regard to this you have the one eye, then you will understand that the former Hyakujō enjoyed 500 lives of grace as a fox.

THE VERSE

Not falling, not obscuring,
Two faces, one die.
Not obscuring, not falling,
A thousand mistakes, ten thousand mistakes.

TEISHŌ ON THE CASE

Like Jōshū and many other Zen masters in ancient China, Hyakujō got his name from the mountain where his monastery was located. Born in

720, during the reign of Emperor Gensō of the T'ang dynasty, he died in 814 at the age of ninety-four. He was a disciple of the great Zen master Baso. It is said that Baso had eighty-three Dharma successors, among whom Hyakujō and Nansen are the most famous. Like Jōshū, Hyakujō experienced a great kensho when he was only eighteen years of age.

Hyakujō was the first formally to compile a list of monastery rules and regulations for Zen practitioners. In English its title would be *Hyakujō's Pure Rules*. These famous regulations continue to exert a great influence on monastic life. Hyakujō's motto, "A day of no work, a day of no eating," is also well-known, and its spirit is still alive in Zen monasteries today.

Ōbaku, who appears in this koan, was the teacher of the famous Zen master Rinzai. He also appears in Case 11 of the *Blue Cliff Record*, where you can appreciate the dignified character of his Zen. Ōbaku is one of the great masters in the history of Zen in China. His real name was Kiun, but he was called Ōbaku after the mountain where his monastery was located. Ōbaku entered the priesthood when he was a small boy and eventually became a Dharma successor of master Hyakujō. Tradition says he was a man of large stature and commanding presence, with a protuberance on his forehead.[5] His voice was said to be loud and sonorous. His celebrated sermons are collected in the chronicle called *The Transmission of Mind as the Essence of Dharma* (Denshin-Hōyō).

As koans go, the story is rather long, and it might be better to read it as a drama. But what connection does this story have with Zen Buddhism? We should know that from the point of view of Buddhism—that is, from Shakyamuni's great enlightened eye—all things, including human beings, have two aspects. One is the phenomenal and the other is the essential. In accordance with the law of cause and effect, all phenomena are constantly changing. The word "hō" (*fa* in Chinese) means law. In Buddhism it also has the meaning of "things." This is because things are changing rapidly and constantly according to the law of cause and effect. They have no definite form. On the other hand, the essential nature of things does not change, no matter how much the phenomena change. Take yourself. Sometimes you might be rich, sometimes poor, sometimes healthy, sometimes sick. If you are young now, you'll soon be old. Some people are born into high estate, others low. But these differences are all phenomenal. Whether you are healthy or sick, your essential nature is always the same. You may think I am talking about two different worlds. Undoubtedly they are two different aspects, but they are two aspects of one substance. From the very beginning, they are intrinsically one.

Now, owing to his delusive answer, the old man, who had also been called Hyakujō, became a fox for 500 lives but was able to return to the human state through the merits of the latter Hyakujō's words. The phenomenal changes were from man to fox and from fox to man, but there is no change in the essential nature. It is always the same, from the very beginning, now, and on into the endless future. It is something like a person being born as a baby, then becoming a child, then a youth, then a person in the prime of life, and finally an old person.

What is one's essential nature? It is not merely an idea or a philosophy; it is an actual fact which can be seen only by the direct experience of enlightenment. Zen always treats things from the aspect of this essential nature. Therefore every koan should be approached in this way.

Getting back to our koan. Ōbaku comes on stage. He was the leading monk of the monastery at the time and was out when the affair happened. He did not return until after the funeral and heard the story of the fox from Hyakujō. Ōbaku asked, "The man of old missed the turning word and fell to the state of a fox for 500 lives. Suppose every time he answered he made no mistakes, what would happen then?" This is a fearful question. Ōbaku is trying to examine his master.

Hyakujō replied, "Just come nearer and I'll tell you."

Ōbaku went up to Hyakujō and slapped the master's face. This is an interesting example of Dharma combat between a master and a disciple. However, as my teacher Yasutani Roshi once told me regarding Ōbaku's action, "You shouldn't think that Ōbaku actually slapped the master's face. He would merely have made the gesture of doing so as a response in Dharma combat. As a disciple, he would have stopped his hand before it reached Hyakujō's face in deference to the position of his master. This was the teaching of my reverend master, Harada Roshi."

Hyakujō clapped his hands with joy. He acknowledged that his disciple had advanced in enlightenment as far as he had and said, "I thought the barbarian's beard was red, but here is a barbarian with a red beard!"

This is a strange expression. What does it mean? In everyday language, it would read something like this: "I think I am a deeply enlightened man, and I acknowledge that you, too, are deeply enlightened." Hyakujō recognized that Ōbaku had presented the genuine activity of his essential nature in a most lively way without even a trace of delusive thought or feeling adhering to it.

ON MUMON'S COMMENTARY

"Not falling under the law of cause and effect—for what reason had he fallen into the state of a fox? The law of cause and effect cannot be obscured—for what reason has he been released from a fox's body? If in regard to this you have the one eye, then you will understand that the former Hyakujō enjoyed 500 lives of grace as a fox."

The former Hyakujō fell into the state of a fox for 500 lives because of his answer that an enlightened person does not fall under the law of cause and effect. But why? He was released from a fox's body by hearing the sermon of the latter Hyakujō, who said that the law of cause and effect cannot be covered up for an enlightened person. But why? If you have the eye to see through the point of the matter, you will understand that the fox life of 500 lives is nonetheless the life of grace.

This is because when Hyakujō was a fox, he was the only fox in the whole universe, and when he was restored to manhood, he was the only man in the whole universe. In spite of phenomenal changes, the essential nature does not change in the slightest from the beginning.

ON THE VERSE

Not falling, not obscuring,
Two faces, one die.
Not obscuring, not falling,
A thousand mistakes, ten thousand mistakes.

As you know, a die (dice in the plural) has six faces and when you throw it, sometimes a one appears, sometimes a four, sometimes a six. Each time a different face may appear, but the die is at all times one and the same.

"Not obscuring, not falling, a thousand mistakes, ten thousand mistakes." Sometimes the form of a fox appears, sometimes the form of a man, but the essential nature is always one. This is very simple logic and easily understood. But Zen requires us to recognize the fact by our living experience, to grasp our essential nature by our mind's eye, so to speak. If you understand only through ideas or concepts, both aspects are wrong. If even a little thinking is mingled in the experience, it is wrong! All wrong!

NOTES

1. Kashyapa Buddha is the sixth of the Seven Buddhas of Antiquity, Shakyamuni being the seventh. Here we may understand that "the time of Kashyapa Buddha" means long, long ago.

2. A turning word (*tengo*) is a word or phrase which has the power to turn delusions into enlightenment.

3. Ino (Chinese: *wei-na;* Sanskrit: *karmandana*) is an official position and title in a Zen monastery, being the monk in charge of rules, regulations, and the registry of monks.

4. In order to make an announcement in the temple, the monks often used a kind of wooden anvil ("byakutsui"), which was about 120 cm tall, cut octagonally and made slimmer toward the top surface. A gavel, which was also cut in octagonal shape, was used to strike the center of the surface of the anvil hard after first moving it several times in a spiral on the anvil's surface.

5. Ōbaku, in order to teach himself true humbleness, constantly prostrated himself before the Buddhist altar, whereby hitting the floor with his forehead so hard that there eventually formed a protuberance, which came to be known as one of his physical features.

Gutei's One Finger

3

Whatever he was asked about Zen, Master Gutei simply stuck up one finger.

He had a boy attendant whom a visitor asked, "What kind of teaching does your master give?" The boy held up one finger too. Hearing of this, Gutei cut off the boy's finger with a knife. As the boy ran away, screaming with pain, Gutei called to him. When the boy turned his head, Gutei stuck up one finger. The boy was suddenly enlightened.

When Gutei was about to die, he said to the assembled monks, "I received this one-finger Zen from Tenryū.[1] I've used it all my life but have not exhausted it." Having said this, he entered nirvana.

MUMON'S COMMENTARY

The enlightenment of Gutei and the boy have nothing to do with the tip of a finger. If you realize this, Tenryū, Gutei, the boy, and you yourself are all run through with one skewer.

THE VERSE

Old Tenryū made a fool of Gutei,
Who cut the boy with a sharp blade.

*The mountain deity Korei raised his hand, and lo, without effort,
Great Mount Ka with its many ridges was split in two!*

TEISHŌ ON THE CASE

Gutei's name was originally a nickname given him because he was always
chanting the *Gutei Butsumo Dharani*. The dates of his birth and death
are not recorded, but he was undoubtedly a contemporary of Ōbaku
and Rinzai. As a sincere Buddhist priest, Gutei earnestly attended to his
daily duties, but when the following incident happened, he was not yet
enlightened.

In the temples and monasteries of ancient China, it was customary for
a guest, in greeting a host, to walk around the seated master and with
head bared, to bow deeply. One day a nun called Jissai, which means
"true world," came into Gutei's room. She walked around his seat three
times. Then, without taking off her bamboo hat, she stood in front of him
and said, "If you can say a word that satisfies me, I will take off my bamboo hat and make a bow." Gutei could say nothing. The nun did not bow
or remove her hat.

It is not so difficult for ordinary people to find something to say in such
a situation. What would you say? You could use any greeting at all, such
as, "Welcome," or "How do you do?" or "I'm glad to meet you." Gutei
thought he should say something smacking of Zen, but he could not
think of a single word, so he remained silent. Sincere as he was, he could
not pass the gate set up by the nun because he had not yet experienced
enlightenment.

The nun challenged him three times and still Gutei could not come up
with a response. As she was preparing to leave, Gutei, worried about the
lateness of the hour, kindly said, "It's already dark. Why don't you stay
here for the night." The nun rejoined, "If you can say something, I'll
stay." Gutei was again dumbstruck. The nun departed.

After she left, Gutei was terribly ashamed and chided himself, "I have
the form of a man, but I lack a man's spirit. I couldn't answer even one
word upon her examination." He made up his mind then to start on a
journey to search for good Zen masters and to undergo severe Zen training with them.

During the last night in his own monastery, Gutei had a strange dream.
The reigning deity of the locality appeared to him and said, "Do not leave.

In a few days, an incarnate bodhisattva will come here and preach to you about the Dharma."

And so it happened. The very next day, the Zen master Tenryū came to the monastery. Gutei welcomed him with great respect and related in detail the story of the nun, his own decision, and the ensuing dream. Upon hearing this, Tenryū stuck up a finger. At that instant, Gutei experienced deep enlightenment.

The point of this koan is just holding up one finger. What does it mean?

There is an ancient Zen text called *Believing in Mind* (Shinjin-Mei), in which the line appears: "One is everything. Everything is one." In the absolute world, the world of enlightenment, the logic of "One is everything, everything is one" reigns. When Tenryū sticks up a finger, that one finger is the whole universe. When we stick up one finger, there is nothing but one finger in the whole universe. When you stand up, there is nothing but standing up in the whole universe. When Gutei saw Tenryū holding up one finger, he realized clearly that the one finger and the whole universe are one. There isn't anything else that remains. There is nothing outside it. That is enlightenment.

ON MUMON'S COMMENTARY

"The enlightenment of Gutei and the boy have nothing to do with the tip of a finger. If you realize this, Tenryū, Gutei, the boy, and you yourself are all run through with one skewer."

Mumon says that the enlightenment of Gutei and the boy have nothing to do with the tip of a finger. The finger was merely the medium. It provided the stimulus or shock which brought Gutei and the boy attendant to enlightenment. Shakyamuni Buddha attained his great enlightenment when he saw the twinkling light of Venus in the eastern sky. Kyōgen came to realization when he heard the sound of a small pebble bouncing against bamboo. The pink blossoms of distant peach trees triggered Reiun's sight into Sight after thirty years of hard Zen practice.

These people all came to enlightenment through various means. In each case mentioned, realization made the person aware that his self nature is empty, limitless, and one with the whole universe. You cannot find enlightenment in the tip of a finger. When you experience satori, you will come to realize the same thing. Then Tenryū, Gutei, the boy, and you yourself will all be run through with one skewer.

ON THE VERSE

Old Tenryū made a fool of Gutei,
Who cut the boy with a sharp blade.
The mountain deity Korei raised his hand, and lo, without effort,
Great Mount Ka with its many ridges was split in two!

What does "Old Tenryū made a fool of Gutei" mean? It is an example of the type of irony of which Zen is very fond. It can be explained by calling to mind Shakyamuni Buddha's declaration that all living beings have Buddha nature. Hakuin Zenji put it another way: "Every living being is intrinsically Buddha." Gutei is, of course, a living being. That being so, what need is there to try to bring him to enlightenment by holding up a finger? Isn't it sheer nonsense to try to make a Buddha out of a Buddha? So this expression could be paraphrased, "You rascal, Tenryū—you are making sport of poor Gutei!" Other interpretations of this phrase are that Gutei makes a fool of old Tenryū, and that old Tenryū and Gutei together make fools of us all. I think you can understand that, in principle, these three interpretations are not different from one another.

"The mountain deity Korei raised his hand, and lo, without effort, Great Mount Ka with its many ridges was split in two!" According to a Chinese legend, Korei, a mountain deity of great strength, divided Great Mount Ka in two—one part Mt. Shuyō, the other Mt. Ka—by the mere touch of his hand, thereby allowing the waters of the Yellow River to flow through. In the same way, Tenryū, by sticking up one finger, broke Gutei's myriad-piled delusions (concepts, philosophies, etc.) into pieces. When one finger is held up, the essential world appears, annihilating all delusions.

NOTE

1. Nothing is known about Master Tenryū except for the following mondo (question-and-answer exchange) held between a monk and him.

A monk asked, "How can I get out of the three worlds?" [In Buddhist philosophy, the three delusive worlds are those of desire, form, and no-form.] Master Tenryū said, "Where are you right now?"

Tenryū is supposed to have had Master Taibai Hōjō as his teacher.

The Barbarian Has No Beard

4

THE CASE

Wakuan said, "Why has the western barbarian no beard?"

MUMON'S COMMENTARY

If you practice Zen, you must actually practice it. If you become enlightened, it must be the real experience of enlightenment. You see this barbarian once face to face; then for the first time, you will be able to acknowledge him. But if you say that you see him face to face, in that instant there is division into two.

THE VERSE

In front of a fool
Do not talk about dreams;
The barbarian has no beard:
It's adding obscurity to clarity.

TEISHŌ ON THE CASE

Master Wakuan Shitai lived from 1108 to 1179. He died at the age of seventy-two, four years before Mumon, the author of the *Gateless Gate*, was born. Wakuan is in the Rinzai line of Zen.

In ancient China, all non-Chinese, and even the Chinese living on the southwest frontier, were called "hu" or barbarian. In this case, the western barbarian could be Bodhidharma, the first patriarch to come to China from India.

If we take the western barbarian to mean Bodhidharma, the case would read, "Why does Bodhidharma have no beard?" Pictures of Bodhidharma are well known, and not only does he always have a beard but a very thick beard indeed! Wakuan was well aware of this. Why then does he say that Bodhidharma has no beard?

Everything has two aspects, phenomenal and essential. The phenomenal Bodhidharma has a beard, but the essential Bodhidharma has no beard. To realize this, you must grasp by experience the essential nature of Bodhidharma.

What is this essential nature? Who has it? What is it like?

All existence has its essential nature—every person, every thing, the whole universe. There is no difference between people's essential nature and the essential nature of things and the universe. It is all the same. When you attain true self-realization, you will acknowledge that this is true. There is no dualistic opposition in the essential nature, such as subject and object, good and bad, Buddha and ordinary man, enlightenment and delusion. The essential nature has no form, no color, no weight, no length, no place, no concepts, no taint or blemish attached to it. It is perfectly pure.

The essential nature cannot be destroyed, even by karmic fire. If the whole universe were to be completely destroyed, the essential nature would continue to exist because it is empty. It is nonsubstantial. It cannot be seen with the eyes, heard with the ears, or touched with the hands. No one can identify the spot where it is.

Just reflect for a moment on your own mind, which is the same thing as your consciousness. You cannot tell where your mind is. Some people point to their head, but that is their brain. It is not the mind. Actually, nobody knows where the mind is, but we do know its functions. It sees, it walks, it thinks. This mind or consciousness of your everyday life is the entrance to the essence of the vast, limitless universe.

We cannot locate our essential nature because it is zero, yet it has infinite capabilities. It can see with eyes, walk with legs, think with a brain, and digest food with a stomach. It weeps when it is sad and laughs when it is happy. Though it is zero, no one can deny its existence. It is one with phenomena. The essential nature and phenomena are one from the very beginning. That is why the *Hannya Shingyō,* or *Prajna Paramita Sutra,*[1] can say, "Form is nothing but emptiness; emptiness is nothing but form."

Yet our essential nature is not a thought or a philosophical concept. It cannot be grasped by our physical senses, but it is an existing reality. It can be comprehended only in direct experience. This experience is kensho or satori, the enlightenment of Zen.

As mentioned above, the gateway to our essential nature is our consciousness. We can enter its boundless world by way of inner concentration. When you touch your beard with your hand, does your mind have a beard? The mind is the agent controlling the movement of your hand. You can see your hand. You can touch your beard. You can recognize everything that is yours—your fingers, your head, etc. But where is the You itself? Not the possessive or genitive you, but the nominative You. You yourself is no other than your mind, and your mind has no beard! So what Wakuan is really saying to us is "Bodhidharma's essential nature has no beard."

You must come to know this through realization. Everybody knows about the phenomenal world, but only a few truly enlightened people know about the essential nature of the universe. Zen always treats reality from this point of view, that is, the essential point of view, and generally speaking, every koan should be approached from this angle.

ON MUMON'S COMMENTARY

"If you practice Zen, you must actually practice it. If you become enlightened, it must be the real experience of enlightenment. You see this barbarian once face to face; then for the first time you will be able to acknowledge him. But if you say that you see him face to face, in that instant there is division into two."

"You see this barbarian once face to face; then for the first time you will be able to acknowledge him." When you live naturally, without delusions, you are a Buddha, seeing with the eyes of Buddha.

"But if you say that you see him face to face, in that instant there is division into two." When you feel that you have seen him face to face, there are two faces. The one face has been divided into two by the concept. When you are occupied with some conceptual activity, you are no longer a Buddha but an ordinary sentient being.

ON THE VERSE

In front of a fool
Do not talk about dreams;
The barbarian has no beard:
It's adding obscurity to clarity.

"In front of a fool, do not talk about dreams." The strange words of Wakuan mean that the fool will take the dream for reality and come to cherish a lot of ideas about it.

"The barbarian has no beard . . ." These words themselves are no other than the beard. You are self-sufficient and complete as you are so long as you have no beard. But if, upon hearing Wakuan's words, you use your brains and doubt even a bit, a beard will sprout and your essential clarity will be obscured by it.

NOTE

1. Usually it is called "Heart Sutra." The full Sanskrit title "Mahaprajna-Paramita-Hrdaya-Sutra" means literally "The Core (in this sense: "heart")-Sutra (of all Sutras) on the great Wisdom of Salvation."

Kyōgen's Man Up a Tree

5

THE CASE

Master Kyōgen said, "It's like a man up a tree, hanging from a branch by his mouth; his hands cannot grasp a branch, his feet won't reach a bough. Suppose there is another man under the tree who asks him, 'What is the meaning of Bodhidharma's coming from the west?' If he does not respond, he goes against the wish of the questioner. If he answers, he will lose his life. At such a time, how should he respond?"

MUMON'S COMMENTARY

Even if your eloquence flows like a river, it is of no use. Even if you can expound the whole body of the sutras, it is of no avail. If you can respond to it fittingly, you will give life to those who have been dead, and put to death those who have been alive. If, however, you are unable to do this, wait for Maitreya to come and ask him.

THE VERSE

Kyōgen is really absurd,
His perversity knows no bounds;
He stops up the monks' mouths,
Making his whole body into the glaring eyes of a demon.

TEISHŌ ON THE CASE

Kyōgen Chikan was a disciple of Isan Reiyū, one of the founders of the Igyō sect of Zen in China. He was a very intelligent and learned man, but his erudition must have been a hindrance, for he did not come to enlightenment early.

Isan, knowing this, said to Kyōgen one day, "What is your essential face before your father and mother were born?" Kyōgen could not answer on the spot, so he went back to his books to check. He searched through all his books, sutras, and lecture notes for a sentence or passage he could use as an answer, but not one satisfied him.

Finally, he went to Master Isan and said, "I don't know the answer. Please tell me what it is."

"It would not be difficult for me to tell you, but if I did you would doubtless reproach me later," the master replied.

This led Kyōgen to reflect that an empty stomach cannot be filled with pictures of food, and so he burned all his books and notes. Despairing of ever being able to come to a true knowledge of Buddhism in this life, he vowed to spend the rest of his days seeking peace of mind in manual labor. In this depressed state, he left Isan and retired to a place in Nan'yō, where the national teacher Echū had once lived in a hermitage. Here Kyōgen also took up the life of a hermit.

One day, as he was clearing the undergrowth, a pebble bounced off the tip of his broom and resounded against a bamboo tree. Hearing the sound, Kyōgen suddenly experienced great enlightenment. He returned to his hut, where he performed ablutions and offered incense in profound gratitude. Then he prostrated himself in the direction in which Isan lived, saying, "Master, your kindness is far deeper than that of my parents. If you had explained these things to me at that time, I would never have had this wonderful joy."

The first stanza of the poem he composed on this occasion is very famous: "One striking sound, and I have forgotten all I knew."

Because Kyōgen's enlightenment had been such a deep experience, his subsequent way of instruction was very strict and severe. In one of his *teishō* he said to his disciples, "It's like a man up a tree, hanging from a branch by his mouth; his hands cannot grasp a branch, his feet won't reach a bough. Suppose there is another man under the tree who asks him, 'What is the meaning of Bodhidharma's coming from the west?' If he does not respond, he goes against the wish of the questioner. If he answers, he will lose his life. At such a time, how should he respond?"

Now you tell me. What do you think he should do?

Every koan presents us with a problem which cannot be solved by thought or reasoning. The common sense of ordinary people will reject it as absurd. Learned people, such as philosophers and scientists, will feel repugnance at the lack of reason in the koan. Such people are often perplexed when confronted by the strange and even abnormal expressions found in the language of the koan. Koans bring us into a land abounding in contradictions of ideas and concepts. We cannot escape by means of rational thinking. There is no other way of freeing ourselves from this confusion than by cutting through it as though it were the Gordian knot. This cannot be done by rational thinking or logical reasoning. It can only be accomplished factually.

What is a fact in Zen? It is the manifestation of essential nature by an action such as standing up, sitting down, eating, drinking, crying, or laughing. In the case of Jōshū's Mu, Mu is the fact. In the case of Gutei's finger, raising a finger is the fact. In this case, the fact is some action of the man in the tree.

ON MUMON'S COMMENTARY

"Even if your eloquence flows like a river, it is all of no use. Even if you can expound the whole body of the sutras, it is of no avail. If you can respond to it fittingly, you will give life to those who have been dead and put to death those who have been alive. If, however, you are unable to do this, wait for Maitreya to come and ask him."

Why does Mumon say that even if your eloquence flows like a river, it is all of no use, or even if you can explain perfectly the whole body of the sutras, it is of no avail? It is because an exposition, however eloquent, is merely the transmission or communication of concepts. It is not a fact, not the essential reality! Suppose you are drinking a cup of tea. Tasting it is giving you enjoyment. In this instance, the taste is the fact. Can you make me enjoy that taste by any amount of explanation? However eloquent your explanation may be, you cannot transmit the taste itself to me. I may understand something of it, but I cannot taste the tea myself.

"If you can respond to it fittingly, you will give life to those who have been dead and put to death those who have been alive." To respond to the problem means to grasp the fact by direct experience. To bring the dead to life means to bring them to enlightenment, that is to awaken them to their essential life. By putting the living to death, Mumon means killing your illusions and cutting through all your conceptual thinking.

"If, however, you are unable to do this, wait for Maitreya to come and ask him." Buddhism teaches that the day will necessarily come when the Buddha's Dharma will completely disappear from the earth. Then Bodhisattva Maitreya, who is now waiting in the Tusita Heaven, will appear as the successor of Shakyamuni Buddha. It is said that he will come some five billion years after the nirvana of Shakyamuni. What Mumon means in using this interminably long period of time is that if you cannot solve the problem, you will never become enlightened. Truly, if you are forever attached to ideas and philosophies, you will never attain enlightenment.

ON THE VERSE

Kyōgen is really absurd,
His perversity knows no bounds;
He stops up the monks' mouths,
Making his whole body into the glaring eyes of a demon.

"His perversity knows no bounds" means that Kyōgen's intention is to kill all the illusions of his disciples and thereby save them. In fact, his perversity is the epitome of kindness. This is an example of Mumon's irony.

"He stops up the monks' mouths, making his whole body into the glaring eyes of a demon." Kyōgen surveys them with glaring eyes, waiting to see if anyone can respond fittingly. But there is not a monk who can utter a word. They are all sitting as silent as shells.

Buddha Holds Up
a Flower

6

THE CASE

Once in ancient times, when the World-Honored One was at Mount
Grdhrakūta,[1] he held up a flower, twirled it, and showed it to the
assemblage.

At this, they all remained silent. Only the venerable Kashyapa broke
into a smile.

The World-Honored One said: "I have the eye treasury of the true
Dharma, the marvelous mind of nirvana, the true form of no-form, the
subtle gate of the Dharma. It does not depend on letters, being specially
transmitted outside all teachings. Now I entrust Mahakashyapa with this."

MUMON'S COMMENTARY

The golden-faced Gautama insolently suppressed noble people and made
them lowly. He sells dog's flesh under the label of sheep's head. I thought
there should be something of particular merit in it. If at that time, however, all those attending had smiled, how would the eye treasury of the
true Dharma have been transmitted? Or if Kashyapa had not smiled, how
would he have been entrusted with it?

If you say that the eye treasury of the true Dharma can be transmitted,
then that is as if the golden-faced old man is swindling country people at

the town gate. If you say it cannot be transmitted, then why did Buddha say he entrusted only Kashyapa with it?

THE VERSE

In handling a flower,
The tail of the snake manifested itself.
Kashyapa breaks into a smile,
Nobody on earth or in heaven knows what to do.

TEISHŌ ON THE CASE

The World-Honored One is one of the ten titles of Buddha, here referring to Shakyamuni. He is said to have been born a prince of the Shakya tribe of northern India, now southwestern Nepal, about the year 565 B.C. Around the age of twenty-nine, he renounced his father's kingdom and undertook a life of severe asceticism. Six years later, exhausted and haggard, he rejected extreme austerity, chose a more moderate way, and began to practice zazen. After practicing for six years, on the morning of December 8th, glancing up at Venus twinkling in the eastern sky, he all of a sudden attained the deepest enlightenment. We accept this as historical fact. Shakyamuni spent the remaining forty-five years of his life teaching others the way of Buddhahood in the truest sense of the word. He is the founder of Buddhism.

Mahakashyapa was a Brahman of Magada. During Buddha's life, he was one of the ten chief disciples and after Shakyamuni's death was his orthodox successor. Kashyapa is famed for assiduously practicing the twelve *dhuta,* or austerities, in order to attain nirvana.

This koan presents the scene of the transmission of the Dharma. Scholars are not in agreement as to the authenticity of the story, but what is more important is understanding the meaning of transmission. The very life of Zen is built on this fact: Buddha's religious experience is transmitted from an enlightened master to a disciple.

Dōgen Zenji tells us: "The subtle Dharma of the seven Buddhas is maintained with its true significance when it is rightly transmitted by an enlightened disciple following an enlightened master. This is beyond the knowledge of the priest of letters and learning." This passage makes it very obvious that the most important thing a Zen student can do is to make sure he or she is studying under an authentic teacher.

In Case 3, we saw that one finger is the whole universe. I have mentioned an old Zen verse which goes: "One thing is the whole, the whole is one thing." The whole universe is, therefore, involved in one finger.

In this koan, Buddha handles a flower. He shows it to the assemblage. In his action, we must recognize the world of the empty-infinite. It cannot be grasped mentally, and if you think you might have understood this world of the empty-infinite, that understanding has nothing to do with Zen. Not only a finger but all things, even a flower, are nothing other than the world of the empty-infinite.

"The eye treasury of the true Dharma, the marvelous mind of nirvana, the true form of no-form, the subtle gate of the Dharma." I am sure these words sound strange to Western ears. It is very difficult to translate the original words into English. It is almost impossible to understand their true meaning even by reading the original Chinese characters. They are all expressions for Buddha nature, which is nothing but the essential nature of our own self.

It is extremely important for us to realize that the essential nature of our own self and the essential substance of the whole universe is one. The fact of this essential nature cannot be transmitted by thoughts or explanations. No words, no matter how clearly we may understand them, will bring us to a realization of this essential nature. Once you have experienced enlightenment, all of these expressions will become as clear as a jewel in the palm of your hand. You will come to see that each of them is nothing but another name for our own essential nature.

ON MUMON'S COMMENTARY

"The golden-faced Gautama insolently suppressed noble people and made them lowly. He sells dog's flesh under the label of sheep's head. I thought there should be something of particular merit in it. If at that time, however, all those attending had smiled, how would the eye treasury of the true Dharma have been transmitted? Or if Kashyapa had not smiled, how would he have been entrusted with it?

"If you say that the eye treasury of the true Dharma can be transmitted, that is as if the golden-faced old man is swindling country people at the town gate. If you say it cannot be transmitted, why did Buddha say he entrusted only Kashyapa with it?"

"Golden-faced Gautama" refers to Shakyamuni, whose face must have been light brown or golden brown. Mumon calls him golden-faced with utmost respect.

"Suppressed noble people and made them lowly." As Hakuin Zenji says in his *Song in Praise of Zazen,* ordinary living beings are intrinsically Buddha. If that is so, why does Buddha appoint only Mahakashyapa as his successor? Doesn't this lower the others and ignore the essential nature of ordinary people? By saying this, Mumon wants to wake us up to our essential nature.

"He sells dog's flesh under the label of sheep's head." Shakyamuni said he has the eye treasure of the Dharma, the marvelous mind of nirvana, the true form of no-form, the subtle gate of the Dharma. These words sound very lofty, but once you have had the actual experience, you will realize each of these expressions is nothing but another name for your own self, something very common. And what is more common than dog's flesh? Mumon says that he thought there should be something of special merit in these words, but they are really nonsense.

This is another example of the sort of irony often resorted to in Zen to present the highest point of view. Mumon is making fun of Shakyamuni. He calls him a swindler, advertising in a loud voice at the town gate in order to sell his goods which are of no value at all.

ON THE VERSE

In handling a flower,
The tail of the snake manifested itself.
Kashyapa breaks into a smile,
Nobody on earth or in heaven knows what to do.

"The tail of the snake . . ." What is the snake? It refers to Shakyamuni. And when he handles a flower, not only the "tail," not only his hand, but also his whole essential nature manifests itself. Holding up a flower is the manifestation of the whole. Every moment is the manifestation of the whole. Life itself is, therefore, nothing but the continuous moment of the whole, and everybody is living the continuous moment of the whole.

But at the time of Shakyamuni only Mahakashyapa could recognize it and broke into a smile, as if to say, "Today Shakyamuni Buddha is giving us a very special sermon!" Nobody on earth or in heaven except Mahakashyapa knew what to do. They just stood there like idiots.

NOTE

1. Mt. Grdhrakūta, or Vulture Peak, where Shakyamuni Buddha preached, is located near the capital of Magada in ancient India.

Jōshū's "Wash Your Bowls"

7

THE CASE

A monk asked Jōshū in all earnestness, "I have just entered this monastery. I beg you, Master, please give me instructions." Jōshū asked, "Have you eaten your rice gruel yet?" The monk answered, "Yes, I have." Jōshū said, "Then wash your bowls." The monk attained some realization.

MUMON'S COMMENTARY

Jōshū, opening his mouth, showed his gall bladder and revealed his heart and liver. If the monk, hearing it, did not really grasp the fact, he would mistake a bell for a pot.

THE VERSE

Just because it is so clear,
It takes us longer to realize it.
If you quickly acknowledge that the candlelight is fire,
You will find that the rice has long been cooked.

TEISHŌ ON THE CASE

This is the same Jōshū we met in Case 1. It is an excellent example of Jōshū's "lips-and-mouth Zen." This koan should be contemplated from two points of view. The first is the actual process of practicing Zen in order to experience enlightenment. The second is the essential nature of the self or being, or of Buddha nature. From the first point of view, what does Jōshū mean by the question, "Have you eaten your rice gruel yet?" Zen masters do not like abstract words or concepts such as Buddha nature, enlightenment, nirvana, and so forth. These terms are only instruments of explanation. But such terms do not actually touch the fact, still less can they grasp it. The verbal exchanges in Zen are, therefore, always concrete. In conceptual form, Jōshū's questions would read, "Have you tasted kensho yet?"

The monk's reply, "Yes, I have," means "Yes, I am already enlightened." Jōshū replies, "Then wash your bowls." Now, what does that mean?

Drawing attention to one's accomplishments is usually nauseating. This is especially true in Zen. When one first experiences enlightenment, one is apt to feel more or less proud and perhaps become a little pompous. This is not completely unreasonable because one has just experienced a world that unenlightened people cannot even imagine. If that pride swells, however, one becomes afflicted with what is known as Zen sickness. It is manifested by certain esoteric mannerisms, such as an excessive use of Zen terms which ordinary people don't understand. Or it may be apparent through rather boisterous laughter, as though one were completely free from all attachment, or by the flamboyant use of ironic or even cynical words. All this is most disgusting in a Zen person. It is, therefore, very important to wash away all the glamor of enlightenment.

The truly great Zen person, who has experienced deep enlightenment and has extinguished all illusory feelings after kensho, should not be distinguishable from the ordinary person, at least not in externals. Through Zen, one should become an ordinary person, a real person, not freakish, eccentric, or esoteric. So, when Jōshū told the monk that if he had finished his meal he should wash his bowls, he meant if you have tasted kensho, wash away its glamor. At this the monk came to a deeper realization.

The other point of view from which this koan should be contemplated is that of the essential nature of the self, or being. As I repeatedly tell you, in the world of essence the logic of the absolute reigns. This means one thing is the whole, the whole is one thing. When you realize this world of essence, you will understand that you and the whole universe are one. When you stick up one finger, there is nothing but the finger in the whole universe. Just the finger. The finger and the whole universe are one. This is seeing in the absolute. This can be true because the finger, having no substance, is empty. This emptiness is nothing but the essential nature of the finger. The substance of all things is emptiness. The subject is empty, the object is empty. And the subject and object are one in emptiness from the very beginning. To ordinary common sense, subject and object oppose each other. There is you, seeing with your eyes, and there is the external object, seen by you. This is true not only for sight but for all our senses. For the truly enlightened eye, however, this dualistic contrast is nothing but an illusion produced by one's thought. I do not know much about Christianity, but I cannot believe that God created a dualistic world. The great enlightenment of Buddha tells us that there are no dualistic contrasts. When you stand up, you simply stand up, there is only standing up in the whole universe, and the substance of standing up is emptiness. Reflect for a moment on the mechanics of movies. What you see on the screen is a continuously flowing movie consisting of a multitude of single images being projected on the screen. Each image is projected for an instant and covers the entire screen. The movie as a whole is the flowing continuity.

In the same way your life is the continuity of standing up, sitting down, laughing, sleeping, waking up, drinking, eating, and, of course, being born and dying. That is the continuity of the whole universe. Now, I presume you understand what Jōshū means when he says, "Wash your bowls." I repeat, our life is nothing but the continuity of these actions, and they are nothing but the continuity of the whole universe.

ON MUMON'S COMMENTARY

"Jōshū, opening his mouth, showed his gall bladder and revealed his heart and liver. If the monk, hearing it, did not really grasp the fact, he would mistake a bell for a pot."

Mumon's first sentence means that when Jōshū says, "Wash your bowls," he is showing us his whole interior, that is, the very truth of Zen, which he has realized. By the second sentence, he means that if the monk's understanding of what Jōshū said was intellectual, failing to grasp the truth, he mistook a pot for a bell or a glass bead for a pearl.

ON THE VERSE

Just because it is so clear,
It takes us longer to realize it.

If you quickly acknowledge that the candlelight is fire,
You will find that the rice has long been cooked.

The fact is very simple. It is just as you see, just as you hear. There is no other secret, no other mystery, no other truth. But it is so simple that most people cannot appreciate the reality and tend to think there must be something deeper, something different. "If you quickly acknowledge that the candlelight is fire, you will find that the rice has long been cooked." Fire refers to the essential nature, candlelight to the action of washing bowls, and the rice again to the essential or Buddha nature. So this stanza means if you acknowledge, on the spot, that the action of washing bowls is nothing other than the manifestation of the essential nature itself, you will find that your essential nature has long been accomplished. Actually, not only washing bowls but standing up, sitting down, eating, drinking, laughing, crying, a stone, a pillar, a flower, a plant—each and everything in the universe is nothing other than the perfect manifestation of the essential nature. If you realize this fact, you will find that your own self nature exists in completeness, from the beginningless past into the endless future.

Keichū Makes Carts

THE CASE

Master Gettan asked a monk, "Keichū made a hundred carts. If he took off both wheels and removed the axle, what would he make clear about the cart?"

MUMON'S COMMENTARY

If you can realize this at once, your eye will be like a shooting star and your spiritual activity like catching lightning.

THE VERSE

Where the active wheel revolves,
Even a master fails.
It moves in four directions: above and below,
South and north, east and west.

TEISHŌ ON THE CASE

We do not know much about Master Gettan Zenka except that he was a relatively close predecessor of Mumon in the Dharma lineage of the Rinzai sect. He once said to a monk: "Keichū made a hundred carts. If he took off both wheels and removed the axle, what would he make clear about the cart?"

Keichū is the name of the man who invented the cart. He is said to have lived during the reign of Emperor Kō of the Hsia dynasty in ancient China and to have become a veteran at cartmaking.

In this case, our essential nature comes on stage in the guise of a cart. Every koan deals with our essential nature, and you must never be bewildered by the garb or trappings it appears in. Here the cart is another name for our essential nature, and Gettan is trying to make us realize it through this medium. He is asking us to apply the question to our own problem. So if you are working on Mu, you must treat the cart as nothing other than Mu. If you are practicing breath counting, the cart is nothing but counting your breaths. If you are practicing *shikantaza*, then the cart is "just sitting," or better still, the cart is the one sitting.

Everything we do from morning to night, from birth to death, is nothing but the cart. The one who sees and whatever is seen by him, the one who hears and whatever is heard by him—these all are carts. In this context, everybody and everything is a cart.

What does it mean to "take off both wheels and remove the axle?" I suppose this will not be difficult to discern intellectually. The wheels and axle mean our concepts and ideas. If you "took off" all your ideas and "removed" all your concepts, what would become obvious to you about your own self? And what would be left?

Or if you "took off" your body and "removed" your mind, what would remain? Some would answer, nothing. Others might say, "God remains." I would like to suggest that the empty-infinite remains. But do not forget that as long as we think or feel, something does remain; it is not the true Mu.

I often use the concept of a fraction as a teaching aid. Usually I condemn the use of concepts in Zen, but sometimes they are a necessary evil. We know that every fraction has a numerator over a denominator. As the denominator, I use a circle containing an eight on its side: ⊗. The circle of course means zero and is empty and void. The eight on its side is the mathematical symbol for infinity. Therefore, the encircled horizontal eight stands for the empty-infinite, and the empty-infinite is a characteristic of our essential nature. It *is* our essential nature.

You may ask why our essential nature is empty. Just consider what we call our mind or consciousness. Does it have any form? No. Any color?

No. Any length or breadth or weight? No. Can we locate it? No, we do not know where it is. The mind has nothing. The mind *is* nothing. It is void and empty, and our essential nature is nothing but the boundless extension or manifestation of this ordinary mind of ours.

While being empty, our mind has, at the same time, limitless and infinite capabilities or activities. It can see, it can hear, it can stand up, it can sit down, it can take a walk. It can feel, it can think, it can imagine, it can forget. Though void, it is limitless and infinite. Therefore, I call it the empty-infinite or the empty-limitlessness, and this is our essential nature. This constitutes the denominator of the fraction.

The phenomenal world is the numerator. Anything will do—a dog, a cat, a finger, a cart (as in this koan), an oak tree, or Mu, or the sound of one hand, or even the whole phenomenal universe itself:α/∞. Ordinary people are at home in this numerator world and think that it alone exists. They are completely unaware of the denominator world.

A most important point to remember is that the numerator and denominator are intrinsically one. I have set up the concept of a fraction and divided oneness into two to try to help you understand that all phenomena have empty-limitlessness behind them, so to speak. As a matter of fact, all phenomena are nothing other than empty-limitlessness itself. The *Hannya Shingyo*, or *Prajna Paramita Sutra*, says "*Shiki soku ze kū, kū soku ze shiki.*" *Shiki* means form and color, namely all phenomena. *Soku* means "nothing but" or "no other than." *Kū* means emptiness or void (the empty-infinite). Thus *shiki soku ze kū* means all phenomena are nothing but emptiness, and *kū soku ze shiki* means emptiness is nothing but all phenomena. The direct experience of this without the help of thinking or reasoning is what we call kensho. Please remember that this fraction is itself a concept, a kind of delusion.

In contemplating the empty-infinite, Buddhism has two approaches, one called Hinayana and the other Mahayana. The Hinayana way is to understand that everything is empty by means of analysis. The Mahayana way is to realize that everything is substantially void by means of experience. We have two Japanese poems which provide an interesting contrast to explain this.

The poem that expresses the Hinayana point of view is:

Since the whole cottage has been built by assembling brushwood,
If we took it to pieces,
Nothing would remain but the field, as before.

The one which expresses the Mahayana point of view is:

Since the cottage has been built by assembling brushwood,
There is nothing but the field,
Even without taking it to pieces.

Now, what does the field mean? Again, it is nothing but the empty-infinite, our essential nature, and what does the brushwood represent? It is the objective world, which includes our body and mental activities—concepts, ideas, thinking, feeling, and so on. When we get rid of this objective world, there remains only standing up, sitting down, going to bed, walking and running, eating a meal when you are hungry, crying when sad, working when you need money. There are no concepts or ideas whatsoever attached to these. When you sit down, there is no philosophy attached. Our life in this world is made up of such actions. Is there anything more? No! And from the standpoint of sitting down or taking a walk, there is no difference at all between Buddhas and us.

When you work on this case, however, you must show me your realization through the cart since this is the medium used here. Actually you can present your essential nature through anything—sometimes a stick, sometimes a dog (as in Jōshū's Mu) and so on. But here it is a cart, so that is how you must show me your realization.

ON MUMON'S COMMENTARY

"If you can realize this at once, your eye will be like a shooting star and your spiritual activity like catching lightning."

Our greatest work is to discover our essential nature. You will search in vain if you seek it in the outside world, or even within yourself, through the path of thought or reason. You must grasp it by real experience. To do this, you must introspect your own self. What is "I"? Who is here? You can see your hand. You can touch your leg, but these are yours, not YOU. Who are YOU? You may answer by pointing to your body, but again that is yours and not YOU. You will only come to know who you are by direct experience, and then your eye will be like a shooting star and your activity like that of a man who can catch lightning with his hand. You will be able to grasp the true meaning of all koans in an instant and penetrate the state of consciousness of others at a glance.

Mumon's most important words are "at once." There must not be any gap at all. It must be instantaneous—or dualistic concepts will creep in. WHACK! Just this!

ON THE VERSE

Where the active wheel revolves,
Even a master fails.
It moves in four directions: above and below,
South and north, east and west.

When you have extinguished all the deluding thoughts you have acquired since birth, the wonderful activity of your essential nature comes into motion. All our delusions come after birth because a newborn infant has no concepts or philosophies. When our essential nature acts, it moves freely and quickly, like a shooting star or a flash of lightning. It moves in all directions, in heaven and on earth, north and south, east and west. And it is so swift that even an accomplished Zen master may miss seeing it.

Daitsū Chishō

9

THE CASE

Once a monk earnestly asked Priest Jō of Kōyō, "Daitsū Chishō Buddha sat in the meditation hall for ten kalpas, but the Dharma of the Buddha did not manifest itself and he could not attain Buddhahood. Why was this?"

Jō replied, "Your question is reasonable indeed."

The monk said, "He sat in zazen in the meditation hall. Why did he not attain Buddhahood?"

Jō replied, "Because he is a non-attained Buddha."

MUMON'S COMMENTARY

I approve the old barbarian's realization, but I don't approve the old barbarian's understanding. When an ordinary person has realized it, he is a saint. If a saint understands it, he is nothing but an ordinary person.

THE VERSE

Far better than realizing the body is to realize the mind and be at peace.
If the mind is realized, there is no anxiety about the body;
If both body and mind are completely realized,
A holy hermit does not wish to be appointed lord.

TEISHŌ ON THE CASE

The priest Jō in this koan is Seijō, a Zen master of the Igyō sect. He was the Dharma successor of the famous master Bashō Esei, a Korean whom we will meet again in Case 44.

The term "Daitsū Chishō" will need some explanation. *Daitsū* means being able to go to all places or go through anything, in other words, pervading the whole universe. *Chishō* means wonderful wisdom. Thus Daitsū Chishō means the wonderful wisdom that pervades the universe. We will at once recognize that this name represents one of the characteristics of our essential nature. This is also true of the names of Buddhas and bodhisattvas. Take Amida Buddha, for example. In Sanskrit, Amida is *Amitayus*, which means limitless life, or *Amitabha*, which means limitless light, also characteristics of our essential nature. Then there is Bodhisattva Kanzeon or Kannon, which in Sanskrit is Avalokitesvara. In Japanese, *kan* means to see with the mind-eye. *Ze* is the world, and *on* means sound, so *ze-on* means the sounds of the world. It is said that Bodhisattva Kanzeon, upon hearing the voices of those who call upon his name, instantly renders mercy to them. This is, of course, the mercy of our essential nature.

The following story of Daitsū Chishō appears in the parable of the magic city in Chapter 7 of the *Lotus Sutra:*

Daitsū Chishō was the king of a certain country and had sixteen sons at the time he entered the priesthood. When he experienced complete enlightenment, he began to preach the Dharma in a mountain area. Upon hearing their father's preaching, all sixteen sons also entered the priesthood. This group constituted the foundation of present-day Buddhism. Each of the sixteen princes eventually became a Buddha, the youngest being Shakyamuni Buddha himself.

It is written that Daitsū Chishō sat in samadhi in the meditation hall for ten kalpas. Ten kalpas means countless ages. One of the sutras defines a kalpa as the period of time it would take an angel who descended from heaven once every hundred years and made one sweep with its robe of feathers across the top of a cubic-mile stone mountain to wear it down level to the ground. Or it is said to be the period of time it would take a bird to consume a cubic-mile container full of sesame seeds if it ate one seed every hundred years. Ten kalpas is, therefore, a very long time.

In spite of such a lengthy practice, the Dharma of Buddha did not manifest itself, and Daitsū Chishō did not achieve Buddhahood. The monk could not understand this, so he earnestly asked Priest Jō, "Why was this?" Jō replied, "Your question is reasonable indeed," which means: yes, it is as you say, he did not attain Buddhahood. Why not? The monk persisted in asking why he did not attain Buddhahood when he actually sat for such a long time in samadhi. Jō answered, "Because he is a non-attained Buddha." This is the point of the koan. Other translations have it, "Because he didn't," or "Because he was not a Buddha." These two versions of the reply miss the point.

As I repeatedly tell you, every koan must be contemplated from the point of view of our essential nature and not from the phenomenal point of view. In this koan we have Daitsū Chishō. What is he? He is a man who will never attain Buddhahood. Who is he? He is Daitsū Chishō, you will say. But who are you? You are John and Jenny and Bob. And each of you will say, "John? That's me," or, "Jenny? That's me," or, "Bob? That's me," or "Daitsū Chishō? That's me." I am John. I am Jenny. I am Bob. I am Daitsū Chishō. Each says "I." Who is that "I"? If you are conscious only of the relative phenomenal "I," it is nothing but the ego. But for the transformed, enlightened consciousness, what is this "I"? You must come to grasp it directly by experiencing enlightenment. Then you will know why neither Daitsū Chishō nor any of you can ever attain Buddhahood.

At the risk of revealing too much, I will explain more clearly. Hit your thigh with your fist. OUCH! That's it. Who is crying out? Not only Daitsū Chishō but all of you are Buddhas from the beginning and will never attain Buddhahood again, no matter how long you sit in samadhi. Can water get any wetter? Can gold become gold again? Can completeness become more complete? Can emptiness become empty? Of course, from the phenomenal point of view, our Buddha nature manifests itself little by little in the process of time. But from the essential point of view, we are Buddhas from the beginning.

As Hakuin Zenji says at the beginning of his *Song in Praise of Zazen*, "All living beings are intrinsically Buddha." It is not until you grasp your own self nature through direct experience that you realize for the first time what a non-attained Buddha means.

ON MUMON'S COMMENTARY

"I approve the old barbarian's realization, but I don't approve the old barbarian's understanding. When an ordinary person has realized it, he is a saint. If a saint understands it, he is nothing but an ordinary person."

The old barbarian here means Shakyamuni Buddha or Bodhidharma.

As I said before, from very ancient times the Chinese have been proud of their race and have referred to others as barbarians. So when Mumon uses the word here, no contempt is implied. Mumon is saying that even though the old barbarian might be Shakyamuni Buddha or Bodhidharma, if he understands the true fact only by thought processes, I do not approve of him at all. He is nothing but an ordinary man. But if an ordinary man has realized it by actual experience, then I admit he is a saint.

ON THE VERSE

Far better than realizing the body is to realize the mind and be at peace.
If the mind is realized, there is no anxiety about the body;
If both body and mind are completely realized,
A holy hermit does not wish to be appointed lord.

I think the meaning of the verse is self-evident. It is far better to realize our essential nature than to resolve the problem of our bodies. By the problem of our bodies is meant all of the problems of our phenomenal world, our physical, economic, and social existence. If you realize your essential nature completely, the problems of the phenomenal world will no longer disturb your peace of mind; you will be filled to your heart's content and will not look for anything more, just as a holy hermit does not wish for worldly honors.

Seizei the Poor

10

THE CASE

A monk, Seizei, eagerly asked Master Sōzan, "I am solitary and poor.
I beg you, Master, please help me to become prosperous."

San said, "Venerable[1] Zei!"

"Yes, Master!" replied Zei.

San said, "You have already drunk three cups of fine Hakka wine and
still you say that you have not yet moistened your lips."

MUMON'S COMMENTARY

Seizei is obsequious in tone, but what is his real intention? Sōzan has the
penetrating eye and thoroughly discerns the monk's state of mind. Be that
as it may, just tell me, where and how has Venerable Zei drunk the wine?

THE VERSE

Poor like Hantan,
Of a spirit like Kōu,
Though they cannot sustain themselves,
They dare to compete with each other for wealth.

TEISHŌ ON THE CASE

Sōzan Honjaku was born in 839 A.D. and died in 901 at the age of sixty-two. A disciple of Master Tōzan Ryōkai, he was one of the greatest masters of the Sōtō sect, which was named after these two masters.

We know almost nothing about the life of Seizei, but we gather from this story that he was an excellent Zen monk indeed.

The words of Seizei, "I am solitary and poor. I beg you, Master, please help me to become prosperous," contain a deep meaning regarding our essential nature. Solitary and poor. Alone and destitute. How true! Every one of us is solitary, for everyone is the only one in the whole universe. One with the whole universe. At the same time, every one of us is extremely poor, for as I repeatedly tell you, in our essential nature there is nothing. There is neither subject nor object. There is nothing to be seen, to be touched, to be handled. It has no form, no color, no weight, no place to stay. In other words, our essential nature is totally void.

On the other hand, this void has limitless treasures. It can see, it can hear, it can cry, it can laugh, run, and eat. In a word, it is limitless. Emptiness and limitlessness are characteristics of our essential nature.

Seizei knows all this, of course, and still he says to Sōzan, "I am alone and destitute. Please help me to become prosperous." He is trying to examine Sōzan's state of consciousness or to fathom the depth of his realization. Discerning his intention, Sōzan calls out, "Venerable Zei!" Seizei replied, "Yes, Master!" Sōzan tells him, "You have already drunk three cups of fine Hakka wine and still you say that you have not yet moistened your lips."

Hakka wine was the best wine in ancient China. Produced by the Hakka family, it was of such high quality that their name became famous throughout the country.

As you know, the answer "Yes, Master!" is a perfect manifestation of the essential nature. What Sōzan means is, "You are perfect just like that. You are using your essential nature fully. Is there any defect in it? No. You have everything from the very beginning. What more do you want?"

ON MUMON'S COMMENTARY

"Seizei is obsequious in tone, but what is his real intention? Sōzan has the penetrating eye and thoroughly discerns the monk's state of mind. Be that as it may, just tell me, where and how has Venerable Zei drunk the wine?"

Seizei says, "I am solitary and poor." He seems to be very humble, but what is the real meaning behind his words? He is trying to examine Sōzan. Sōzan has the enlightened eye and thoroughly discerns Seizei's state of consciousness and his secret intention. He says, therefore, "You have already drunk three cups of fine Hakka wine." Where and how did Seizei drink the best wine to the full? It was, of course, when he answered, "Yes, Master!" to Sōzan's call. That is, the perfect appearance of his essential nature. He has drunk fully of the wine.

ON THE VERSE

Poor like Hantan,
Of a spirit like Kōu,
Though they cannot sustain themselves,
They dare to compete with each other for wealth.

Hantan is the name of a man who lived in second-century China. He wanted to become a prefect, but the illness of his mother prevented it. He became, instead, a fortune-teller, and like many of the fortune-tellers in Japan, he was apparently unable to use his powers to make money for himself. Hantan lived in great poverty. It is said that his family never knew the taste of millet and that his wife and children lived in a small pushcart as he pursued his itinerant life, with only the trees as a roof over their heads at night.

Kōu was a Chinese warrior hero in the third century B.C. His spectacular career was eventually brought to an end by his defeat at the hands of Ryūhō, the founder of the Han dynasty. He was, nevertheless, famous for his courage and bravery. His splendid horse, Sui, also seemed to have caught his master's fighting spirit. Kōu's romance with his beautiful mistress, Gu, is a well-known chapter in Chinese history. It is said that when defeated and in imminent danger of death, Kōu threw a party at which he sang the following song, which later became quite famous:

Strength to drive through a mountain,
Spirit to cover the whole earth!
Yet the time is unfavorable,
Sui wants to advance no more;
Gu, oh, Gu! What shall I do with you!

Sōzan and Seizei are extremely poor (in their consciousness)—just like Hantan. They are truly void in their mind and as brave as Kōu in their spirit. Their inner world is as vast as space, and the two of them are competing for the wealth of this inner world. There is an interesting Japanese *haiku* which says:

> *At the end of the year,*
> *I don't even have a piece of straw*
> *To strangle myself with.*

In my opinion, the writer of these lines is still rich enough. He has much wealth, for he possesses a consciousness of "I" or "myself." I wish he would throw away this consciousness of "I" too!

You should know that poverty is the best condition for proceeding along the way of Zen because, in most instances, wealth prevents us from being sufficiently serious to practice Zen. It is said that people in the Buddhist heavens do not practice zazen because they have almost no life problems. Feeling continually satisfied, they do not possess the will to attain enlightenment and therefore become caught in the karmic cycle of the six realms. They are unable to free themselves from the law of causation.

I cannot help thinking that rich people in this world are in the same situation. From the Zen point of view, you should be grateful for your poverty.

Yōka Daishi says in his *Song of Enlightenment* (*Shōdōka*):

> *The sons of Shakyamuni are known to be poor,*
> *But the poverty is of the body;*
> *Their spiritual life knows no poverty.*
> *Though the poverty-stricken body is wrapped in rags,*
> *The spirit holds within itself an invaluable treasure.*
> *That invaluable treasure is never impaired,*
> *However much one uses it,*
> *And beings are thereby benefitted ungrudgingly,*
> *As required by the occasion;*
> *The triple body and fourfold wisdom are perfected within it.*
> *The eightfold emancipation and sixfold miraculous powers are*
>   *impressed on it.*

The triple body,[2] fourfold wisdom,[3] eightfold emancipation,[4] and sixfold miraculous powers[5] are terms in Buddhist philosophy. Their basic meaning is simply the wonderful manifold activity of our essential nature, which is why Yōka Daishi can say, "Poverty is of the body; the spiritual life knows no poverty."

NOTES

1. "Venerable" is used here to translate *shari* (*ajari* in full form, *acarya* in Sanskrit), an honorific title for the monk who leads the disciples, correcting their manners and deeds.

2. The Dharmakaya (Dharma body), the Sambhogakaya (Reward body), the Nirmanakaya (Corresponding body).

3. The fourfold wisdoms are: The wisdom of the great round mirror; the wisdom of identity; the wisdom of perceiving the phenomenal world clearly; the wisdom of doing works.

4. The eight kinds of emancipation are: liberation when subjective desire arises, by examination of the object, or all things, and realization of their filthiness; liberation when no subjective desire arises by still meditating as above; liberation by concentration on the pure to the realization of a permanent state of freedom from all desire; liberation in realization of the infinity of space or the immaterial; liberation in realization of infinite knowledge; liberation in realization of nothingness or nowhereness; liberation in the state of mind where there is neither thought nor absence of thought; liberation by means of a state of mind in which there is final extinction of both sensation and consciousness. (Taken from *A Dictionary of Chinese Buddhist Terms* [Soothill & Hodous—Kegan, Paul, Trench, Trubner & Co.].)

5. These are psychic powers such as the heavenly eye, the heavenly ear, knowing another's thoughts, and so forth.

Jōshū Examines the Hermits

11

THE CASE

Jōshū went to a hermit's hut and asked, "Anybody in? Anybody in?" The hermit thrust up his fist. Jōshū said, "The water is too shallow for a ship to anchor." Thereupon he left.

Again he went to a hermit's hut and asked, "Anybody in? Anybody in?" The hermit, too, thrust up his fist. Jōshū said, "Freely you give, freely you take away. Freely you kill, freely you give life." He made a profound bow.

MUMON'S COMMENTARY

Each hermit thrust up his fist the same way. Why is one accepted and the other rejected? Tell me, what is the cause of the confusion? If on this point you can say a turning word, then you can see that Jōshū's tongue has no bone. Now he raises up, now he thrusts down in perfect freedom. But though this is so, it is also true that Jōshū himself has been seen through by the two hermits. Furthermore, if you can say that there is a distinction of superiority and inferiority between the two hermits, you have not yet the eye of realization. Neither have you the eye of realization if you say there is no distinction of superiority and inferiority between them.

THE VERSE

His eye is a shooting star,
His activity like lightning;
A sword that kills man,
A sword that gives man life.

TEISHŌ ON THE CASE

We have already met Jōshū in Cases 1 and 7. The hermits referred to were Zen monks in ancient China who, having experienced the highest stage of enlightenment, settled down in a small hermitage in the mountains, or in a grove, to continue the practice of Zen by themselves. This was not uncommon at the time of Jōshū, who visited two such practitioners and tried to examine them to fathom the depth of their Zen realization. It was also an occasion for him to polish his own realization.

Now imagine Jōshū visiting a hermitage. He opens the door. As it is probably a small place, the hermit can be seen sitting just inside. Jōshū calls to him, "Anybody in? Anybody in?" This is not to be taken as a usual greeting. What Jōshū means is, "Is the subject at home? He's not out, is he?" Of course the subject is what is called Buddha nature or essential nature, which is our true self.

Jōshū's words seem to have still another meaning in the original Chinese: "Is there anything here? If you have anything, show it to me." The hermit thrusts up his fist, as if to say, "The subject is right here. Just this." Remember, Gutei stuck up his finger. A finger, a fist—is there any difference?

Jōshū responds, "The water is too shallow for a ship to anchor" and departs. A rendering of Jōshū's words could be, "What a trifling realization. It's of no use. The water is too shallow for a gigantic ship like me to anchor. I'll have nothing to do with you." What a terrible scolding! We must not think that Jōshū left without casting a glance at the hermit's face, however, to see his response to the abuse. If the hermit showed any sign of having been offended or irritated even a little by the words of scorn, his Zen practice must have been shallow indeed. If his consciousness was as steady and immovable as the fist itself, his face would not have shown even a trace of irritation.

At the same time, Jōshū would have been examined by the hermit, who on his part must have clearly perceived Jōshū's intention. It was like two mirrors reflecting each other. So when Jōshū was examining the hermits, they must have been examining him too! That is why Mumon says, "It is also true that Jōshū himself has been seen through by the two hermits."

When you sit with this koan, you must enter as far as possible into the state of consciousness of each hermit as well as that of Jōshū. Then you will grasp what was going on between them. Perhaps one day you will be able to see through all three of them.

To return to the case, Jōshū then visits another hermit and says the same thing. "Anybody in? Anybody in?" And the second hermit thrusts up his fist just like the first. Then Jōshū says, "Wonderful! Freely you give, freely you take away. Freely you kill, freely you give life. What a master you are!" and he makes a profound bow. Here, too, as he was leaving, Jōshū would have glanced at the hermit's face to see his response to the praise. If the hermit showed even the slightest sign of pleasure at his words, Jōshū would have discovered the degree of the hermit's state of consciousness.

ON MUMON'S COMMENTARY

"Each hermit thrust up his fist the same way. Why is one accepted and the other rejected? Tell me, what is the cause of the confusion? If on this point you can say a turning word, then you can see that Jōshū's tongue has no bone. Now he raises up, now he thrusts down in perfect freedom. But though this is so, it is also true that Jōshū himself has been seen through by the two hermits. Furthermore, if you say that there is a distinction of superiority and inferiority between the two hermits, you have not yet the eye of realization. Neither have you the eye of realization if you say there is no distinction of superiority and inferiority between them."

"Jōshū's tongue has no bone" means that Jōshū himself can freely give and freely take away. He can freely kill and freely give life. He can deal with all Zen practitioners in perfect freedom.

"If you say that there is distinction of superiority and inferiority between the two hermits, you have not yet the eye of realization. Neither have you the eye of realization if you say there is no difference between them." To our logical thinking these words are sheer nonsense; there is either a difference or no difference. If you try to solve such a contradiction by logic, you will end up frustrated, so do not try. Here it can be clearly seen again that we cannot grasp a koan, or Zen, by means of our conceptual way of thinking. We must enter a deeper level of consciousness, a level beyond all contradictions, a level beyond this and that, yes and no. This is the level on which Jōshū lives and acts. We must learn to appreciate his superlative skill and ability in testing the depth of a Zen student's state of consciousness.

I should like to add a word of explanation here. When you are truly enlightened, you will realize that the minds or consciousnesses of the two hermits are the same, for they are one. They are not even the same, but just one. They are the substance of our true self, our essential nature, the denominator of the fraction I have mentioned.

Mumon says that if you claim there is any distinction of superiority and inferiority between the two hermits, you do not yet have the eye of realization. Mumon goes on to say, however, that if you state there is no distinction of superiority and inferiority, you still do not yet have the eye of realization.

When you are truly enlightened, you will realize that no two consciousnesses can be exactly the same. By this I mean the phenomenal or relative consciousness. Difference and identity can co-exist in the essential world, but they will be contradictory in logic. There is no contradiction in the essential world. Of the two hermits, which is superior? Only a great Zen master like Jōshū can tell.

ON THE VERSE

His eye is a shooting star,
His activity like lightning;
A sword that kills man,
A sword that gives man life.

When discerning others, Jōshū's eye darts forth as quickly as a shooting star. He can evaluate the consciousness of another at a glance, as rapidly as lightning. He can deprive Zen practitioners of all their delusions with a word, sharp as a sword. At the same time, he can make them experience enlightenment by a word, as if giving them new life.

Zuigan Calls Himself "Master"

12

THE CASE

Every day Master Zuigan used to call to himself, "Master!" and would answer, "Yes!" Again, he would call, "Thoroughly awake! Thoroughly awake!" and he would answer, "Yes! Yes!" "Don't be deceived by others, any day or any time." "No! No!"

MUMON'S COMMENTARY

Old Zuigan himself buys and sells. He has many puppet gods and devils with which he plays. But why? Look! One is calling. One is answering. One keeps awake. One is not deceived by others. But if you get stuck there, that's not it. If you were to imitate Zuigan, it would be the understanding of a fox.

THE VERSE

The reason those who learn the Way don't realize the truth
Is simply that they perceive the discriminating consciousness they've
*   had all along.*
It is the origin of endless life and death;
Fools take it for the essential self.

TEISHŌ ON THE CASE

The dates of Master Zuigan Shigen's birth and death are not known but are presumed to have been some time between 850 and 910 A.D. He was a disciple of Gantō, a very famous Zen master whom we shall hear about in the next case. Zuigan used to call himself "Master!" both before and after his enlightenment, and right up to the time of his death. From beginning to end his koan was just "Master!" Every day he would call to himself, "Master!" and answer, "Yes!" Then he would cry, "Thoroughly awake! Thoroughly awake!" which means "Don't be obscure. Be clearly aware of yourself." Then he would reply "Yes! Yes!" to himself.

What is the "master"? It is, of course, your essential nature, which is also called Buddha nature or the primal face before your parents were born. In Zen, it is sometimes Mu, or the sound of one hand, or *Masagin* (three pounds of flax, see Case 18), or *Kanshiketsu* (dried shit-stick, see Case 21). Sometimes the essential nature appears as a finger, sometimes as a flower, or in this case, as the "master."

Consider who is calling. What connection is there between the one who is calling and the master who is being called? We think of the one calling as "I." We think, "I am calling." But what is this "I"? You may think that what you conceive of as "I" is nothing but your phenomenal or relative consciousness—your ego, which does not surpass the world of the six senses of sight, hearing, smell, taste, touch, and discursive intellect. In fact, most ordinary people conceive an image of an ego and take this phenomenal, relative consciousness for their sole "I." Then they think it has some kind of form called a "soul," which is freed from the body when they die and flies up to heaven or down to hell. But as you know, your consciousness has neither form nor color and occupies no place.

Buddhist psychology teaches us that there are several levels of consciousness. Below the six senses there is a seventh consciousness, called the consciousness of transmission or of a constant awareness of "I." Below that is the eighth consciousness, which in Sanskrit is called *ālaya-vijñāna*, that is, the storehouse of consciousness. All the experiences and impressions received by the six senses are transmitted by the seventh to the eighth and stored there. Under the eighth consciousness there expands the vast ocean of the ninth consciousness, which is called the consciousness of the pure and clear essential nature. This is nothing other than our primal face. It is the inside of the whole universe. This ninth consciousness, the vast ocean of consciousness which is common to all of us, cannot be caught by the six senses. It cannot be pictured by concepts or ideas and cannot be understood by thought. It can only be grasped through the experience of enlightenment or self-realization.

When you experience enlightenment, you will realize that all the six senses and the seventh and eighth consciousnesses are nothing other than the ninth, as though they were waves on the water of a vast ocean. When you die, the six senses are destroyed and disappear along with the body. But the seventh, eighth, and ninth consciousnesses are never destroyed. They exist constantly and eternally.

When Zuigan calls "Master!" you may think that the one who calls is his superficial "I" and the master called to is his true essential nature. That is a misconception. From the Zen point of view, you should know that the one calling Zuigan and the one called to are both Zuigan's essential nature. It is sometimes expedient to name the superficial consciousness "ego," but the truth is that the ego does not have substantial existence. It is merely a concept or a kind of delusion. When you have once attained true self-realization, you will realize that what you think of as the ego is nothing but a kind of wave of, or glorious light from, your essential nature.

In the *Bodhisattva's Vow,* by Tōrei Zenji, we find the following passage:

On each moment's flash of thought will grow a lotus flower,
And on each lotus flower will be revealed a Buddha.

I am always telling you to wipe out your thoughts, to sweep away your concepts and ideas, calling them the enemy, as this is useful for guiding Zen practice. But actually I should call them the temporary enemy, the enemy for the time being. As long as you are controlled or pulled around by concepts, including that of ego, they are your enemy because they are the obstacles to obtaining enlightenment. But if you once attain true self-realization, you will acknowledge that all concepts are nothing but the glorious light of your self-nature.

Even after we are enlightened, however, we are apt to lose sight of the master, but if we are aware of the essential nature, aware of *being* the essential nature, we will always enjoy peace of mind. So, after enlightenment we must endeavor not to let our awareness of the essential nature diminish.

That is why Zuigan called himself "Master!" every day (maybe every moment) and why he himself replied, "Yes!" He cried, "Thoroughly awake! Don't be obscure!" "No, I will not!" he answered himself. "Don't be deceived by others, any day or any time." "No, I never will."

That was the way Zuigan practiced Zen after enlightenment as well. In the "others" mentioned here, even Shakyamuni Buddha and Bodhidharma must be included. Even though Shakyamuni Buddha may come and say "You are wrong," or "Your enlightenment is not true," you should not be confused but should rely on your realization.

ON MUMON'S COMMENTARY

"Old Zuigan himself buys and sells. He has many puppet gods and devils with which he plays. But why? Look! One is calling. One is answering. One keeps awake. One is not deceived by others. But if you get stuck there, that's not it. If you were to imitate Zuigan, it would be the understanding of a fox."

Calling "Master!" is a mask which Zuigan buys himself. The answer "Yes!" is also a mask that he sells himself. "Thoroughly awake!" is one of the masks, and "Don't be deceived by others!" and "No, I will not!" are masks too. But, if you stick to the way of Zuigan, self-realization is as far from you as before. If you try to imitate him, it will be nothing but the understanding of a fox, which means it will be the conceptual understanding of an unenlightened person.

ON THE VERSE

The reason those who learn the Way don't realize the truth
Is simply that they perceive the discriminating consciousness they've
    had all along.
It is the origin of endless life and death;
Fools take it for the essential self.

The reason those who are searching for the truth cannot realize it is simply that they perceive only the relative consciousness and take it for a fixed entity. They think it has some kind of form called the spirit, which, when a person dies, leaves the body and goes somewhere. However, that very concept is the origin of our endlessly going through life and death—which means all delusions—the origin of our endless transmigration. Fools mistake that for the essential nature.

Tokusan Carries
His Bowls

13

THE CASE

One day Tokusan came down to the hall carrying his bowls. Seppō asked him, "Old Master, the bell has not yet rung nor the drum sounded. Where are you going with your bowls?" Tokusan immediately went back to his room. Seppō told this to Gantō. Gantō said, "Great Tokusan though he is, he has not yet realized the last word."

Hearing of this, Tokusan sent his attendant to summon Gantō and then asked him, "Don't you approve of this old monk?" Gantō secretly whispered his intention. Tokusan remained silent.

Sure enough, the next day when Tokusan ascended the rostrum, his talk was quite different from usual. Gantō went to the front of the Zen hall and rubbing his hands together, laughed loudly and said, "Wonderful! How happy I am that our Old Man has realized the last word. From now on he'll be subject to no one on earth."

MUMON'S COMMENTARY

As for the last word, neither Gantō nor Tokusan have ever heard it, even in a dream. When I examine this point, I find they are just like puppets on a shelf.

THE VERSE

If you grasp the first word,
You will realize the last word.
The last word and the first word,
These are not one word.

TEISHŌ ON THE CASE

Tokusan Senkan was born around 782 A.D. and died in 865 at the age of eighty-three. As a young man, he was an able Buddhist sutra scholar, renowned especially for his interpretation of the Diamond Sutra. He did not believe in the principle of Zen, that is, becoming Buddha through realization of one's self-nature by directly pointing to the mind. He held Zen Buddhism in great contempt. Since at that time the Zen sect was spreading in South China, he started to travel south to refute it. On the way, he attained enlightenment under the guidance of Master Ryūtan. An account of his enlightenment is given in Case 28.

Seppō Gison and Gantō Zenkatsu, who appear in this case, are both disciples of Tokusan. Seppō lived from 822 to 908, and Gantō from 828 to 887. At the time of this episode, Tokusan was eighty-one years old, Seppō forty-one, and Gantō thirty-five. Although younger than Seppō, Gantō was further advanced in Zen practice, so he was Seppō's elder brother in the Dharma. He had already experienced great enlightenment, while Seppō was still on the way.

Seppō eventually attained greatness through hard, strenuous practice, became a Dharma successor to Tokusan, and produced more than 150 excellent Zen masters. Gantō also became a Dharma successor to Tokusan. He escaped the great persecution of Buddhism in 845 as a ferryman on a lake. His life ended with a great shout, let out in a state of complete composure as temple looters put the sword to his neck after everyone else had fled. Hakuin Zenji (1685–1768) was later to resolve his perplexity over this shout and exclaimed, "Oh, Gantō is still alive, strong, and healthy!"

The point to notice in this koan is how Tokusan and Gantō cooperate in striving to lead Seppō to experience great enlightenment.

One day Tokusan came down from his room to go to the hall to eat. He was carrying his bowls and perhaps he was tottering along. He might also have been a little hungry. One ancient book says that the meal was late that day. Seppō was *tenzo*, the monk in charge of the kitchen and responsible for the meals. When he saw Tokusan coming along he said, "Where are you going, Old Master? The bell has not yet rung, nor has the drum sounded." These are the usual signals for mealtime in a monastery. Tokusan said nothing and quietly returned to his room.

What a splendid state of mind! Tokusan was not aware of it himself, but he had matured wonderfully with age. Can you appreciate it? Seppō was not able to. Here was Tokusan unconsciously showing him the supreme world of Zen by his action, but Seppō could not recognize his master's state of mind.

Similarly Mahakashyapa realized what Shakyamuni really meant when he twirled a flower in front of the assembled monks. But Seppō could not recognize it in Tokusan. Seppō seems, moreover, to have been a little proud of putting Tokusan in his place and told Gantō about it.

Hearing this gave Gantō an idea about how to lead Seppō to enlightenment, so he said, "Is that so? Our old man Tokusan, great as he is, has not realized the last word of Zen." Literally, the last word would seem to mean the highest state of consciousness in Zen. Gantō's device was to prod Seppō, who was lingering along the way, by making him wonder whether there might be a last word. What is it? He must strive to achieve it in deeper realization.

When Tokusan heard what Gantō had said, he called for him and asked, "Don't you approve of me?" Then Gantō whispered his real intention to Tokusan. What do you suppose he whispered? We must fathom Gantō's depth to find out. In any case, Tokusan approved.

The next day, Tokusan ascended the rostrum and delivered a talk which was quite different from the usual one. Seppō was in the assembly, listening. Gantō went to the front of the Zen hall, rubbed his hands together and said laughingly, "How happy I am to know that the old master has wonderfully realized the last word of Zen. From now on, nobody in the world will be a match for him." Gantō was still trying to incite Seppō to deeper realization, but in spite of all these efforts, Seppō was not able to attain it at that time. It was some years later that Seppō finally came to great enlightenment under Gantō's guidance.

ON MUMON'S COMMENTARY

"As for the last word, neither Gantō nor Tokusan have ever heard it, even in a dream. When I examine this point, I find they are just like puppets on a shelf."

The last word? Not only Tokusan and Gantō but even the Buddhas and the patriarchs themselves do not know what it is, for it is beyond perception. The last word is that which is spoken without using lips and tongue. It has no meaning. It is nothing. It is less than nothing, so to speak. But how about the first word?

Mumon's statement that upon examining the actions of Tokusan and Gantō, they seem to be puppets is merely feigned ill will. In his heart he is praising them highly. They have neither pride nor shame; no thought at all in their consciousness, only sincere kindness and the desire to help Seppō come to enlightenment. You should learn to appreciate the irony often found in Zen writings.

ON THE VERSE

If you grasp the first word,
You will realize the last word.
The last word and the first word,
These are not one word.

The opening two lines tell us that the first and last words are the same, but the third and fourth lines tell us that these two words are not one. Do you know what this means?

If you interpret the verse literally and conclude it means simply that the first and last words are not the same, then no special comment is needed, but we should appreciate the verse more deeply.

If two things are exactly the same, there is no need to say they are one, for one is a concept based on the premise that there are two. To say that A is the same as A, or that A and A are one, is nonsense. A is not one with A. A is not one with any identical thing, not even itself. A transcends the concept of oneness. Thus, the verse tells us, "These are not one word."

Nansen Kills the Cat

14

THE CASE

Once the monks of the eastern and western Zen halls in Master Nansen's temple were quarrelling about a cat. Nansen held up the cat and said, "You monks! If one of you can say a word, I will spare the cat. If you can't say anything, I will put it to the sword." No one could answer, so Nansen finally slew it. In the evening when Jōshū returned, Nansen told him what had happened. Jōshū thereupon took off his sandals, put them on his head, and walked off. Nansen said, "If you had been there, I could have spared the cat."

MUMON'S COMMENTARY

What is the meaning of Jōshū's putting his sandals on his head? If you can give a turning word concerning this matter, you will be able to see that Nansen's command was not meaningless. But if you can't, look out! Danger!

THE VERSE

Had Jōshū been there,
He would have given the command instead;
Had he snatched away the sword,
Even Nansen would have begged for his life.

TEISHŌ ON THE CASE

This is a very famous koan. Nansen is Master Nansen Fugan, and, as usually happened, he got his name from the mountain on which he lived. His family name was Ō, so he was also called Ō Roshi.

Nansen was born in 748 and left home at the age of nineteen to become a monk. He became one of the greatest Dharma successors of Master Baso. Once, when Baso was conversing about the harvest moon with Hyakujō, Seidō, and Nansen, his three best disciples, he said, "The sutra is in the hands of Seidō, Zen is in the hands of Hyakujō, only Fugan surpasses the world of things." Nansen Fugan died in 834 at the age of eighty-seven. We will speak of him in more detail in Cases 19, 27, and 34.

In Nansen's monastery there must have been two Zen halls, one to the east of the compound and one to the west. One day monks from the two halls were quarreling about a cat. We are not told just what the problem was, but it may have had something to do with the cat's Buddha nature. Perhaps Nansen was listening in, unobserved. In any case, he appeared with a sword in his right hand and taking the cat in his left, he held it up to his monks and said, "You monks! If one of you can say a word, I will spare the cat. If you can't say anything, I will put it to the sword." No one could answer, so Nansen killed it.

For ordinary people who know nothing about Zen, it would not be difficult to say something at such a time. But for those who are studying Zen, it will be a bit difficult because they have some conceptions about Zen. They will try to say some Zen-like "turning words."

If you had been there at the time, what would you have said? Just try to say the "turning words" to save the cat.

Here I would like to deliberate on one point: What does the cat mean or stand for?

As you know, Zen dislikes abstract concepts. It does not use definite labels or words, for they tend to bring about fixed notions, and the true life of things is lost. In order to prevent this, Zen takes anything at hand and tries to express the essential nature through that object—a dog, a cat, a tree, a fox, a finger—anything will do. In this case, it is a cat. Now, what does the cat mean? It is the symbol of the origin from which all relative thought arises. All thoughts that come from the premise of the opposition of the subject and object are delusions. To kill the cat means to cut off the origin of all delusive thoughts. This is precisely what Nansen did.

Jōshū was away when all this happened and did not return to the monastery until evening. Nansen told him what had taken place and probably asked him, "What do you think about it?" Jōshū put his sandals on his head and walked away.

Jōshū, of course, was deeply enlightened and had swept away not only all delusive thoughts but also all remembrance of enlightenment. He had no ideas, no concepts, not even a trace of enlightenment. He was a truly emancipated man, who presented the inner world of his consciousness to Nansen. The latter showed his approval by his reply, "If you had been there, I could have spared the cat."

If you try to imagine what Jōshū was saying in his heart, it might be: "Master, you are talking about killing a cat, but I don't understand what you mean. Now I must go." But this is only our imagination. In Jōshū's heart there was nothing, not even thoughts such as these. He did not say a word. By his action alone he showed his state of consciousness and gave the master his answer to the koan. In that action there was no discriminative thinking, not even the thought that sandals belong on the feet and not the head. But I do not want you to think that wearing sandals on your head is characteristic of Zen! If your thinking is like that, then you are on the fox level. As I said before, our aim in Zen is not to become strange or peculiar but to become a true person.

Nansen's sword kills everything, and Jōshū gives everything life. They represent the two sides of Zen activity. One side, represented by Nansen, extinguishes or cuts off delusions which arise fundamentally from opposing subject and object. The significance of this is to cut off all evil. There is a Zen saying, "There is not even a grain of dust in the essential world."

The other side of Zen activity is to give life to everything. Jōshū presents this side uniquely by his extraordinary action. Its significance is to practice all good. There is a Zen saying, "Nothing remains outside the Buddha's Dharma." In order to promote man's spiritual advancement, both are indispensable.

ON MUMON'S COMMENTARY

"What is the meaning of Jōshū's putting his sandals on his head? If you can give a turning word concerning this matter, you will be able to see that Nansen's command was not meaningless. But if you can't, look out! Danger!"

What do you think it means to put sandals on your head? Can you give a turning word? A "turning word" means a word that has the power to make a person turn around in his consciousness and, by the help of this word, come to enlightenment. But if you cannot say an appropriate word, then look out! You too may be killed by Nansen! Danger!

ON THE VERSE

Had Jōshū been there,
He would have given the command instead;
Had he snatched away the sword,
Even Nansen would have begged for his life.

What this means is that if Jōshū had been there, he might have snatched the sword from Nansen's hand and pointed it at his throat, saying, "What kind of Zen-stinking talk is that?" Then Nansen would have begged for his life. The verse seems to appreciate Jōshū more than Nansen, but this is only rhetorical. Nansen is no less great than Jōshū.

Tōzan's Sixty Blows

15

THE CASE

When Tōzan came to Unmon for instruction, Unmon asked, "Where have you come from?" Tōzan said, "From Sado." Unmon said, "Where were you during the summer retreat?" Tōzan said, "At Hōzu Monastery, south of the lake." Unmon said, "When did you leave there?" Tōzan said, "On the twenty-fifth of August." Unmon said, "I spare you sixty blows."

The next day Tōzan came up to Unmon and asked, "Yesterday you spared me sixty blows though I deserved them. I beg you, sir, where was I at fault?" Unmon said, "Oh, you ricebag! Have you been wandering about like that, now west of the river, now south of the lake?" At this, Tōzan had great realization.

MUMON'S COMMENTARY

At that time, if Unmon had given Tōzan the essential food of Zen and awakened him to an active Zen spirit, his family gate would not have become so desolate. Tōzan struggled with himself in agony all through the night and at daybreak came to Unmon again. Unmon gave him a further push to break through. Although Tōzan attained realization immediately, he still could not be called bright. Now I ask you, does Tōzan deserve sixty blows with the stick or not? If you say he does, then all the trees, grasses, thickets, and groves should be beaten. If you say he does not, then Unmon is telling a lie. If you grasp this clearly, you are breathing through one mouth with Tōzan.

THE VERSE

The lion has a puzzling way of teaching its cubs:
The cubs crouch, leap and spring back swiftly;
Unintentionally, he gave a checkmate again,
The first arrow was light, but the second went deep.

TEISHŌ ON THE CASE

Unmon Bun'en appears in five cases of the *Gateless Gate:* 15, 16, 21, 39, and 48. His family name was Chō. Unmon was a successor of Seppō, and died about the year 950. Unmon is famous for the strict and severe way he guided his disciples, for this was the way he had learned from his own master, Bokushū, who always kept the door of his *dokusan*[1] room closed. Bokushū would judge whether or not a student was ready for an interview by the sound of his footsteps as he approached the *dokusan* room. If he thought there was some hope, Bokushū would say, "Come in!" As soon as the student entered, the master would seize him roughly by the collar and yell, "Say it!" If the student hesitated even for a moment, Bokushū would push him out the door and slam it.

Unmon had this experience in his first two *dokusan* with Bokushū. The third was even more traumatic because as he was pushed out the door, his leg was caught and broken. "Ouch!" he cried, and in that instant Unmon suddenly attained great enlightenment. Just "Ouch!", nothing else, no subject or object, neither relative nor absolute, just "Ouch!" This was Unmon's great enlightenment.

The Tōzan who appears in this case is the same Tōzan Shusho we find in Case 18, the *masagin* koan. In Chinese Zen history there are two masters with this name: Master Tōzan Gohon, the founder of the Sōtō sect, and the Tōzan of the present case, who was also called Shusho and became a master in the Rinzai sect. He died about the year 990. At the time of this koan, he was as yet unenlightened and had come to Unmon for guidance.

"Where have you come from?" Unmon asked him. This was not simply a commonplace greeting but a prying question. The master was sounding out Tōzan to see whether he was enlightened, and if so, how deeply.

"From Sado," answers the monk. No one can tell from this whether there has been realization or not, so Unmon continues, "Where did you spend the summer?" Tōzan answers, "At Hōzu Monastery, south of the lake." "When did you leave there?" "On the twenty-fifth of August." It appears to Unmon that there is no enlightenment whatsoever. Tōzan is incapable of deviating from the path of an ordinary conversation. In other words, he is still blind.

As you know, questions and answers in *dokusan* are limited to the confines of Dharma and should not deal with anything like social greetings or travel routes. In asking such questions, Unmon was trying to discern Tōzan's consciousness, but the monk did not understand this. Tōzan might have been riding on a very fine horse, all the time unaware he was even on a horse. His route was always the highest way, but he did not know it. In short, he was recognizing only things outside of himself.

I would like to point out that a deeply enlightened person might answer Unmon's questions in the same way as Tōzan. There would then be other indications, however, by which a true Zen master could recognize enlightenment—such as the manner of walking or talking, or a light in the person's eyes. In any event, Tōzan did not show the slightest degree of enlightenment.

Unmon said, therefore, "I spare you sixty blows." The Japanese reading is three *ton*. *Ton* means twenty, so three *ton* blows is sixty. The real meaning of Unmon's statement is, "You deserve to be beaten with sixty blows, but I will spare you so as not to dirty the stick." This remark is more stinging than even sixty blows! But we must remember that it was a very kind stinging on Unmon's part. Tōzan, of course, could not be expected to know why the master scolded him so bitterly. He did not think his answers had been that impolite.

Tōzan was not able to sleep. The following morning at dawn he went to Unmon and asked, "Yesterday you spared me sixty blows. I beg you to tell me, where was I at fault?"

Tōzan is quite simple and sincere. There is no ego in him at all; he is like a child asking in all earnestness for an answer, and that is an ideal state of mind for the practice of zazen.

Unmon replied, "Oh, you ricebag! Have you been wandering about like that, now west of the river, now south of the lake?" This means, "Oh, you good-for-nothing! What are you trying to find, wandering all over the world, going from one Zen master to another?" Many Zen students like to go from master to master, looking for something with which to become enlightened. It takes most of them a long while to find out that they must grasp it within themselves. In any event, with this remark Tōzan attained great enlightenment.

ON MUMON'S COMMENTARY

"At that time, if Unmon had given Tōzan the essential food of Zen and awakened him to an active Zen spirit, his family gate would not have become so desolate. Tōzan struggled with himself in agony all through the night and at daybreak came to Unmon again. Unmon gave him a further push to break through. Although Tōzan attained realization immediately, he still could not be called bright. Now I ask you, does Tōzan deserve sixty blows with the stick or not? If you say he does, then all the trees, grasses, thickets, and groves should be beaten. If you say he does not, then Unmon is telling a lie. If you grasp this clearly, you are breathing through one mouth with Tōzan."

If Unmon had given Tōzan "the essential food," which means blows of the stick, or a shout of "Kwatz!" instead of talking to him, Tōzan would have become enlightened much sooner.

"His family gate would not have become so desolate" means that Unmon's sect would not have become as deserted as it is now. There is no remnant of this sect in Japan today; it ceased to exist several hundred years ago in China.

"Though Tōzan attained realization immediately, he still could not be called bright." As you know, all living beings are intrinsically Buddha. Even though Tōzan came to realization immediately, it was nothing more than acknowledging what he had within himself, so how could that be called particularly brilliant or clever?

Comments or criticisms in Zen are always given from the highest point of view, which transcends that of the patriarchs and even that of Buddhas. Here Mumon seems to be leveling severe criticism at Unmon and Tōzan, but really it has nothing to do with them. He merely wants to warn all Zen students.

"Does Tōzan deserve sixty blows with the stick or not? If you say he does, than all the trees, grasses, thickets, and groves should be beaten." As you know, everything, every action of ours in the phenomenal world, is nothing but the perfect manifestation of the substantial world, which is nothing but our essential nature. Everyone and everything in the whole world is perfect and guiltless. In this respect, Tōzan did not commit any fault. All his answers were correct. If you say he is guilty, then not only everything in the monastery but also everyone in the world must be guilty, for there is not even the tiniest bit of a difference between Tōzan and the rest of us.

"If you say he does not, then Unmon is telling a lie." If Tōzan is not guilty, then Unmon is a liar and deserves a beating himself.

"If you grasp this clearly, you are breathing through one mouth with Tōzan." This means your enlightenment will be as clear as Tōzan's.

ON THE VERSE

The lion has a puzzling way of teaching its cubs:
The cubs crouch, leap and spring back swiftly;
Unintentionally, he gave a checkmate again,
The first arrow was light, but the second went deep.

It is said that the lion, about a week after the birth of her cubs, pushes them off of a cliff into a ravine. In this way, she gets to know their strength and will only raise those that can climb back up. Unmon treated Tōzan just like this parent lion. Tōzan went back to Unmon again the next morning and asked, "Where was I at fault?" like the cub which returns to its parent.

"Unintentionally, he gave a checkmate again." The first checkmate was: "I spare you sixty blows," and the second was: "Oh, you ricebag! Have you been wandering about like that, now west of the river, now south of the lake?"

"The first arrow was light, but the second went deep." The first arrow was not effective enough, but the second hit the target and penetrated deeply.

NOTE

1. *Dokusan* refers to a private interview with the master in which the student's views are tested.

The Sound of the Bell
and the
Seven-Panel Robe

16

THE CASE

Unmon said, "The world is vast and wide like this. Why do we put on our seven-panel robe at the sound of the bell?"

MUMON'S COMMENTARY

Generally speaking, in practicing and studying Zen, it is most detestable to follow sounds and pursue colors. Even though you may become enlightened through hearing sounds and come to realize mind by seeing colors, that is the ordinary way of things. People do not know that for real Zen monks, when they are riding on sounds and becoming one with colors, everything is clear, moment by moment, everything is full of wonder, action after action. When you hear a sound, however, just tell me, does the sound come to the ear or the ear go to the sound? Even though you have extinguished both sound and silence, what will you realize here? If you hear with the ear, you cannot realize it. When you hear with the eye, for the first time it will become intimate.

THE VERSE

With realization, all things are of one family,
Without realization, everything is separate and different;
Without realization, all things are of one family,
With realization, everything is separate and different.

TEISHŌ ON THE CASE

Since I told you about Unmon in the previous *teishō* I shall omit any detailed references to him here. I would just like to point out that after the Sixth Patriarch, Enō, Zen Buddhism in China divided into five sects: Sōtō, Rinzai, Igyō, Hōgen, and Unmon. Unmon is the founder of the sect bearing his name and is considered one of the greatest Zen masters in China.

One day Unmon said, "The world is vast and wide like this. Why do we put on the seven-panel robe [ceremonial *kesa*] upon hearing the sound of the bell?"

The world is very spacious and when you open your eyes, the whole world comes into them. Nothing will interrupt your seeing. At that moment, each one of you is one with the whole world. You are nothing else but the whole world, the whole world is nothing other than you. When you have no consciousness of "I," everything is yours; there is nothing that is not yours. That is what Unmon meant when he said, "The world is so vast and wide like this!" The world is truly very spacious, and you are completely free of all restrictions. You can stand up, sit down, eat when you are hungry, lie down when you feel tired. You can do anything freely and at will. But why do monks, hearing the sound of the bell, put on ceremonial robes (seven-panel *kesa*) and come to the hall?

The *kesa* is the outer robe worn by regular Buddhist priests. The *rakusu*, which many of us wear in the zendo, is a kind of miniature *kesa*. *Kesa* are differentiated by the number of cloth panels sewn together. The five-panel *kesa* is made of five strips of cloth and is the robe which monks wear for their daily activities. The seven-panel *kesa* is a dress coat worn for minor ceremonies. *Kesa*, which have nine to twenty-five panels, are for full-dress occasions.

Every morning in the monastery, when the appointed time comes, the bell is rung. Upon hearing it, the monks put on their seven-panel *kesa* and go to the hall to participate in the morning ceremony. But why? Ah, this "why"! It is the wonderful charm, the magical talisman which brings a Zen student to enlightenment. This "why" is the miraculous means of putting away the "why" of reasoning with all its thoughts and ideas. And to pursue the "why" you must surpass the "why."

When you hear the bell, you should know that the sound is empty in itself. When you put on a robe, you must realize that the action of putting it on, the robe, and you yourself are all totally void. Some of you are familiar with the last line of the mealtime sutra, "We and this food and our eating are equally empty." If you can acknowledge this fact, you will realize that when you put on your robe there is no reason or "why" in it. Why do you put on a suit and go out at eight o'clock every morning? Why do you eat lunch at noon? Why do you go to bed at ten in the evening? Why? Why? Try to search out this "why." There is no reason for the "why" in anything! When we stand up, there is no reason "why." We just stand up! When we eat, we just eat, without any reason "why." When we put on the *kesa*, we just put it on. Our life is a continuous just . . . just . . . just.

ON MUMON'S COMMENTARY

"Generally speaking, in practicing and studying Zen, it is most detestable to follow sounds and pursue colors. Even though you may become enlightened through hearing sounds and come to realize mind by seeing colors, that is the ordinary way of things. People do not know that for real Zen monks, when they are riding on sounds and becoming one with colors, everything is clear, moment by moment, everything is full of wonder, action after action. When you hear a sound, however, just tell me, does the sound come to the ear or the ear go to the sound? Even though you have extinguished both sound and silence, what will you realize here? If you hear with the ear, you cannot realize it. When you hear with the eye, for the first time it will become intimate."

"In practicing and studying Zen, it is most detestable to follow sounds and pursue colors." To put it a little more clearly, as long as you think or feel yourself to be the subject and pursue sounds and colors as objects outside of yourself, you will never attain enlightenment.

"People do not know that for real Zen monks, when they are riding on sounds and becoming one with colors . . ." Riding on sounds and becoming one with colors means being one with the whole objective world. When you are absorbed in the song of a bird or seeing the color of a flower there is nothing but the song or color in the whole universe. At that time the song is not a song, nor is the color a color anymore. For real monks, everything is clear, moment by moment; everything is free, action after action—for everything is just as it is.

"When you hear a sound, however, just tell me, does the sound come to the ear or the ear go to the sound?" Neither! When you are hearing, there is neither ear nor sound. To hear without ear and sound is true hearing!

"Even though you have extinguished both sound and silence, what will you realize here?" Sound represents the whole objective world, and silence represents consciousness or mind. When you have extinguished both sound and consciousness, there is no hearing. What is there?

"If you hear with the ear, you cannot realize it. When you hear with the eye, for the first time it will become intimate." Hearing with your whole being, not just with the organ of the ear, is expressed by Unmon with the two words "*in-mo*," which mean, "just this." When you become truly one with the objective world, you will for the first time realize your essential nature, the reality of the universe itself, which at any time and anywhere is "just this," "just that," "just it." Nothing more, nothing less.

ON THE VERSE

With realization, all things are of one family,
Without realization, everything is separate and different;
Without realization, all things are of one family,
With realization, everything is separate and different.

"With realization, all things are of one family." All is one, one is all. Everything is one, one is everything. This is the vista of the enlightened world. Recall for a minute the fraction I have told you about. In the denominator world, the world of the zero-infinite, all is one, and every numerator contains the denominator, so one is all.

"Without realization, everything is separate and different." This is what we see in our ordinary world. All things stand opposed and separate. There is no inner relation between them. To the unenlightened person, the world of abstract equality (the world of the zero-infinite, or of absolute emptiness) is completely unknown.

"Without realization, all things are of one family." This is the blind equality, perverted equality. To unenlightened eyes, man and woman are the same, teacher and student are the same, parents and children are the same, king and beggar are the same.

"With realization, everything is separate and different." This is the most difficult to understand. Everything and everyone is alone and single.

Everything is the only one in the whole universe, alone and single. Everything in the universe has two phases. In the first, everything is completely the same. We call this absolute sameness. In the second phase, everything is completely different from everything else. All things are separate and disconnected. They are alone and single. This we call absolute difference. These two aspects are what we realize in enlightenment.

The National Teacher's
Three Calls

17

THE CASE

The national teacher called his attendant three times, and three times his attendant responded. The national teacher said, "I thought I was standing alone with my back to you, but now I find that you are standing alone with your back to me."

MUMON'S COMMENTARY

The national teacher called three times and his tongue dropped to the ground. The attendant responded three times, emitting the answer with light. The national teacher was old and lonely. He held the cow's head and forced it to eat grass. The attendant would have none of it; delicious food has little attraction for a man who has had enough to eat. Just tell me, where are they standing alone with their backs to each other? When the country is prosperous, persons of talent are esteemed; children of rich families are too proud to eat plain food.

THE VERSE

We must carry an iron yoke with no hole,
It is not a slight matter, the curse is passed on to our descendants;
If you want to support the gate and sustain the house,
You must climb a mountain of swords with bare feet.

TEISHŌ ON THE CASE

"National teacher" (*kokushi* in Japanese) refers to a teacher of the emperor. The national teacher in this case is Nan'yō Echū (or Chū), a Dharma successor of the sixth patriarch, Enō. The attendant is thought to be Tangen Ōshin, Echū's sole Dharma successor. He also appears in Case 18 of the *Blue Cliff Record*.

Echū, after he had attained great enlightenment, succeeded to the sixth patriarch's Dharma. He then retreated to a small temple called Kōkanji, which was located in the Tōsu Valley of Mt. Byakugai. Here he continued to practice zazen single-mindedly for forty years with a Zen priest friend named Seizazan.

Emperor Shukusō, hearing what a great Zen master Echū was, sent messengers several times to invite him to the palace to be the national teacher. After refusing innumerable times, Echū finally decided to accept the invitation. His friend, Seizazan, opposed the decision, feeling it was too early to leave the mountain. "I am finished with you from now on," he told Echū and remained alone, practicing zazen. History tells us nothing about him after that.

In this connection, I would like to say something about practicing zazen alone. I strongly discourage it in all cases, particularly for students who have not completed what we call in Japanese *shitsunai no shirabe*. Literally this means "the investigation in the room," which is carrying on koan study under your master. To practice zazen alone is so difficult that it is almost impossible. Most students who do so go wrong. For effective zazen, it is very important to practice sitting with a group, at least occasionally, if you want to get results.

The true practice of zazen is very severe. The present koan is a good example of this. To attain kensho (self-realization) is not so difficult; for some people only one *sesshin* (Zen retreat) is sufficient. But kensho is only the entrance to our final goal in doing zazen, namely the accomplishment of our character. This involves a purification which is most difficult and requires a great deal of time. There is really no end to the practice of Zen. You cannot accomplish a perfect character in forty years. Practicing a million years is still insufficient.

The sutras are very clear in saying that it took Amida and Shakyamuni thousands of millions of kalpas to become Buddhas. As I told you before, a kalpa is an almost immeasurably long period of time. What does this inconceivably long period of time tell us? It says that from one point of view, our essential nature can be polished endlessly, and from another point of view, the stains and layers of dirt which have accumulated on our essential nature are immeasurably thick.

In the *Sange-mon*, the purification verse recited every morning in Zen practice, it is said: "From time immemorial, I have created all evil karma; this is on account of my beginningless greed, anger, and folly, which are born of my body, mouth, and thought." As I have so often told you, our dualistic ego is to blame for this. The origin of evil karma is fundamentally the discriminating consciousness of subject and object, you and me, which is no other than the dualistic ego.

Returning to the koan, it is said that the emperor not only greeted and said good-bye to Echū personally but such was his esteem for Echū that he always pushed his teacher's cart. The T'ang dynasty was an era of eminent Zen masters, and among them, national teacher Echū was conspicuously great. Everyone studying Zen at that time made great efforts to go to him for instruction at least once in their lives. The number of his disciples must have been staggering, but he is said to have left only one Dharma successor, Tangen, who is thought to be the attendant in this koan. Echū must have been a severe teacher indeed!

> The national teacher called, "Attendant!"
> The attendant answered, "Yes!"
> "Attendant!" "Yes!" "Attendant!" "Yes!"

After the third time, the national teacher said, "I thought I was standing alone with my back to you, but now I find that you are standing alone with your back to me!" The national teacher is showing that everything is independent and alone, in and with the whole universe. He means, "I thought I was standing alone in the whole universe with you lost behind me, but now I find that you are standing alone in the whole universe and that I am lost behind you." With this the national teacher is recognizing the attendant's realization of the essential world.

When the national teacher calls, "Attendant!" his calling is the essential nature itself appearing in full view on the surface; there is nothing in the whole universe but the calling. The attendant cannot appear on the surface. He is concealing himself behind the national teacher's shadow. Therefore, the national teacher says, "I am standing alone in the whole universe with you lost behind me."

In the same way, when the attendant responds, "Yes!" it is his essential nature itself appearing on the surface; there is nothing but "Yes!" in the whole universe. The national teacher is concealing himself behind the back of the attendant. So the national teacher says, "I find that you are standing alone in the whole universe and that I am lost behind you."

The national teacher recognized that the attendant had realized the world of the essential nature, so what he was really saying was, "I recognize that you have realized you are standing alone in the whole universe, just as I am." This is Echū's confirmation of the attendant's enlightenment. When one thing or person manifests itself on the stage, there can be nothing else. Everything and every person is completely solitary.

ON MUMON'S COMMENTARY

"The national teacher called three times and his tongue dropped to the ground. The attendant responded three times, emitting the answer with light. The national teacher was old and lonely. He held the cow's head and forced it to eat grass. The attendant would have none of it; delicious food has little attraction for a man who has had enough to eat. Just tell me, where are they standing alone with their backs to each other? When the country is prosperous, persons of talent are esteemed; children of rich families are too proud to eat plain food."

"The national teacher called three times and his tongue dropped to the ground. The attendant responded three times, emitting the answer with light." "His tongue dropped to the ground" means he spoke too much. The national teacher called the attendant three times, but one time would have been enough. Why was it necessary to call three times? He moved his tongue superfluously. The national teacher was far too solicitous. By answering "Yes," the attendant allowed the light of his essential nature to shine forth.

"The national teacher was old and lonely. He held the cow's head and forced it to eat grass." The national teacher is old and feeling alone and wants to make the attendant realize his essential nature more clearly, so he calls him three times. It is just like a herdsman forcing grass down a cow's throat.

"The attendant would have none of it; delicious food has little attraction for a man who has had enough to eat." The attendant has attained the deepest enlightenment and does not want anything else, so he simply responds, "Yes!" It is like a person who has eaten his fill and has no appetite for dessert.

"When the country is prosperous, persons of talent are esteemed."
When a country is in the midst of peril, a brave hero is longed for, but
when peace prevails, it is the intellectually gifted who are highly esteemed, and such people have no interest in doing trifling work.

"Children of rich families are too proud" means that children of rich
families are too used to luxuries to take pleasure in common things such
as plain food or cheap toys. Both this passage and the previous one refer
to the attendant, who is wholly satisfied with his own being.

ON THE VERSE

We must carry an iron yoke with no hole,
It is not a slight matter, the curse is passed on
    to our descendants;
If you want to support the gate and sustain the house,
You must climb a mountain of swords with bare feet.

This verse is telling us that it is a tremendous task to support true Buddhism. The iron yoke with no hole means an unbearable burden. The
gate is the gate of Buddhism, the true way of Buddha, and the house is, of
course, the house of Buddhism. Mumon is telling us that supporting this
decaying house is just like carrying an iron yoke without a hole, or climbing barefoot a mountain covered with protruding blades. Our descendants will never have peace or rest, bearing forever the heavy burden they
inherit.

Tōzan's Masagin

18

THE CASE

A monk asked Master Tōzan in all earnestness, "What is Buddha?"
Tōzan said, "*Masagin!* (Three pounds of flax!)"

MUMON'S COMMENTARY

Old Tōzan realized a bit of clam Zen. Slightly opening the two halves of the shell, he exposed his liver and intestines. This may be so, but tell me, where do you see Tōzan?

THE VERSE

Masagin *juts forth!*
Words are intimate and the mind is even more intimate.
He who speaks about right and wrong
Is a man of right and wrong.

TEISHŌ ON THE CASE

The Tōzan in this case is Tōzan Shusho, who was a Dharma successor of Unmon. We met him in Case 15.

A monk asked, "What is Buddha?"

If we try to answer this question by means of an explanation, we would have to say a great many things indeed. But for the moment, let us take this Buddha to be the Buddha mind, our essential nature or our primal face before our parents were born. It is the Buddha Hakuin Zenji speaks about when he says, "All living beings by nature are Buddha."

Without true enlightenment, we cannot meet our own inner Buddha. Even though we remain unenlightened, however, if we have no lump of ego, our mind will naturally harmonize with the Buddha mind.

By this I mean that if our consciousness is not dualistic and discriminating, we will be able to do things smoothly and naturally, like a fish swimming in water or a bird flying in the sky. At such times, we are not far from Buddha himself. If even a little dualistic consciousness appears, however, our peace of mind is broken.

Now, the monk in this case, though we can suppose that he has some belief in his inner Buddha, has not yet realized it clearly, so he asks Tōzan, "What is Buddha?" Tōzan says, "*Masagin!*"

In Japanese *masagin* means three pounds of flax. Literally, it means three *kins* of *ma*. *Ma* is flax, *sa* is three, and a *kin* (or *gin*) is a measure of weight, so we translate *masagin* as three pounds of flax. But what does three pounds of flax have to do with Buddha? Where is the connection?

Just cry out, "*Masagin!*" At that moment, is there anything but "Masagin"? As a matter of fact, just the first syllable "ma" is enough, or "sa" or "gin," or even more simply just "n." Whatever you say, it is just that. Nothing else. When you say "ma," what else is there? When there is nothing else, "ma" is Mu, and it is the perfect manifestation of the whole universe. The whole universe is occupied by "ma," and nothing remains outside of it.

This is the same as the "Whack!" in Case 67 of the *Blue Cliff Record*. In that koan, Fudaishi ascended the platform and sat down to explain the *Diamond Sutra*. Then he hit the stand with a resounding whack— *Ka-chin!* as we say in Japanese—and came down from the platform. He had finished the lecture on the sutra.

As I said before, another name for *masagin* is Mu. When you open the enlightened eye, you will realize at once that *masagin* is nothing other than the one who is standing up, sitting down, eating meals, reciting sutras, sleeping, crying, and so on. Really, *masagin* is another name for your essential nature right here and now.

Some commentators say that when the monk came to Tōzan, he was weighing out flax, so that when he was asked, "What is Buddha?" he replied, "Three pounds of flax." It does not matter whether that was the case or not, but if we think that Tōzan is telling us that Buddha is three pounds of flax or that three pounds of flax is Buddha, Buddha is lost entirely. For neither *masagin* nor *ma* nor *sa* nor *gin* have anything to do with the weight of flax.

How great and wonderful is *masagin!* But its secret will remain hidden if you try to penetrate it with thoughts or meanings. Only the truly enlightened eye can discern its greatness.

ON MUMON'S COMMENTARY

"Old Tōzan realized a bit of clam Zen. Slightly opening the two halves of the shell, he exposed his liver and intestines. This may be so, but tell me, where do you see Tōzan?"

This means that when Tōzan opens his lips and cries "*Masagin!*", he exposes his whole being, his essential nature. With "*Masagin!*" he is presenting all the Dharmas of all Buddhas. Is that not the perfect presentation of the whole?" "Aha!" This, too, can be the perfect exposition of our essential nature. Where do you see Tōzan? Here! *Masagin!* Whack!

ON THE VERSE

Masagin *juts forth!*
Words are intimate and the mind is even more intimate.
He who speaks about right and wrong
Is a man of right and wrong.

Masagin! Whack! That's it! There is no front and back, upper and lower. It just juts forth—*Masagin!*

"Words are intimate and the mind is even more intimate." Intimate means, "That's it." *Masagin!* That's it. Whack! That's it. The words "even more" are only rhetorical. There is no me outside of *masagin*, and there is no *masagin* outside of me. Just One, without subject or object, without awareness of anything.

"He who speaks about right and wrong is a man of right and wrong." Speaking about the yes or no of *masagin* has nothing whatsoever to do with it. *Masagin* is a fact, not a concept. You should never give any meaning to *masagin* or you will instantly deprive it of its life. And the life of *masagin* is the true life of Buddha, the true life of our essential nature. There was an old Zen master who said that even the word Buddha is a stain on the clean ground of mind.

What is Buddha? *Masagin! Masagin* is *masagin.* You are you. When you realize that, you will meet your true self face-to-face. That is enlightenment. That is what "intimate" means.

Tōzan thrusts forth the real Buddha in front of you as *masagin.* If you want to realize *masagin* absolutely, work on *masagin* just as you work on Mu. If you keep working on *masagin* as though your very life depended on it, suddenly your true inner life will spring forth. That is *masagin!* The fact is self-evident. If a person argues and searches for something more than the fact, he is a man of dualistic concepts. He will never grasp the fact.

Ordinary Mind Is the Way

19

THE CASE

Jōshū earnestly asked Nansen, "What is the Way?" Nansen answered, "The ordinary mind is the Way." Jōshū asked, "Should I direct myself toward it or not?" Nansen said, "If you try to turn toward it, you go against it." Jōshū asked, "If I do not try to turn toward it, how can I know that it is the Way?" Nansen answered, "The Way does not belong to knowing or not-knowing. Knowing is delusion; not-knowing is a blank consciousness. When you have really reached the true Way beyond all doubt, you will find it as vast and boundless as the great empty firmament. How can it be talked about on a level of right and wrong?" At these words, Jōshū was suddenly enlightened.

MUMON'S COMMENTARY

Nansen was asked a question by Jōshū, and Nansen's base was shattered and melted away. He could not justify himself. Even though Jōshū has come to realization, he will have to delve into it for another thirty years before he can realize it fully.

THE VERSE

The spring flowers, the moon in autumn,
The cool breezes of summer, the winter's snow;

If idle concerns do not cloud the mind,
This is man's happiest season.

TEISHŌ ON THE CASE

Like Case 14, this koan is a mondo, or question and answer, between Master Nansen and his disciple Jōshū. Both of these men attained their first enlightenment at the age of eighteen and spent their subsequent years deepening their realization. When Nansen was fifty, his practice reached its peak in the stage of great enlightenment called in Japanese *daigo tettei*. Jōshū entered the priesthood while still young. It is presumed he penetrated the depth of his essential nature, as seen in this koan, sometime after his fiftieth year.

The subject of this mondo is the Chinese character *tao*, which in Japanese has two meanings, *michi* and *dō*. Both mean "way"; but for the way of everyday life, *michi* is used. It is the relative way and sometimes means a road or a method or a means. It is the way of everyone and everything, a thief, a king, a rat, or a truck.

The other meaning, *dō*, is used to refer to the absolute Way. It is another name for Dharma. It is the Chinese Tao and *dō* in the Japanese arts. I am sure you all know about *ken-dō*, the way of swordsmanship; *kyu-dō*, the way of archery; *sho-dō*, the way of calligraphy; *sa-dō*, the way of tea; *ka-dō*, the way of flowers; and *ju-dō* and *aiki-dō*, which are popular in the West now. All of these *dō* or ways have a factor in common with Zen—concentration of mind, being absorbed within oneself. Just recall the fraction I mentioned earlier. As you will remember, the denominator is the zero-infinite. The numerator is anything in the phenomenal world. The denominator is *dō*, the absolute Way, so every numerator, which is over the denominator, also turns out to be the Way.

Of course, Jōshū was well aware of this fact because he had experienced realization many times. Still, his mind was not sufficiently at peace. There was a trace of uneasiness in his heart. So humbly he went to his teacher Nansen and asked with great sincerity, "What is the Way?"

"The ordinary mind is the Way," his master told him.

Ordinary mind, what is that? It is nothing but our ordinary consciousness, our ordinary everyday life. It is just getting up, washing your face, eating breakfast, going to work, walking, running, laughing, crying; the leaves on the trees, the flowers in the field, whether white, red, or purple; it is birth, it is death. That is the Way. We do not even have to use the word "mind." The ordinary is the Way!

For those who are practicing Mu, Mu is the Way. Mu is the ordinary mind. Again, everything you do, that is the Way, that is Mu. When you get up, that is the Way, that is Mu. Until you have realized it definitively by experience, however, you will be unable to make heads or tails out of these words. It seems that Jōshū was no exception, so he asked again. "Should I direct myself toward the Way, or not?" Where will I look for it?

Nansen answered, "If you try to turn toward it, you go against it." Which means: the more you seek it, the more it will elude you. If you hunt for it, you will never find it. If you do not search for it, but truly identify yourself with one thing—it could be Mu, or perhaps *masagin,* or the famous sound of one hand—you are in accordance with the Way. This is so, even if you are as yet unenlightened. That is why I am always urging you, "Just do Mu. Become one with Mu. Melt yourself into Mu. Let yourself be absorbed in Mu."

When you are truly one with something, you are one with yourself, and the time will necessarily come when you will realize your own self nature.

We find Dōgen Zenji giving us this teaching in his *Fukan zazengi (Universal Recommendation of Zazen).* He says, "Stop the activities of mind-consciousness. Stop thinking in concepts and ideas, and cease desiring to become Buddha."

Back to the koan. We find Jōshū still asking, "If I do not try to turn toward it, how can I know that it is the Way?" I am sure all Zen practitioners can understand the anguish behind this question. There seems to be nothing unreasonable in the question.

Nansen tells him, "The Way does not belong to knowing or not-knowing. Knowing is delusion. Not-knowing is a blank consciousness." The supreme Way is an absolute fact that transcends knowing and intellection. The absolute fact cannot be calculated, cannot be measured relatively, nor can it be gained after birth. Not-knowing means total ignorance and stupidity, which, of course, has nothing to do with Zen or enlightenment.

Nansen goes on to say, "If you have really reached the true Way beyond all doubt, you will find it as vast and boundless as the great empty firmament. How can it be talked about on the level of right and wrong!"

Even after experiencing several enlightenments, Jōshū still had traces of mist. Then suddenly, at Nansen's words, he attained perfect enlightenment. All vestiges of doubt were finally swept away.

Until we realize the Way by satori, we cannot help but be agonized by our own delusions. It is like binding ourselves with rope. To free ourselves from the agonies of the dualistic world, we must forget ourselves in samadhi at least once in our lives. The famous Chinese sage Confucius said:

> *The Way is at hand, but people are looking for it afar;*
> *Farmers are using it every day without being aware of it.*
> *We cannot be separated from the Way even for an instant;*
> *What we can be separated from is not the Way.*

In this respect, the Way in Confucianism seems to have something in common with the Way in Buddhism.

ON MUMON'S COMMENTARY

"Nansen was asked a question by Jōshū, and Nansen's base was shattered and melted away. He could not justify himself. Even though Jōshū has come to realization, he will have to delve into it for another thirty years before he can realize it fully."

Nansen's essential position was shattered by Jōshū's question. That is because Nansen could not answer any question without leaving his essential ground, which is the state of absolute emptiness, and entering the phenomenal world of dualistic opposition. One must leave the essential world, the world of Mu, when one wants to teach or instruct others.

"Even though Jōshū has come to realization, he will have to pursue his study for another thirty years before he can realize it fully." Mumon seems to be looking down on Jōshū contemptuously, but this is not so. Mumon is speaking freely from his standpoint as a critic, who must always look at everything from the highest point of view.

ON THE VERSE

The spring flowers, the moon in autumn,
The cool breezes of summer, the winter's snow;
If idle concerns do not cloud the mind,
This is man's happiest season.

We have various delights in the four seasons. What more do we want?

"If idle concerns do not cloud the mind" means that when we are detached from all useless matters such as delusive and discriminating feelings or thoughts, our mind is at peace. Then every day is truly good. We then enjoy each day as the happiest day of our lives.

A Man
of Great Strength

20

THE CASE

Master Shōgen said, "Why is it that a man of great strength does not lift up his leg?" He also said, "It is not with the tongue that we speak."

MUMON'S COMMENTARY

It should be said that Shōgen poured out all that he had in his intestines and belly. But there is nobody who can recognize this. However, even someone who realized this immediately would be given a bitter blow by me. Why? Look! If you want to know whether it is pure gold or not, you must look at it in the midst of fire.

THE VERSE

Raising a leg, I upturn the Scented Ocean;
Lowering my head, I look down on the four dhyana heavens.
There is no place to put this whole body,
Please finish this poem in your own words.

TEISHŌ ON THE CASE

Master Shōgen Sūgaku is in the descending line of Rinzai. He is closely associated with Japan because his great-grandchild in the Dharma, Daiō

Kokushi, brought the Rinzai sect to Japan. Many of you probably know that Daiō is the founder of Daitoku-ji Temple in Kyōtō.

Shōgen received the Dharma successor's robe from his teacher, Master Mitsuan Kanketsu. This robe is the external proof of orthodox succession. When Shōgen grew old and the time came for him to choose a Dharma successor, he made up three phrases with which to examine his disciples. Eventually these phrases became quite famous and are known as "Shōgen's Three Turning Words". In this case we have the first two:

(a) Why is it that a man of great strength does not lift up his leg?

(b) It is not with the tongue that we speak.

The third, although we will not consider it here, is:

(c) Why is it that the crimson lines of a clearly enlightened person never cease to flow?

These are called "turning words" because they have the power to turn one's delusions into realization. Shōgen examined all his disciples with these three turning words, but not one could pass the test. He put the robe away and died without a successor. Thirty or forty years later a Zen master by the name of Sekkei was ordered by the emperor to go to Shōgen's monastery. Having been chosen as worthy, he got the robe out of its case and showed it to the assembled monks. Thus Sekkei succeeded Shōgen.

Now for the koan. When we think of a man of great strength, we picture a Japanese *sumō* wrestler or a world champion heavyweight boxer. Surely the wrestler or boxer would be able to lift up his own leg. So what does Shōgen mean when he says that a man of great strength does not or cannot lift up his leg? It seems strange, even irrational, to our ordinary common sense.

If you take the man of great strength to be a man of great enlightenment, as Harada Roshi and Yasutani Roshi do, it will not be too difficult to understand this koan. As you know, a deeply enlightened person is one who has extinguished all delusions and all the concepts and feelings that arise from the dualistic opposition of you and me, subject and object. That person is not aware of himself when he does something. When he eats, he just eats and is not conscious that he is eating. When he walks, he just walks. He has no awareness of his legs.

But, you may say, it is the same for any ordinary healthy person who is not conscious of his legs when he walks. He just puts one foot ahead of the other again and again, without any awareness of his legs or of walking. Then there is the man whose legs pain him when he walks; he is fully aware of his legs when he is using them. Now I ask you, is there any difference between a person who is unaware of his legs and a person who is keenly aware of his painful legs?

As I have told you many times, every koan must be viewed from the point of view of our essential nature, which is the world of Mu. In Mu, in the essential nature, there is neither Buddha nor ordinary people. If, therefore, it is true that a deeply enlightened person or a person in perfect health does not lift up his leg, then it must be the same not only for ordinary people but also for people whose legs pain them. We must realize that from the essential point of view, no one lifts up his legs when he stands up or walks. If you know what the essential nature is, at least intellectually, you will not find it too difficult to understand what the present koan means.

Shōgen goes on to say, "It is not with the tongue that we speak." This means that when we speak we do not move the tip of our tongue. Just as we do not lift our leg, so we do not move our tongue. When speech flows, we are not aware that we are speaking, nor are we aware that our tongue is moving. Our essential nature does not move an iota, and this is true even in the case of the stutterer who is most painfully aware of his tongue in his stammering.

ON MUMON'S COMMENTARY

"It should be said that Shōgen poured out all that he had in his intestines and belly. But there is nobody who can recognize this. However, even someone who realized this immediately would be given a bitter blow by me. Why? Look! If you want to know whether it is pure gold or not, you must look at it in the midst of fire."

"Shōgen poured out all that he had in his intestines and belly." By this, Mumon means that Shōgen revealed the whole Dharma—all his essential world—when he said that a man of great strength does not lift his leg. This was accomplished by long and severe Zen practice.

In the remainder of his commentary, Mumon says there might be someone who would dare to come before him and say, "I have realized it completely." But Mumon would not approve of him; he would hit him. Why? Take a look! If *you* were standing in front of Mumon, he would point at you and say, "There you are, holding concepts like that!"

ON THE VERSE

Raising a leg, I upturn the Scented Ocean;
Lowering my head, I look down on the four dhyana heavens.
There is no place to put this whole body,
Please finish this poem in your own words.

According to Indian cosmology, the Scented Ocean surrounds Mount Sumeru in the center of the universe. Above Mount Sumeru there are three kinds of world: the world of desire, the world of form, and the world of no form. In the world of form there are four dhyana heavens, and Mumon refers to the four collectively. More precisely, the world of form represents the whole universe.

Mumon means that our whole being, that is, our essential nature, is as vast as the universe, and its strength is truly boundless. When you lift a leg, the whole universe is turned upside down. When you lower your head, you cover the whole universe. Nothing remains outside of you. The action of kicking is the whole universe. Nothing remains outside of it. When you lower your head, that action is the only one universe; nothing remains outside of you. Your being is so vast there is nowhere to put it! Now please finish the last part about your essential nature yourself. Do you have any ideas?

Unmon's Kanshiketsu

21

THE CASE

A monk asked Unmon in all earnestness, "What is Buddha?" Unmon said, "*Kanshiketsu!* (a dried shit-stick)"

MUMON'S COMMENTARY

It should be said of Unmon that he was too poor to prepare even the plainest food and too busy to write a draft. Suddenly he took up the shit-stick to support the gate (of Buddhism). You can see how the Dharma has decayed.

THE VERSE

Lightning flashing,
Sparks shooting from a flint;
A moment's blinking—
It's already missed.

TEISHŌ ON THE CASE

This koan is very simple. There is nothing complicated about it. It is an example of Unmon's terse and pithy mondo. Intellectuals may be perplexed by its simplicity. As a koan, it resembles Case 18, "Tōzan's Masagin." Here we have Unmon's *kanshiketsu*. *Kanshiketsu*, so simple and naked, but if you are doing your zazen in perfect absorption, upon hearing this question and answer you can attain realization in an instant.

You met Unmon in Cases 15 and 16 and learned about the strict way he was guided and how later he directed his own disciples in the same manner. I also told you about the Unmon sect being one of the five Zen sects. At this point I would like to say a little more about this.

The founders' individual characteristics gave each Zen sect its own distinctive features. For example, the characteristic of the Sōtō sect is careful and meticulous practice. From olden times there has been a saying "Sōtō, the farmer." This refers to Sōtō's stress on detail in training and practice, like the farmer who cultivates plants with minute attention and care.

The characteristic of the Rinzai sect is its sharpness and commanding air. The saying about this sect is, "Rinzai, the general." The imposing and commanding air of the Rinzai sect comes from Master Rinzai himself, who is often compared to a majestic general riding on horseback.

The expression used to describe the characteristic of the Unmon sect is "a red flag fluttering in the distance [on top of a far mountain]." It can be seen clearly from a great distance, but is very difficult to reach. Unmon is the skillful and superb master of words—often, as in this koan, using just one. The words and phrases in his Dharma combat are extremely subtle and of appealing excellence. There is an old saying that each one of Unmon's phrases contains three. I would like to explain this to you.

A Zen master has said that there are three kinds of Zen phrase. The first is typified by the phrase "The box and its lid." If the box and its lid are made by a fine craftsman, they fit tightly and well. Not even a drop of water can get in. In just such a way, a good Zen master's words will match the student's inquiries. They fit like a glove on a hand. The second is typified by the phrase "Cutting off all delusions." This means that a good Zen master's words have the power to cut off the student's delusions and dualistic concepts like the sharpest sword. Although the majority of students are unable to recognize the fact, all koans have the power to cut off delusions so that students can attain the enlightened eye. Even though their heads have already been cut off by the master's words, most students do not realize that their lives have been lost. The third phrase is "Waves following waves." Standing on the beach, you can see how closely and faithfully the waves follow each other. In Japan, high waves are referred to as male and low ones as female. They pursue each other incessantly. In the same way, the words of a great Zen master will always follow the individual degree of consciousness of the students. He can thus give most suitable guidance to all. It is said that one phrase of Unmon's teaches in all three ways.

In the present koan a monk asked Unmon, "What is Buddha?" And Unmon answered, "*Kanshiketsu!*" Do you see how that answer fulfills the requirements of the three phrases mentioned above? First of all, it fits the question very snugly. Second, *kanshiketsu* has the power to cut off all conceptual thoughts. Third, the answer must have fitted the degree of consciousness of the monk.

Kanshiketsu! A dried shit-stick! In the secular world, a dried shit-stick is a dirty thing. It seems to have been used instead of toilet paper in ancient China. No one would ever bring it into the living room! But Unmon's *kanshiketsu* isn't dirty. Neither is it discolored or smelly. Someone has said, "As this monk is attached to the conceptual holiness of Buddha, Unmon takes up the shit-stick to deprive him of the concept." *Kanshiketsu* has no odor, no concept, no ideas attached to it. It is Mu! It is Whack! It is *masagin.*

Is *kanshiketsu* the same as *masagin?* Is *kanshiketsu* the same as our essential nature? Is there any difference? You must scrutinize this yourself, even if it takes you thirty years. Then one day you will realize that *kanshiketsu* is nothing other than the whole universe! This will bring you the greatest peace of mind. But to tell you the truth, all this has nothing in particular to do with *kanshiketsu.* Just "ka" is enough, or even only "n." Just cry "ka" with your whole being and you will see that there is nothing but "ka" in the whole universe. Nothing remains outside of it. It is your essential nature; it is the whole universe, and you must come to this realization by living experience.

ON MUMON'S COMMENTARY

"It should be said of Unmon that he was too poor to prepare even the plainest food and too busy to write a draft. Suddenly he took up the shit-stick to support the gate (of Buddhism). You can see how the Dharma has decayed."

Poor! Poverty is the best and most important condition for the practice of zazen. Possessions, both material and spiritual, are rebels that obscure our essential nature. Material possessions, moveable and immoveable, and spiritual possessions like our beliefs, thoughts, and knowledge are kinds of property that are apt to become hindrances to attaining enlightenment. That is why I say that poverty is the best condition for practicing zazen. But on the other hand, if we do not rely on these things, they will not hinder us but will become useful after enlightenment, especially when we want to serve others.

Unmon has eliminated all kinds of possessions and become totally poor. He has no concepts, no philosophies, no ideas, nothing at all. In his world there is not even a speck of a cloud. Mumon therefore says he has not prepared even the plainest food to eat, which means Unmon has not prepared answers to the question. Moreover, he is too busy to write a draft properly. So, as a temporary expedient, he randomly takes up the shit-stick and thrusts it out: "*Kanshiketsu!*"

"You can see how the Dharma has decayed." This is a cynical expression. From the essential point of view, however, everything is perfect and complete as it is. What is there for us to do? Thrusting out a shit-stick must be nothing but the deterioration of Buddhism.

ON THE VERSE

Lightning flashing,
Sparks shooting from a flint;
A moment's blinking—
It's already missed.

Kanshiketsu! This one voice is just like a flash of lightning or sparks from an iron flint. It disappears in an instant. If you try to see it or try to think about it even for a brief period, it passes away. You can't grasp it. If you want to realize it—*kanshiketsu!* That's it!

Kashyapa's Flagpole

22

THE CASE

Ananda asked Kashyapa in all earnestness, "The World-Honored One transmitted the brocade robe to you. What else did he transmit to you?" Kashyapa called, "Ananda!" Ananda replied, "Yes, Master." Kashyapa said, "Knock down the flagpole at the gate."

MUMON'S COMMENTARY

If you can give a turning word befitting this, you will see that the meeting at Mount Grdhrakūta is definitely still in session. If not, it is because Vipashyin Buddha has been keeping something in mind from the remotest times, and even now he still cannot attain the mystery.

THE VERSE

The answer is more familiar than the question;
How many discuss this with glaring eyes!
Elder brother calls, younger brother answers—the family disgrace!
Here is the spring that belongs to neither yin nor yang.

TEISHŌ ON THE CASE

Kashyapa is the Mahakashyapa who appears in Case 6. It is said that when he was born, the room was filled with golden light, all of which streamed into the baby's mouth. He received the name Kashyapa, which means to swallow light, and later became one of the richest men in India. He was older than Shakyamuni Buddha and, as a venerable Brahman, had many disciples around him. Kashyapa opposed Shakyamuni's early teaching because it differed from traditional Brahmanism, but he eventually acquiesced and became so ardent a disciple that Shakyamuni chose him as his Dharma successor (see Case 6). It is said that Kashyapa dressed so poorly and looked so thin that some of his disciples found him despicable. Whenever he preached, Shakyamuni Buddha had him share his seat.

Ananda, Shakyamuni's cousin, is said to have been born on the night Buddha attained his great enlightenment. He grew into a handsome and popular young man and therefore had many trials to suffer because of women. Shakyamuni often helped his young disciple with this problem. Ananda became his favorite disciple and served the master for twenty years as his attendant.

Ananda was highly intelligent and had an extraordinary memory. Not only was he able to quote from memory all the sermons he had heard Shakyamuni give, but by some mysterious ability he was also able to quote the first sermon Shakyamuni gave after his enlightenment. Ananda would have been a newborn baby at the time this sermon was delivered. After Shakyamuni's death, 500 enlightened disciples held an assembly at Vaibhāra to compile all the Master's sermons. Ananda's presence was earnestly desired because he could remember them all, but since he was not as yet enlightened, he was unqualified. For one desperate week he engaged in energetic practice and attained self-realization. Kashyapa examined him by commanding, "If you are enlightened, come into the cave through the keyhole." Ananda did so (but I do not know how!) and joined the meeting.

Ananda recited all the sermons for the assembly, and those present agreed that they were exactly as the master had uttered them. It is for this reason that most of the sutras begin with "Thus I have heard . . ." This is a good example of what I was telling you before: possessions such as intelligence and a good memory are powerless in your practice. But if you do not depend on them, they will not work against you. Indeed, they could be helpful to others.

After attaining realization, Ananda continued his practice under Kashyapa for twenty years, believing that his own enlightenment and those of the Buddhas and patriarchs were all the same. But gradually he began to

doubt and wondered if there were something else besides his own experience. Therefore he asked Kashyapa, "Did the World-Honored One transmit anything besides the brocade robe to you?"

Calling it brocade is an expression of respect for the robe. Actually it
was made of coarse cloth. It is the Buddhist surplice, material testimony
that the true Dharma had passed from Shakyamuni to Kashyapa. I suggest you reread the account of this in Case 6.

Kashyapa replied to Ananda's question by calling out, "Ananda!"
Ananda replied, "Yes, Master!" That's all. Everything is complete. Nothing remains outside the call and the reply. "Ananda!" That call is the only
one in the whole universe. It is one with the universe. "Yes, Master!" That
reply is the perfect manifestation of the whole. Every one of us should be
able to attain realization upon hearing it. When Kashyapa called Ananda,
there was not a speck of delusion. When Ananda replied, the whole
universe was totally used up by the one voice. Nothing remained outside of it.

Kashyapa said, "Knock down the flagpole at the gate." A flag was
raised on the pole at the gate when a sermon was being preached or when
Dharma combat was in progress. Kashyapa's command could mean that
the mondo is over; nothing remains, so the flagpole is unnecessary. Knock
it down. Or you may take it to mean that the flagpole stands for all
thoughts, concepts, and philosophies. Kashyapa noticed that Ananda still
harbored some concepts and commanded him to get rid of them. It is said
that Ananda instantly attained deep realization.

Every one of us calls and replies in our daily life. But almost none of
us can realize the true meaning of this. If there had been no delusions,
Ananda should have attained perfect realization the instant he heard the
call and gave the reply. But he did not. Kashyapa then gave him a last
blow: "Knock down the flagpole!" With that blow, Ananda knocked out
all remaining concepts and came to the realization that he is Buddha himself from the very beginning, standing empty and alone in the whole
universe.

ON MUMON'S COMMENTARY

"If you can give a turning word befitting this, you will see that the meeting at Mount Grdhrakūta is definitely still in session. If not, it is because

Vipashyin Buddha has been keeping something in mind from the remotest times, and even now he still cannot attain the mystery."

"If you can give a turning word befitting this" means that if you truly realize the call and reply, you will be able to say something to make the other realize the essential world.

"You will see that the meeting at Mount Gṛdhrakūta is definitely still in session" means that you will realize that your essential nature still exists as it did in Shakyamuni Buddha's time—that is, from the eternal past.

"If not, it is because Vipashyin Buddha has been keeping something in mind from the remotest times, and even now he still cannot attain the mystery." It is said that there are six Buddhas who preceded Shakyamuni: (1) Vipashyin Buddha, (2) Sikhin Buddha, (3) Vishvabhu Buddha, (4) Krakucchanda Buddha, (5) Kanakamuni Buddha, and (6) Kashyapa Buddha. What Mumon is saying is that even the first Buddha, which is none other than our essential nature, if he has a speck of a concept, will never become enlightened. Even the smallest particle of thought will become your ego and cause you to fall into hell.

ON THE VERSE

The answer is more familiar than the question;
How many discuss this with glaring eyes!
Elder brother calls, younger brother answers—the family disgrace!
Here is the spring that belongs to neither yin nor yang.

"The answer is more familiar than the question," but if you see with enlightened eyes, what difference is there between the call and reply? "Ananda!" "Yes, Master!" That's it! Neither has any color. Emptiness has no color whatsoever.

"Elder brother calls, younger brother answers—the family disgrace." Kashyapa's call and Ananda's reply are both, from Mumon's point of view, useless and unnecessary. By calling and replying, they are raising unnatural waves on the tranquil and peaceful water. To transmit enlightenment by calling and replying is not only useless but stinking. Isn't it the shame of the Buddhist family? As you know, we are intrinsically Buddha. We are doing that (calling and replying) every day from morning till night, without any nasty smell of Zen or satori.

"Here is the spring that belongs to neither yin nor yang." According to the Chinese philosophy, yin and yang are the feminine and masculine elements of the universe. What Mumon wants to say is, "Within me there is a spring which has nothing to do with seasons, time, and space." Such a spring is the everlasting spring, the spring of the essential world, which is beyond relativity. There we can enjoy the true spring, which is true peace of mind.

Think Neither Good
Nor Evil

23

THE CASE

The sixth patriarch was once pursued by the monk Myō as far as Mount Daiyu. The patriarch, seeing Myō coming, laid the robe and bowl on a rock and said, "This robe represents the faith. How can it be competed for by force? I will allow you to take it away."

Myō tried to lift it up, but it was as immovable as a mountain. Terrified and trembling with awe, he said, "I came for the Dharma, not the robe. I beg you, lay brother, please reveal it to me."

The patriarch said, "[At the very moment you were chasing after me] without thinking good or evil, what was the primal face of Monk Myō?" In that instant, Myō suddenly attained deep realization, and his whole body was covered with sweat. In tears, he bowed and said, "Besides the secret words and secret meaning you have just revealed to me, is there anything else deeper yet?"

The patriarch said, "What I have now preached to you is no secret at all. If you reflect on your own true face, the secret will be found within yourself."

Myō said, "Though I have been at Ōbai with the other monks, I have never realized what my true self is. Now, thanks to your instruction, I know it is like a man who drinks water and knows for himself whether it is cold or warm. Now you, lay brother, are my master." The patriarch said, "If that is the way you feel, let us both have Ōbai for our master. Be mindful and hold fast to what you have realized."

MUMON'S COMMENTARY

It should be said of the sixth patriarch that his action sprang from urgent circumstances. His kindness is like that of a grandmother who peels a fresh litchi, removes the seed, and puts it into your mouth so that all you have to do is swallow it.

THE VERSE

It can't be described! It can't be pictured!
It can't be sufficiently praised! Stop trying to grasp it with your head!
There is nowhere to hide the primal face;
Even when the world is destroyed, it is indestructible.

TEISHŌ ON THE CASE

The sixth patriarch, Daikan Enō, is the sixth Dharma successor of the Great Master Bodhidharma. Born in Shinshū in Canton Province in South China in the year 637, he died in 713 at the age of seventy-six. His family name was Ro and his given name Nō. The son of a local official who died while Nō was still a child, the boy lived with his mother in extreme poverty, gathering firewood on the mountainside to sell in town.

One day while visiting a certain house, Nō heard a sutra being chanted. Upon hearing the phrase, "Dwelling nowhere, Mind comes forth," he suddenly attained a deep realization. He asked the master of the house, "What is the sutra you are reciting?"

"This is the *Diamond Sutra*," the master answered.

Nō asked him, "Where did you learn it?"

"I learned it at the monastery of Zen Master Kōnin in Ōbai Prefecture," was the reply. Hearing this, Enō decided to go to Master Kōnin in Ōbai for the true Dharma of Buddhism.

But this meant that he would have to leave his mother alone, and at first he was reluctant to tell her. When he finally did, his mother, who had deep faith in Buddhism herself, encouraged him in his resolution. Fortunately, some of their neighbors promised to look after Enō's mother for him, and so he left for Ōbai.

The fifth patriarch asked him, "Where have you come from?"

"From Reinan (south of the mountain)," Enō answered.

"What did you come for?" the patriarch asked.

"To become Buddha," Enō told him.

"You cannot become Buddha because the people of Reinan have no Buddha nature." These words have a deep meaning, but for the time being we may take them as simply examining words by which the patriarch was trying to shake Enō.

But Enō was not bewildered, "Though there is south and north for man, how can there be a south and north for Buddha nature?"

The patriarch, having found some promise in this reply, purposely spoke roughly to him, "Go down and work in the rice-cleaning shed." Enō obediently did as he was told and stayed at that work for eight months.

At that time the patriarch was in the process of deciding who his Dharma successor would be. There were about 700 monks studying under him, and one day he addressed the assembly: "I think my life in this world will soon come to an end. Therefore, I wish to decide who my Dharma successor will be. If any of you are confident, come to my room and present me with what you have realized so far."

Now, among his disciples, the senior monk, Jinshū, was the most intelligent and an excellent scholar. Everyone, including Jinshū himself, thought that there was no one who could compete with him. Nevertheless, he did not have sufficient confidence to present the verse he composed expressing his state of realization to the master face-to-face. One book says he went to the master's door ten times but could not bring himself to knock. Finally, he wrote out the verse on a piece of paper and hung it in a corridor where the master frequently passed. The verse ran like this:

The body is the Bodhi-tree,[1]
The mind is like the stand of a clear mirror.
Wipe it clean from time to time,
Never let dust and rubbish adhere to it.

When the patriarch read this, he knew it was the work of Jinshū. The verse is very useful for directing Zen students who are aiming at enlightenment, but it is not the manifestation of the world of enlightenment. The patriarch did not express his true judgment, however, but simply said, "This verse is splendid. Anyone who conducts his practice according to this verse will make no mistake."

Enō, who was still working in the shed, heard about all this. He felt the verse was the expression of an unenlightened person and decided to compose his own, using Jinshū's metaphors. Since he was illiterate, Enō had to ask someone else to write it down for him. He then hung it in the corridor beside Jinshū's verse. Enō's verse said:

The Bodhi is intrinsically no tree;
Nor has the clear mirror any stand.
There is not one thing from the beginning,
Where can dust and rubbish adhere at all?

I think you can recognize immediately the difference between the two verses and the state of realization of the two men. In Japanese, we call Jinshū's point of view *shushōhen*, which means the ascending process of Zen practice aiming at the complete actualization of Buddha nature. Enō's point of view is called *hombunjō*, which means the essential nature of existence. From the very beginning, Jinshū was no match for Enō.

The patriarch saw the verse and, recognizing it as the work of the young rice-cleaner, decided to choose him as his Dharma successor. For some reason, though, he did not praise the verse publicly but pulled it down and tore it up, saying, "A foolish thing like this is useless." At midnight, however, he went to the rice shed and examined Enō with great severity. In the end, he admitted Enō's enlightenment and transmitted to him the great Dharma which he had received in a direct line of succession from Shakyamuni Buddha. As I said before, the symbol of this transmission was the golden robe. Along with it, he gave Enō the following advice: "Don't stay on this mountain. Hide yourself from society for at least ten years, nourishing the sacred seedling long and well. Otherwise great suffering will come to you as a result of others' jealousy. I will show you how to escape." And he guided Enō to the river, which they crossed by boat, the patriarch himself handling the oars.

The following morning the patriarch did not preach. When the attendant asked him why, the patriarch merely replied, "The Dharma has gone away." A great tumult followed this disclosure, and there was much speculation as to who had received the Dharma. When Enō's absence was eventually discovered, several of the monks took off immediately to catch him and retrieve the robe and the Dharma. The present koan begins here.

The monk in the koan is Myō, who was once a general. He pursued

Enō as far as Daiyu Mountain, where he caught up with him. When Enō saw Myō coming, he laid the robe on a rock and said, "This robe represents the faith. It should never be competed for by force. Take it away if you want to."

Myō tried to lift it up but could not. It was as heavy as a mountain. Terrified and trembling with awe, Myō said, "I came for the Dharma, not the robe. I beg you, lay brother, please reveal the Dharma to me."

Enō said to him, "In the very moment when you were running after me and trying to catch up with me, without any thought of good or bad, what was your primal face before your parents were born?" At that instant, Myō was seized by a deep enlightenment. His whole body was bathed in perspiration. With tears of gratitude flowing down his cheeks, he bowed to the new patriarch and said, "I have understood the secret words and the secret meaning you have just revealed to me. But tell me, is there anything else deeper still?"

As pieces of eggshell cling to a newborn chick, so delusive thoughts and feelings still clung to Myō. He still harbored doubts.

Now, the word "secret" has two meanings. One is "that which is hidden from us," and the other is "intimate." In Buddhism, "secret" means that which is most intimate to us. It is what is self-evident to us but which we cannot explain or teach to others. Nor can it be taught to us by others.

The patriarch said, "What I have told you is no secret at all. It is not hidden to anyone. If you reflect on your own face (your true self, your essential nature), the secret will be found within yourself." This means: Reflect upon your own self nature. There you will find the true secret, the true intimacy, the self-evidence of the inner self. It is being cold, being hot, being glad, being sad, being sorry, being hungry, being sleepy, getting up, walking, laughing, eating, drinking, etc. It is nothing but the activity of your true self. At this point, Myō shed all the remaining eggshell. He prostrated himself and said, "Though I've been under the fifth patriarch at Ōbai with the other monks, I have never seen my true face. But now, thanks to your instruction, I have realized my essential nature for the first time. It's just like a man who drinks water and knows for himself whether it is hot or cold. Now you are my teacher, please accept me as your disciple."

The patriarch replied, "If that is the way you feel, let us both have Ōbai for our master. Keep hold of what you have realized and nourish it well." This last part of the instruction is most important. After having attained enlightenment, we must cherish the Dharma and do our best to bring the sacred infant to maturity. This is the highest duty of a Zen student. And the way to do this is *shikantaza,* just sitting.

In obedience to his predecessor, the sixth patriarch hid himself for ten or fifteen years. We meet him again at Hosshōji in Kōshū, in Case 29. The once illiterate Enō became such a capable teacher that a compilation of his preachings was made, now called *The Rostrum Sutra.* No one else has been honored by having his preaching called sutra except, of course, Shakyamuni Buddha himself.

ON MUMON'S COMMENTARY

"It should be said of the sixth patriarch that his action sprang from urgent circumstances. His kindness is like that of a grandmother who peels a fresh litchi, removes the seed, and puts it into your mouth so that all you have to do is swallow it."

The sixth patriarch's wonderful skill in posing the question, "In the moment when you were thinking of neither good nor evil, what was Myō's primal face?" sprang from urgency. He has the kindness of a grandmother, who, in preparing her grandchild's meal, does everything but eat it for him.

ON THE VERSE

It can't be described! It can't be pictured!
It can't be sufficiently praised! Stop trying to grasp it with your head!
There is nowhere to hide the primal face;
Even when the world is destroyed, it is indestructible.

Our primal face cannot be painted by any artist, no matter how talented he may be. Nor can it be praised sufficiently by writers or poets, however great their ability. We cannot grasp our primal face by concepts or ideas, so stop thinking and pondering about it. The primal face is always and everywhere manifesting itself clearly and distinctly to us if we have the eye to see.

"Even when the earth is destroyed, it is indestructible." Of course, if you understand Mumon's words as a primal face apart from the universe, this will not be true. In this connection, I suggest you refer to Case 29 of the *Blue Cliff Record.* The case reads like this:

A monk asked Daizui, "In the great karmic fire, when everything perishes with the entire universe, will this perish or not perish?" Daizui said, "It will perish." The monk said, "If that is so, will I pass away with it?" Daizui said, "You will pass away with it."

Here there seems to be some contradiction between Mumon's last phrase and Daizui's confirmation. Which is true? Each of you should ponder this problem for yourself.

NOTE

1. "Bodhi" indicates the highest Way, although "Bodhi-tree" means a linden tree in the ordinary sense of the word.

Leaving Speech and Silence Behind

THE CASE

A monk asked Fuketsu in all earnestness, "Both speech and silence are concerned with *ri* and *mi*. How can we transcend them?" Fuketsu said, "I constantly think of Kōnan in March, where partridges are chirping among hundreds of fragrant blossoms."

MUMON'S COMMENTARY

Fuketsu's activity of mind is like lightning. He gains the road and immediately walks along. But why does he rest upon the tip of the ancient one's tongue and not cut it off? If you realize this deeply, a way will be found naturally. Just leave all words behind and say one phrase.

THE VERSE

Fuketsu does not speak in his usual style;
Before he says anything, it is already manifested.
If you go on chattering glibly,
You should be ashamed of yourself.

TEISHŌ ON THE CASE

Fuketsu Enshō Zenji is the fourth descendant of Rinzai Zenji. He was born in 896 and died in 973 at the age of seventy-eight. As a youth he studied the Confucian classics but failed the examination for public office. He then turned to Buddhism, first the Tendai sect and then Zen. His first teacher was Master Kyōsei, who was Seppō's disciple. He later studied under Nan'in and eventually became a great teacher in Rinzai Zen. This is his only appearance in the *Gateless Gate,* but he appears more frequently in the *Blue Cliff Record.*

The first line of the koan requires a bit of explanation. "Both speech and silence are concerned with *ri* and *mi*." The word *ri-mi* can be found in "Rimitaijōbon (Chapter of the Essential Purity of Ri-Mi)" in the *Hōzōron* (Treatise on the Jewel Treasury), ascribed to Sō Jō (Monk Jō). Jō was a fourth-century monk and one of the four great translators of the Buddhist scriptures under Kumarajiva, who died about 412, more than a hundred years before Bodhidharma came to China.

In the second chapter of the *Hōzōron,* Jō says, "To enter is *ri,* to come out is *mi.* When we enter *ri,* the dust of the outer world has no place to adhere. When we come out to *mi,* the inner mind has nothing to do with it." Literally, *ri* means separate and *mi* means minute or extremely subtle. These terms could be understood to mean that if we separate from the phenomenal world and enter into the inner world, that is called *ri.* When we come out of the inner world, that is called *mi.*

One way of thinking about *ri* and *mi* would be in terms of the denominator and numerator of the fraction I often refer to. Alternatively, it could simply be that *ri* means the subject or consciousness, and *mi* means the object or outer world. In either case, speech is of *mi,* the phenomenal world, and silence is of *ri,* separated from the phenomenal world.

At any rate, both speech and silence are connected with subject and object—in other words, with the dualistic world. The monk in this case knew that as long as we are confined to the world of dualistic concepts, we cannot free ourselves from the sufferings of the six evil realms.

It was in relation to all this that we find the monk asking Fuketsu, "How can we transcend *ri-mi,* the world of dualistic concepts?"

As I often bring to your attention, ordinary people think that subject and object are in opposition and that the objective world is standing before our consciousness as the completely different outer world. They suffer pain and agony because the outer world does not obey their will, and circumstances do not go as they wish. We should know that subject and object are intrinsically one. This is the most fundamental point of Buddhist teaching. It is the true satori of Zen. To intuit, experience, and realize this fact is the main reason for doing zazen.

If you realize clearly that subject and object are one, you may say either that there is only the subject in the whole universe without any object whatsoever or that there is only object without any subject. Taking the former stand would lead one to say, "In heaven above and earth below, there is only I, alone and sacred." The latter point of view would lead us to say, "No subject" or "No I (*muga*)." "Only I, alone and sacred" and "No I" are the same. People who have not experienced the absolute world of oneness are always perplexed in the dualistic world of subject and object, of *ri* and *mi*.

What do speech and silence mean here? Superficially, we all know that speech is speaking with our lips and tongue. If we think about it a bit more deeply, however, speech is the expression of thoughts and not only involves the mouth but also the eyes and gestures and actions as well. Thus we can speak in many ways. To put it even more comprehensively, when we have concepts or ideas, or images or pictures in our consciousness, that is speech. To have none of these is silence.

To our ordinary common sense, I suppose there is no other way to free ourselves from speech and silence than to die. But we are not considering death. It does not solve the problem. Incidentally, to commit suicide is one of the gravest sins in Buddhism. A person's essential nature can never be killed or otherwise perish. Anyone who harbors the slightest thought that this is possible sins gravely. The light of such a person's essential nature is hidden from his eyes.

The monk wanted to see how Fuketsu would solve this difficult problem, so he asked, "Both speech and silence are concerned with *ri* and *mi*. How can we transcend them?" He seems to be saying that even if you have a tiny bit of a concept or picture in your mind, you fall into the dualistic world of subject and object. If you have nothing in your consciousness, you are like a dead man, totally useless. How can we be free from lapsing into this dualistic pitfall?

Fuketsu, however, was not concerned with *ri-mi* and could show very clearly his true way of living. "Once I went to the south of the Yangtze River (Kōnan) and looked at the spring scenery there. It was very wonderful. Hundreds of sweet-scented flowers were in full bloom, and partridges chirped and sang among them. I've been constantly thinking of it ever since."

In Fuketsu's consciousness there is neither subject nor object, neither "only I, alone and sacred" nor "no I." He is completely free from *ri* and *mi* and speech and silence. We are not told whether the monk realized Fuketsu's world or not, but that is not important. What is important is that we all attain great enlightenment by Fuketsu's answer.

ON MUMON'S COMMENTARY

"Fuketsu's activity of mind is like lightning. He gains the road and immediately walks along. But why does he rest upon the tip of the ancient one's tongue and not cut if off? If you realize this deeply, a way will be found naturally. Just leave all words behind and say one phrase."

Fuketsu's way of guiding people is not only as quick as lightning but the most appropriate for the monk's stage of understanding. But Mumon says that from his point of view, it is still dull. Why does he rest on the tip of the ancient one's tongue and not cut it off? In other words, why did he not cut off the concepts of *ri* and *mi* for the monk, for they are really the words of an ancient priest (Sō Jō)? Mumon seems to be protesting to Fuketsu, but he is really spurring us on to open our Dharma eye. If you clearly realize this koan, you will be able to realize perfect freedom and true peace of mind in your daily life. Just try; see if you can say a phrase or some words without using your brain and mouth! There are several koans in the *Gateless Gate* and *Blue Cliff Record* which are in this category. The next case in this text, and Cases 70, 71, 72, and 73 in the *Blue Cliff Record* are similar.

ON THE VERSE

Fuketsu does not speak in his usual style;
Before he says anything, it is already manifested.
If you go on chattering glibly,
You should be ashamed of yourself.

Fuketsu, as a Dharma descendant of Rinzai, is usually very strict in dealing with his disciples. But here he is mildness itself, ". . . where partridges are chirping among hundreds of fragrant blossoms."

And still these words are superfluous! "Before he says anything, it is already manifested." All living beings are intrinsically Buddha. Before we move our lips, everyone is bestowed with perfect Buddha nature. What else is necessary?

"If you go on chattering glibly, you should be ashamed of yourself." Saying such superfluous things as "subject and object are one," "our essential nature transcends all dualistic concepts," or "I am thinking of sweet-scented blossoms" is nonsense. You should be ashamed of yourself because you do not seem to have realized your essential nature even a bit!

Now I would like to tell you more about the monk Jō. He was such a talented writer that the then emperor ordered him to leave the monastery and return to lay life to serve as an imperial secretary. Jō refused and was condemned to death. He was only thirty-one years of age. He asked for one week's reprieve, during which time he wrote the *Hōzōron*. When it was finished, he calmly submitted to the execution. At the point of death, Jō wrote the following poem:

> *Four elements have no master from the beginning;*
> *The five skandhas are intrinsically void.*
> *When the neck goes under the sharpest blade,*
> *It is as if you cut through the spring breeze.*

The five skandhas (aggregates or elements) are form, sensation, conception, discrimination, and awareness. The opening words of the *Prajna Paramita Sutra* are: "Avalokitesvara Bodhisattva practicing deep prajna paramita clearly saw emptiness of all the five skandhas, thus completely relieving misfortune and pain."

Another example of composure in the face of death is Bukkō Kokushi, the founder of Engakuji. His monastery was invaded by soldiers when he was still in China. He was sitting in zazen at the time, and one of the soldiers came up from behind to cut off his head. With great composure, Bukkō composed and recited the following poem:

> *There is no ground on which to put a single staff;*
> *How happy it is to find both the subject and the object empty.*
> *Of great rarity is the giant sword of Gen,*
> *It is just as if the spring breeze is cut off in a flash of lightning.*

The soldier put down his sword and retreated with his accomplices.

I am sure you can see the similarity between the two poems, and I believe that nothing except zazen can give us this composure in the last moment of our life.

The Sermon of the
Third Seat

25

THE CASE

Master Kyōzan went to Maitreya's abode in a dream and was led to
the third seat. A venerable monk struck the anvil with a gavel and said,
"Today the third seat is due to speak." Kyōzan stood up, struck the
stand with the gavel, and said, "The Dharma of Mahayana is beyond
the four propositions and transcends the hundred negations. Listen!
Listen!"

MUMON'S COMMENTARY

Just say, did he preach or did he not? If you open your mouth, you miss.
If you shut your mouth, you miss too. Even if you neither open nor shut
your mouth, it is a hundred and eight thousand miles away.

THE VERSE

The broad daylight, the blue sky—
He speaks of a dream in a dream;
Suspicious! Suspicious!
He is trying to deceive the whole assembly.

TEISHŌ ON THE CASE

The Zen master in this koan is Kyōzan Ejaku, the sixth descendant of the sixth patriarch, Enō. He was born in 814, about the time of Hyakujō's death, and died in 890 at the age of seventy-seven. He was a contemporary of the famous Zen master Seppō. In Japan, this was the era of Kōbō Daishi, or Kūkai (774–835), founder of the Shingon sect, and Dengyō Daishi, or Saichō (767–822), founder of the Tendai sect.

Kyōzan's parents repeatedly refused to allow him to become a monk. When he was seventeen, he presented his parents with the third and fourth fingers of his left hand as a gesture of his earnestness. They thereupon gave him permission to enter the monastery. After various pilgrimages, he went to Master Isan Reiyū and remained with him for fifteen years.

Isan and Kyōzan are co-founders of the Igyō sect, one of the five Zen sects of ancient China. Igyō is a combination of the names of Isan and Kyōzan. These two maintained such an ideal relationship of master and disciple that the main characteristic of the Igyō sect came to be contained in the following words: "Father and son chant in accordance with each other." There was no gap between the master and his disciple. Isan appears in Case 40 of this text.

An interesting story is told about Kyōzan when he was living at Tōhei. Isan had sent him a letter and a bronze mirror. He ascended the rostrum and, showing the mirror to the assembled monks, said, "Now listen, all of you. Isan has sent me a mirror. Just tell me, is this Isan's mirror or mine? If you say it is mine, didn't it come from Isan? And if you say it is Isan's, isn't it here with me? If you can give me a Zen word, I'll keep it. If you can't, I'll break it." He said this three times, but there was no one who could answer, so he broke the mirror.

If I had been there, I would have said, "Show me the mirror," and I would have taken it, looked at the face reflected in it and said, "Oh, this is mine!"

There is another interesting story about Kyōzan. Once a great Indian Arhat (a Hinayana Buddhist who has attained the highest enlightenment) came flying to China and met Kyōzan. Kyōzan asked him, "When did you leave India?" "This morning" was the reply. "You left India this morning and just arrived here now! What took you so long?" "Well, I was sightseeing here and there." Kyōzan scolded him, "You have some occult power, but you have never even dreamed of the great occult power in true Buddhism."

This great occult power that Kyōzan was speaking of has nothing to do with flying around the world. It is simply eating when you are hungry, drinking when you are thirsty, and taking a rest when you are tired. It is said that when the Arhat returned to India he praised Kyōzan highly, saying, "I went to China to meet Manjusri,[1] but I was lucky enough to meet a little Shakyamuni." In this way Kyōzan came to be nicknamed Little Shakya.

The present koan is a story about Kyōzan's dream. In this case, Mu, zazen, standing up, sitting down, eating, drinking, Jack, Mary, and so forth appear on stage under the name of dream. We should know that not only are our delusions and the phenomenal world dreams, but also our enlightenment and the essential world itself are nothing but dreams. The fact of today will be a dream tomorrow. Minute by minute, second by second, everything previous to right now is a dream. And, of course, now is a dream too. When we dream, however, we are not aware that it is a dream. At that moment it is real for us.

As you all know, there are good dreams and bad dreams, happy dreams and unhappy dreams. One of the sutras says, "Shakyamuni Buddha was born and practiced zazen and attained great enlightenment and preached sermons and died; these processes are all dreams." These are examples of good dreams. On the other hand, the six realms or the three evil paths (hell, the world of hungry ghosts, and the world of animals) are examples of bad dreams. Ordinary people have mostly tiny, useless dreams, although there are a few who can awaken to the wonderful, joyous dream of enlightenment. Buddhas and patriarchs are those who dream great dreams and preach about them in a dream.

So Kyōzan dreamed a dream. He dreamed he went to Maitreya's abode and was led to the third seat. A senior monk struck the wooden anvil with a gavel and announced, "Today the sermon will be given by the third seat." Kyōzan stood up, struck the stand with the gavel, and said, "The Dharma is beyond the four propositions and transcends the hundred negations. Listen! Listen!"

Some of these words deserve an explanation. The Bodhisattva Maitreya, who appeared in Mumon's commentary on Case 5, is to be the next Buddha. He is now waiting in the Tusita Heaven and will come five billion, 670 million years after Shakyamuni's nirvana. The four propositions (or the four terms) and the hundred negations mean all kinds of concepts and thoughts. The four propositions are explained in several versions, one of which is: (1) one, (2) different, (3) being, (4) nonbeing. Another version is: (1) being, (2) nonbeing, (3) both being and nonbeing, (4) neither being nor nonbeing. The hundred negations are arrived at in different ways. For example, each of the four propositions contains all four, which gives us 16. Then, introducing the past, present, and future, we multiply by three and get 48. These are doubled since they have already arisen or are about to arise, which makes 96. Then the original four are added again, giving us the hundred negations. A hundred simply means infinite in number.

Kyōzan stood up and struck the stand with the gavel, WHACK! "The Dharma of Mahayana is beyond all thought and expression!" More precisely he was saying, "WHACK!" Just this! What is the Dharma of Mahayana? Just WHACK! Just standing up and sitting down, laughing or crying. Mountains are high and rivers are wet. To what can the nasty concepts of the four terms and hundred negations adhere? But unless you grasp this by living experience, it will never become your own treasure.

"WHACK! Listen!" Kyōzan's preaching was perfect. Later, when Isan heard this story, he praised Kyōzan, saying, "He has entered the stage of sainthood."

The ordinary Zen man does not know anything about this sainthood. Buddhist philosophers know only the 52 stages by which one arrives at Buddhahood. In true Buddhism, we must ascend these 52 stages after we have attained Buddhahood, or perfect enlightenment. Among the past patriarchs and great Zen masters, there are many who can only be called ordinary men with enlightenment. Generally speaking, people can be classified into four groups: (1) the ordinary person without enlightenment, (2) the ordinary person with enlightenment, (3) the saint without enlightenment, (4) the saint with enlightenment. The ultimate aim for all of us Zen practitioners should be to become the fourth kind of human being.

ON MUMON'S COMMENTARY

"Just say, did he preach or did he not? If you open your mouth, you miss. If you shut your mouth, you miss too. Even if you neither open nor shut your mouth, it is a hundred and eight thousand miles away."

WHACK! The Dharma of Mahayana is beyond all concepts and thoughts. Is this preaching or not? If you say something, you miss. If you keep silent, you miss too. Moreover, even if you neither open nor shut your mouth, you are far away from the true Dharma. That means if you have even a bit of a concept or thought in your mind, you are one hundred and eight thousand miles away from the real fact.

There are several koans in this category. We have pointed out the similarity with *masagin* in Case 18, as well as with Case 67 of the *Blue Cliff Record,* which was quoted there. Another is Case 92 of the *Blue Cliff Record:*

> One day the World-Honored One ascended the rostrum. Manjusri struck it with a gavel and said, "Contemplate clearly the Dharma of the King of the Dharma. The Dharma of the King of the Dharma is just this."

There is also Case 7 of the *Book of Equanimity:*

> Yakusan Igen had not ascended the rostrum for quite a while. The head monk said, "All the monks have been anxious for instruction for a long time. Please, Your Reverence, won't you give a sermon?" Yakusan ordered the bell and drum. The assembly gathered. Yakusan ascended the rostrum, and after sitting there for a while, he descended and returned to his room. The head monk followed him and asked, "You consented to give a sermon. How is it that you uttered not a word?" Yakusan said, "For sutras there are sutra specialists. For sastras there are sastra specialists.[2] Why do you wonder at this old monk's behavior?"

ON THE VERSE

The broad daylight, the blue sky—
He speaks of a dream in a dream;
Suspicious! Suspicious!
He is trying to deceive the whole assembly.

"The broad daylight, the blue sky." Everything is perfectly clear. WHACK! That's all!!

"He speaks of a dream in a dream. Suspicious! Suspicious! He is trying to deceive the whole assembly." Dream? Where is the dream? Isn't a dream a real fact? Isn't everything in a dream real? If you speak of a dream, is there anything but a dream? Take care not to be deceived by Mumon.

NOTES

1. A bodhisattva who represents the Buddhist wisdom and realization.
2. Buddhist scriptures are divided into three parts:
   (a) Sutras—the Buddha's own preaching and discourses;
   (b) Vinaya—the moral code, rules and regulations of the Sangha or community of monks;
   (c) Sastras—commentaries and articles written by the Buddha's disciples and followers.

Two Monks Roll Up the Blinds

26

THE CASE

A monk once went to Daihōgen of Seiryō before the midday meal to ask for instruction. Hōgen pointed to the bamboo blinds with his hand. At that moment, two monks who were there went over to the blinds and rolled them up in the same manner. Hōgen said, "One has gained, one has lost."

MUMON'S COMMENTARY

Just tell me, which one has gained and which one has lost? If you have one eye opened concerning this point, you will know where National Teacher Seiryō failed. Nevertheless, you should not inquire into this problem in connection with gain or loss.

THE VERSE

The blind being rolled up, bright clarity penetrates the great empty space.
Yet the great empty space still does not match the principle of our sect;
It is far better to throw away emptiness and everything completely,
And with a tight fit, never to let the wind pass through.

TEISHŌ ON THE CASE

Master Daihōgen or Hōgen Mon'eki of Seiryō monastery was the founder of the Hōgen sect. Literally, Daihōgen means Great Dharma eye, his name as a Zen master. Mon'eki was his personal name. He was the fifth descendant of Master Tokusan, whom we met in Case 13, carrying his bowls. Hōgen died in 958 at the age of seventy-four.

In olden days, Zen monks did *angya* either to attain or to deepen their enlightenment experience. *Angya* means to travel about searching for excellent Zen masters in order to engage in mondo (questions and answers) with them. Once when Hōgen was doing *angya* he stayed at a small monastery overnight.

The master of the monastery asked him, "What do you hope to get by doing *angya?*"

"I do not know," Hōgen answered.

The master said, "Not knowing is the closest fit." Upon hearing this, Hōgen suddenly attained deep enlightenment. The next morning, the master saw him off to the gate. Noticing a big stone in the garden, he pointed to it and asked Hōgen, "You monks usually say the whole universe is just one mind. Just tell me, is this stone within the mind or outside the mind?"

"Within the mind," Hōgen replied.

"It will be awfully difficult for you to travel around with such a big stone inside of you!" the master retorted.

Hōgen was shocked by this remark and decided to stay at the monastery to study. The master was Rakan (or Jizō) Keishin Zenji, who appears in Cases 12 and 20 of the *Book of Equanimity*. Eventually Hōgen became his Dharma successor.

Hōgen was famous for his skill in guiding his disciples. In Japanese, his method is called *sokutaku dōji*, which could be translated, "simultaneous picking and pecking." It is said that when the chick has grown enough to be hatched from the egg, it picks at the shell from within, trying to break it open. Meanwhile, the mother hen pecks at the same point from outside. If this picking and pecking is done simultaneously and at the same spot, the shell is broken and the chick safely hatched. Applying this to Zen guidance, it means the master's "peck" should be neither too soon nor too late for the disciple's "pick." Hōgen was skillful in this respect, and his method became one of the characteristics of his sect.

Let us consider the present koan. Once a monk went up to Hōgen's room before the midday meal to ask for instruction. There were two monks there attending Hōgen. He pointed to the bamboo blinds, which were unrolled. The two attendants, guessing what he wanted, went to the blinds and rolled them up. They both did it exactly the same way. Nevertheless, Hōgen said, "One has gained and the other has lost," which means one is good and the other is not.

This koan can be contemplated from two points of view, one shallow and the other deep. Hōgen said one had gained and the other lost, but he did not say which was the good one and which the bad. If either of the two had shown any sign of being disturbed, he would have been the one that lost. If one of them had lacked confidence in his realization, he might have become uneasy thinking that perhaps the master was referring to him as the one who lost. But a monk who is truly confident about his realization will always maintain a steady state of mind and will not be shaken or disturbed, even a little. Hōgen scrutinized their faces closely. Looking at the koan from this point of view, we see the similarity to Case 11, where Jōshū examined the two hermits.

The other point of view from which to contemplate this koan is to consider what Hōgen truly meant when he said one had gained and the other lost. In the world of the essential nature, is there anything, after all, to be called gain or loss, good or bad? As I tell you so often, in the world of Mu there are no such dualistic oppositions. Hōgen uses them as turning words to try to bring them to the realization of the essential world. His words may cause them to doubt. By doubting, and doubting deeply, they will reach the state of mind where there is no gain or loss. Let us not forget that not only the two monks but all the rest of us as well are being urged by Hōgen to realize this world of absoluteness where there are no dualistic concepts at all. That is the world of our essential nature.

Usually this koan is seen from the two angles mentioned above. I would like to add another view, one which seems to me to be the deepest from the Zen perspective. A monk came to Hōgen to ask for instruction. Seeing him, Hōgen gestured to the bamboo blinds with his hand. What was Hōgen's true meaning in doing so? He said nothing. The two attending monks guessed that the master wanted to have the blinds rolled up. Is that true? No. He just pointed to the bamboo blinds. Nothing more, nothing less. This is nothing other than the manifestation of his essential nature, just as was Gutei's raising up of a finger. As to his saying, "One has gained, one has lost," the same is true. There is no meaning at all. Just, "One has gained, one has lost." Nothing more, nothing less. Master Hōgen did not move his lips or tongue a bit when he said these words but was manifesting his entire body perfectly. I prefer this last view to the former two.

To return to the story I told you about at the beginning of the *teishō*, when Hōgen was leaving the monastery after his overnight stay, Master Jizō came to see him off. Pointing to a large stone in the garden, he asked Hōgen if the stone was inside or outside his mind. Hōgen replied, "Inside!" whereupon the master commented that it must be a very heavy load to carry around all the time. If I had been Hōgen, I would have answered the master's question as to whether the stone was inside or outside the mind with, "I have no time for such silly talk! Ask the stone!" Or I might have said, "Do you have such a strange thing as a mind? Show it to me!" Or perhaps I would have told him, "I don't have outside or inside with me at the moment!" Or I could have said, "The stone is not outside me, yet I can walk very lightly with it, like this. Bye-bye!" and I would have laughed loudly and walked away.

ON MUMON'S COMMENTARY

"Just tell me, which one has gained and which one has lost? If you have one eye opened concerning this problem, you will know where National Teacher Seiryō failed. Nevertheless, you should not inquire into this problem in connection with gain or loss."

"Just tell me, which one has gained and which one has lost?" If we take these words literally, none of us would know how to answer because we were not present at the scene. To take them literally, however, is merely superficial. Mumon's real intention is to tease us out of our thoughts so we come to realize the essential world.

"If you have one eye opened concerning this problem, you will know where National Teacher Seiryō failed." One eye means the enlightened eye. When one opens the eye of enlightenment and sees the essential world, he will see that Hōgen failed. That is because he spoke of gain and loss, which do not exist at all in the world of absolute reality.

ON THE VERSE

The blind being rolled up, bright clarity penetrates the great empty space.

Yet the great empty space still does not match the principle of our sect;
It is far better to throw away emptiness and everything completely,
And with a tight fit, never to let the wind pass through.

To roll up the blind means to banish delusions or dualistic concepts by practicing Zen—sometimes by breath-counting, sometimes by just sitting, and sometimes by working on Mu or other koans. If you persevere to your utmost, you will come to the empty state of mind, where all concepts and thoughts are completely extinguished, just as when the blinds are rolled to the top and the vast empty sky becomes apparent in all its brightness and clarity.

Yet complete emptiness is still not the highest degree of self-realization. If we become attached to the world of emptiness, it will become a pitfall which traps us.

"A tight fit" has to do with our essential nature, of course. I am sure you know that "the wind" refers to our thoughts. When we are in such a state of mind, even if Buddha or Maitreya or Bodhidharma should appear and say something to us, no matter what it is, our peace and steadfastness will not be shaken in the slightest degree. But we must continue daily to roll up the blind by wholeheartedly persevering in our zazen practice.

Not Mind, Not Buddha

THE CASE

A monk asked Nansen in all earnestness, "Is there any Dharma that has not been preached to the people?" Nansen said, "There is." The monk said, "What is the Dharma which has never been preached to the people?" Nansen said, "This is not mind; this is not Buddha; this is not a thing."

MUMON'S COMMENTARY

Nansen was merely asked a question, and he exhausted all his possessions at once and was reduced to nothing.

THE VERSE

Speaking too much degrades virtue,
No words are truly effective;
Even though the great ocean should change,
It can never be communicated to you.

TEISHŌ ON THE CASE

We have already met Master Nansen in Case 14, where he killed a cat. He was the teacher of Jōshū, who appeared in Cases 1, 7, 11, 14, and 19, and will appear again in Cases 31 and 37. Nansen was a disciple of the great teacher Baso, who left more than eighty Dharma successors. Three of them were conspicuously eminent: Nansen Fugan, Hyakujō Ekai, and Taibai Hōjō.

Besides the ones in the *Gateless Gate,* there are numerous koans about Nansen in the *Blue Cliff Record* and the *Book of Equanimity.* In the former, Nansen appears in Cases 28, 31, 40, 63, 64, and 69. In the latter, he is in Cases 9, 23, 69, 91, and 93. All of these are of the utmost interest and importance. In all of them we can see what is most characteristic in Nansen's way of guiding his disciples.

Let us look at Case 69 of the *Book of Equanimity* for a moment. It reads as follows: "Once Nansen addressed the assembly, saying, 'None of the Buddhas of the three worlds, past, present, and future, know it really *is.* Instead, the cat or ox knows it *is.*'"

This case contains an important reference to Dōgen Zenji. While still a young monk, he had read a vast number of sutras but had not found the answer to the most fundamental question: Since the sutras say that our self nature is intrinsically Buddha, why then is it necessary for us to practice discipline and become Buddha? Dōgen Zenji visited many venerable masters seeking the answer to this question, but always in vain. Finally he went to Eisai Zenji, who was the first to bring Rinzai Zen to Japan from China. Eisai's prompt reply was, "None of the Buddhas, of the past, present, and future know it really is. Instead the cat or the ox knows it is."

When he heard this, Dōgen was deeply affected, and sweat poured out all over his body. This was his first experience of self-realization. What does this teaching mean? You must contemplate it as a koan.

In returning to the present koan, I would like to quote Case 28 of the *Blue Cliff Record,* which is basically the same but a little longer.

> Nansen went to Master Nehan of Hyakujō and was asked by him, "Is there any Dharma which the saints in the past have never preached to the people?" Nansen answered, "There is." Hyakujō asked "What is the Dharma that has never been preached to the people?" Nansen said, "This is not mind; this is not Buddha; this is not a thing." Hyakujō said, "You have preached like that." Nansen said, "As for me, it is just like this. How about you?" Hyakujō said, "I am not a great Zen master. How can I know whether there is preaching or no-preaching?" Nansen said, "I don't understand." Hyakujō said, "I have preached too much for you."

This is a very interesting mondo, isn't it? You can see that it is somewhat more detailed than in the *Gateless Gate.* In any event, it seems that this was Nansen's favorite question. If you think you understand what Nansen meant when he said, "The exceptionally secret Dharma is not mind, not Buddha, not a thing," then you are not only totally mistaken but you have not even found the point of the koan.

I will give you a hint. Put the emphasis on "This!" THIS is not mind; THIS is not Buddha; THIS is not a thing! THIS is all! Nothing remains apart from it. You must realize THIS directly at this very moment! WHACK! THIS!

ON MUMON'S COMMENTARY

"Nansen was merely asked a question, and he exhausted all his possessions at once and was reduced to nothing."

What was his answer? THIS! is not mind. THIS! is not Buddha. THIS! is not a thing. Thus Nansen spewed out all his insides. Nothing remained. He was reduced to absolute zero. THIS is the whole! He has vomited up everything. Nothing else remains.

ON THE VERSE

Speaking too much degrades virtue,
No words are truly effective;
Even though the great ocean should change,
It can never be communicated to you.

Speaking too much means discussing or explaining too much. The more we speak, the more we separate ourselves from reality.

"No words are truly effective." THIS! That's it! WHACK! That's it! There is an effect. It is the presentation of the whole. It defies all explanation.

"Even though the great ocean should change," into a field, for example, or a mountain, "IT can never be communicated to you." No matter what happens, it is quite impossible to give IT to you. IT is entirely one with you from the very beginning, so how can IT be communicated to you any more completely? Water cannot become any wetter! The sword cannot cut itself off!

Ryūtan's Name
Echoed Long

28

THE CASE

One day Tokusan kept asking Ryūtan for instruction till nightfall. Ryūtan finally said, "The night is late. Why don't you go to bed." Tokusan thanked him, made his bows, raised the door curtain and left. Seeing how dark the night was, he turned back and said, "It's pitch black outside." Ryūtan lit a lantern and handed it to Tokusan. Just as Tokusan reached for it, Ryūtan blew it out. At that Tokusan came to sudden realization and made a deep bow.

Ryūtan asked, "What have you realized?" Tokusan replied, "From now on, I will not doubt the words of the old master who is renowned everywhere under the sun." The following day Ryūtan ascended the rostrum and declared, "There is a man among you whose fangs are like trees of swords and whose mouth is like a bowl of blood. Strike him and he won't turn his head. Someday he will settle on the top of an isolated peak and establish my Way there."

Tokusan brought his sutra commentaries and notes to the front of the hall, held up a torch and said, "Even if you have exhausted abstruse doctrine, it is like placing a hair in vast space. Even if you have learned the vital points of all the truths in the world, it is like a drop of water thrown into a big ravine." He then burned all his commentaries and notes. After making his bows, he left.

MUMON'S COMMENTARY

Before Tokusan had crossed the border, his mind was full of resentment and his mouth speechless with anger. He wanted to go all the way south, intending to refute the doctrine of the special transmission outside the sutras. When he got to the road to the province of Rei, he asked an old woman if he could buy a *tenjin* from her. The old woman said, "Your Reverence, what are all those books you are carrying in the cart?" Tokusan said, "Those are commentaries on the *Diamond Sutra*." The old woman said, "In that sutra, it says the past mind can't be caught; the present mind can't be caught; the future mind can't be caught. Your Reverence, with which mind are you going to take the *tenjin?*" This one question tightly shut Tokusan's mouth, but hearing the old woman's words, he still did not completely die away. He asked her, "Is there a Zen master near here?" She replied, "Master Ryūtan lives about five *ri* away."

After Tokusan arrived at Ryūtan's, he was entirely defeated. It must be said that his former and latter words are not consistent. It seems that Ryūtan, forgetting his own unsightliness, took too much pity on Tokusan. Seeing a live charcoal in Tokusan, he immediately threw muddy water over his head to extinguish it. Looking at the whole affair coolly, I think it is just a farce.

THE VERSE

Seeing the face is better than hearing the name;
Hearing the name is better than seeing the face.
Even though he saved his nose,
Alas, he lost his eyes!

TEISHŌ ON THE CASE AND MUMON'S COMMENTARY

Ryūtan Sūshin Zenji was a fifth-generation successor of the sixth patriarch, Enō. It is said that he was a son of a rice cake shop-owner. Every day he delivered rice cakes to Master Dōgo. His relation with Buddha deepened, and he finally became a monk. The details of his life are unknown except for several mondo and preachings about Zen, but it is presumed that he lived around 850 A.D.

We met Tokusan Senkan Zenji in his later years in Case 13, where he was carrying his bowls to the Dharma hall. As I told you in that *teishō*, Tokusan was a specialist in the *Diamond Sutra*. He was proud of the fact that no one could compete with him in its interpretation and delighted in his nickname, Shū Kongō Ō. Shū was his family name, Kongō means diamond, and Ō is king. Hence his name means "Shū, King of the Diamond Sutra."

According to Buddhist doctrine, an incalculable period of time is necessary for ordinary people to become Buddha. Zen Buddhism says it can happen instantaneously through self-realization. Tokusan thought this was utter nonsense.

"If that is Zen teaching, then Zen is not Buddhism," he reasoned. "It must be the teaching of devils in disguise. I will go south, where this teaching is flourishing, and destroy it all." He packed up the notes and commentaries he would need to make his refutations in Dharma combat and started on his way.

Here Mumon's commentary begins. Chronologically, it precedes the case, so we shall start with it. When Tokusan had not yet come out of the border, that is, when he had not yet left home, his mind was full of resentment, and he was unable to open his mouth, so great was his indignation. These deep feelings indicate the intensity of his anger towards Zen, which advocated realization of Buddhahood independent of sutra knowledge. Great sutra scholar that he was, Tokusan set off to vanquish the foe.

While on the road to the province of Rei, he became a bit hungry and decided to get something to eat. He found a small snack shop in the area run by an old woman. Tokusan asked her for a *tenjin*. Now *tenjin* has a double meaning. Literally, it means "pointing to the mind," but it also refers to something to eat, probably a sweet similar to the Japanse *manjū*.

When the learned sutra scholar asked the old woman for a *tenjin*, there is no doubt as to his meaning. He was hungry. But the old woman responded by asking him a question, "Your Reverence, what are you carrying in the cart?" He told her proudly, "They are notes and commentaries on the *Diamond Sutra*. I am Shū Kongō Ō. Nobody can compete with me in the interpretation of its teaching." "Is that so?" the old woman said. "Then I would like to ask you a question. If you can answer it, I'll treat you to a *tenjin*. If not, I won't even let you buy one!"

"Ask me whatever you like," the great scholar offered. The old woman said, "I hear that it is said in that sutra, 'The past mind can't be caught; the present mind can't be caught; the future mind can't be caught.' With what mind are you going to eat the *tenjin*? (=What mind are you going to point to?)"

Tokusan was dumbstruck. Not one of his scholarly words was of any use to him. The greatest specialist on the *Diamond Sutra* could not answer a question concerning one of its phrases put to him by an old woman. How incompetent intellectual understanding can be! We are not told whether Tokusan got his *tenjin* or not.

When he finally found his tongue, Tokusan surmised there must be a good Zen master in the area who was exerting great influence on the neighborhood. He asked, "Is there a Zen master near here?" "Master Ryūtan lives about five *ri* [one *ri* is 360 steps] away," the old woman replied.

So Tokusan went to Ryūtan's. *Ryū* means dragon, and *tan* means deep water. At the gate of the monastery, Tokusan called out loudly, "The name Ryūtan has echoed to me for a long time, but upon arriving I can find neither dragon nor water." Master Ryūtan peeked through a crack in the door and answered, "You have your Ryūtan now." What an interesting exchange of Zen greetings! That evening in the master's room Tokusan threw away his pride and asked for instruction.

Here we take up the main case of the koan. The two discussed Buddhist doctrine and Zen far into the night, and Tokusan was completely persuaded of the Zen view. Finally Ryūtan said, "The night is late. Why don't you go to bed." So Tokusan made his bows with thanks, and lifting the curtain that hung in the doorway, he saw that it was dark outside. Turning back he said, "It's pitch black outside."

Ryūtan lit a lantern and handed it to Tokusan. Just as Tokusan reached for it, Ryūtan blew it out. At that Tokusan came to sudden realization and made a deep bow.

Why did Tokusan come to realization so soon after he met the master? The answer is very simple: he was ready for it. Previous to that moment, knowingly or unknowingly, Tokusan's practice had been accumulating and had matured sufficiently so that the hard ball of doubt broke with one probe from the master. When he blew out the candle, Ryūtan was actually blowing out the darkness!

Ryūtan asked, "What have you realized?" Tokusan replied, "From now on, I will never doubt the words of the old master who is renowned everywhere under the sun." The old master is, of course, the world-famous Ryūtan himself, and what Tokusan is really saying is that he does not doubt Ryūtan. In other words, he has deeply realized Ryūtan's view that all living beings are Buddha from the beginning.

The following day when he ascended the rostrum, Ryūtan said, "There is a fellow among you whose fangs are like trees of swords and whose mouth is like a bowl of blood." These are compliments paid to an extraordinarily great man. "Strike him and he won't turn his head." This means that he is extremely confident and steady. "Someday he will settle on the top of an isolated peak and establish my Way there." This prediction later came true.

Tokusan brought his notes and commentaries on the *Diamond Sutra* to the front of the hall, pointed to them with a torch, and said, "Even though you may come to understand all abstruse doctrine, it is like putting a hair in vast space. Even though you may have learned all the most important truths in the whole world, it is like a drop of water thrown into a huge ravine." Then he burned all the papers, bowed, and departed.

ON THE VERSE

Seeing the face is better than hearing the name;
Hearing the name is better than seeing the face.
Even though he saved his nose,
Alas, he lost his eyes!

"Seeing the face is better than hearing the name." For Zen practice it is most important, indeed indispensable, to see our real face once. It is not enough to hear rumors about it. The face can refer to two things, to Master Ryūtan, who was so famous, and to our own primal face or essential nature. The rumor refers both to Ryūtan and to all writings and philosophical ideas about Zen or Buddhism. They are merely rumors of enlightenment.

"Hearing the name is better than seeing the face." When you attain enlightenment, there is nothing special about it. Your eyes are horizontal, your nose is vertical. Hearing a name or a rumor can be better than actually seeing it. Tokusan had heard of the famous Ryūtan and had imagined a great, dignified Zen master, but he found only a poor old monk. Enlightenment is just like that.

"Even though he saved his nose," means even though he attained a little enlightenment.

"Alas, he lost his eyes!" What a pity to become utterly blind! This is another of those ironical Zen phrases. It requires a little explanation. In Zen there are five kinds of blindness: (1) ordinary blindness—unenlightened people who know nothing about the truth; (2) bad blindness—persons attached to wrong philosophies or religions; (3) blindness before enlightenment—people in right faith who are studying and practicing in the right way but are still unenlightened; (4) right blindness—the eye of great enlightenment, which sees nothing in the whole universe; (5) true blindness—the eye in which the light of enlightenment has utterly disappeared. This is Buddha's eye.

I think that Tokusan's blindness was of approximately the fourth variety. His enlightenment was still not perfect.

Not the Wind, Not the Flag

29

THE CASE

The wind was flapping a temple flag, and two monks were having an argument about it. One said, "The flag is moving." The other said, "The wind is moving." They argued back and forth but could not reach the truth. The sixth patriarch said, "It is not the wind that moves. It is not the flag that moves. It is your mind that moves." The two monks were struck with awe.

MUMON'S COMMENTARY

It is not the wind that moves; it is not the flag that moves; it is not the mind that moves. Where do you see the essence of the patriarch? If you have a close grasp of the matter, you will see how the two monks, intending to buy iron, got gold, and that what the patriarch impatiently said was a failure on the spot.

THE VERSE

The wind moves, the flag moves, the mind moves;
All have missed it.
They only know how to open their mouths,
And do not know that their words have failed.

TEISHŌ ON THE CASE

The sixth patriarch is Master Enō, who appeared in Case 23. There we learned about his deep enlightenment while still a young man and his journey to Ōbai to study under Master Kōnin. Enō was put to work in the rice-cleaning shed, but after he posted his famous verse which showed the depth of his enlightenment, he was secretly chosen to be the master's Dharma successor. You will remember that Master Kōnin gave Enō the following advice: "Do not stay on this mountain. Hide yourself from society at least ten years and nourish the sacred seedling long and well; otherwise great suffering will come to you from people's jealousy. I will show you how to escape." He guided Enō to the river, which they crossed by boat, the master himself handling the oars.

About fifteen years after these events, Enō reappears in this koan. The setting is Hosshōji, a temple in the province of Kō. It is recorded that the Abbot Insō knew when Enō first came to the temple that he was not an ordinary person. Insō asked him, "Aren't you the layman Ro who succeeded to the Dharma and robe of the fifth patriarch, Ōbai?" Enō, thinking it the right time to reveal his identity, showed Insō the robe. The abbot paid him great respect. Enō then had his head shaved and became a priest.

In those days, when the abbot was to give a sermon or Dharma combat was to be held, a flag was raised at the temple gate to announce the event. One day, two monks saw the flag fluttering in the wind and started a discussion as to whether the wind or the flag was moving. Soon they were quarreling, one insisting that it was the wind, the other that it was the flag. Enō, hearing them and thinking it all sheer nonsense, said, "You venerable monks! Why are you arguing so bitterly? It is neither the wind nor the flag but your mind that moves."

The problem in this koan seems to be whether the wind is blowing or the flag is blowing, but we must understand that the moving wind and the moving flag are not the reality or the fact; they are merely labels. The wind does not say, "I am moving." The flag does not say, "I am moving." Master Enō said, "The mind is moving." But what is the mind? Enō's remark is, so to speak, a kind of compromise with the two monks. He did not reveal what he really meant. If he had, the monks would not have understood at all and would have been left in complete ignorance. So Enō came down a step and spoke on their level, but even then they did not understand.

Instead of Enō, we find Mumon preaching this point. In his commentary he says, "It is not the wind that moves; it is not the flag that moves; it is not the mind that moves." There is an interesting story about Mumon's commentary.

In ancient China there was a nun named Myōshin who was a disciple of the famous Zen master Kyōzan. You can read about him in Case 25. This nun was in charge of the guest houses of the Kyōzan monastery. One day seventeen monks from the Shoku district came to visit. In the evening they were discussing this koan about the wind and the flag, and they all missed the point. The nun, who had been listening to their conversation behind a sliding door, said in a loud voice, "How pitiable these seventeen blind donkeys are! They've never even dreamed of Buddha's Dharma!" Instead of being angered, the monks were humbled by these words and asked Myōshin to teach them.

In a strong and authoritative voice, Myōshin said, "It is not the wind that moves; it is not the flag that moves; it is not the mind that moves." Upon hearing this, all the monks came to enlightenment. They made obeisance in gratitude and became Myōshin's disciples, returning home without even seeing Kyōzan. This is quite a celebrated anecdote in Zen history; there is no other record of so many people attaining realization simultaneously.

There is another interesting story in the same category as this koan. During the Tokugawa period in Japan, a venerable Zen master of the Sōtō sect by the name of Sonnō lived in Sendai. One day one of his disciples came to visit, bringing melons as a gift. The master, much pleased with both the gift and his disciple, suggested they try some of the fruit. Sonnō said, "It's very sweet." "Yes," replied his disciple, "It's very sweet." Then the master smilingly asked, "What do you think, is the melon sweet or the tongue sweet? If the melon is sweet, the sweetness has nothing to do with the tongue. If the tongue is sweet, the sweetness has nothing to do with the melon. Where does the sweetness actually come from? Try to tell me that!"

The disciple thought for a while and then replied, "It comes from the causal contact of the tongue and the melon." The master retorted, "That answer is merely from the theoretical standpoint of Buddhism. It contains no experience of the Zen monk!" The monk asked him, "If so, where does it actually come from? Please give me a turning word."

Master Sonnō gave him the following instruction: "Where does it come from? Even the Buddhas and patriarchs cannot tell you. If you search for 'where,' you will find the whole universe is the melon and that there is no tongue outside the melon. Or you will find that the whole universe is the tongue and that there is no melon outside the tongue. In the world of reality, there is neither subject nor object. The real fact transcends both mind and things. We call it the essential activity of no-thinking, which has been transmitted from Buddha to Buddha, from patriarch to patriarch. From now on you must exert yourself all the more intensely." The monk was deeply impressed.

Now let us look at the koan in the present case. Is the situation not the same? If you say the wind is moving, the wind is all and is quite alone in the universe. There is no flag or mind outside the wind. If you say the flag is moving, the flag is the only thing in the universe. There is no wind or mind outside the flag. If you say the mind is moving, the mind is all. Nothing exists outside of it. The true fact transcends all these three, and what is that? You must search for it deeply by yourself.

As I have often told you, the whole universe is one; the universe and I are one, but, since in delusion we acknowledge subject and object, dualistic concepts and thoughts arise. There is no object outside of the subject, there is no subject outside of the object. The essential world, which is void, is nothing other than the world under the law of causation. Ordinary people regard as two what is essentially one. There is no two at all. In a dream we may see many things: mountains, rivers, trees, grass, animals, and birds. We see these as external objects. Upon awakening, we find that we did not see these things at all. We saw nothing but ourselves after all, didn't we? Our actual world is not the least bit different from the dream. Mountains, trees, rivers, grass, and so on are nothing but our true self. We call it "the only Mu in the whole universe," or "our own self," or "the other self," and there is only one between heaven and earth. Or we may say, "There is only I, alone and sacred, in heaven above and the earth below." When you realize the world of oneness, the present koan will become clear to you naturally.

Now with these explanations, you may come to form some concept of oneness, but you can never be satisfied by a mere concept or even understanding. When you are truly one, truly one with the other, you transcend even the oneness itself, because oneness is nothing but a concept.

ON MUMON'S COMMENTARY

"It is not the wind that moves; it is not the flag that moves; it is not the mind that moves. Where do you see the essence of the patriarch? If you have a close grasp of the matter, you will see how the two monks, intending to buy iron, got gold, and that what the patriarch impatiently said was a failure on the spot."

As Mumon says, the truth is that neither the wind nor the flag nor the mind moves. When the patriarch says, "It is your mind that moves," how are we to understand him? Though the patriarch was, of course, well acquainted with the fact of the essential world, for the sake of expedience he came down to the level of the two monks and said, "The mind moves." In this respect, it may seem that Mumon's comment is right. "It is not the wind that moves; it is not the flag that moves; it is not the mind that moves." But from my point of view, Mumon, too, was mistaken to comment as he did because the true fact transcends all moving and non-moving. It is just . . . what?!

ON THE VERSE

The wind moves, the flag moves, the mind moves;
All have missed it.
They only know how to open their mouths,
And do not know that their words have failed.

This means that they are all wrong in the same way; that is, they know how to open their mouths but do not know that their words miss the mark. In Zen, the mark is none other than the real fact.

Mind Is Buddha

30

THE CASE

Taibai asked Baso in all earnestness, "What is Buddha?" Baso answered, "The very mind is Buddha."

MUMON'S COMMENTARY

If you grasp it on the spot, you wear Buddha's clothes, eat Buddha's food, speak Buddha's words, do Buddha's deeds; you are Buddha himself. Though this may be so, Taibai has, alas, misled not a few people into mistaking the mark on the balance for the weight itself. How can he realize that even the mere mention of the word "Buddha" should make a man rinse his mouth for three days? If one is such a man, when he hears someone say, "The very mind is Buddha," he will cover his ears and run away.

THE VERSE

The blue sky, the bright day.
It is most detestable to hunt around;
If, furthermore, you ask, "What is Buddha?"
It is like shouting your innocence while holding the loot.

TEISHŌ ON THE CASE

Master Baso Dōitsu is the Dharma grandson of the sixth patriarch, Enō. Master Baso was a great teacher and produced many fine Zen masters, among whom Hyakujō, Nansen, Taibai, and Bukkō are particularly famous. It is said he passed away in 788 A.D. Though it is not clear just how old he was at the time, it is believed that he was about eighty.

Master Taibai Hōjō went to Baso asking for guidance after studying Buddhist philosophy for more than thirty years. When he heard Baso say, "The very mind is Buddha," he attained deep enlightenment. After that he retreated to a mountain and deepened his realization by continuing *shikantaza* (just sitting) for about thirty years.

It is said that Taibai always sat with an eight-inch rod on his head. If his posture sagged or he dropped off to sleep, the rod would fall off, so he always had to keep himself alert. That was his way of doing *shikantaza*. Master Tenryū was one of his disciples, and Gutei, Tenryū's disciple who is famous for raising one finger, was his Dharma grandson.

Master Baso knew that Taibai was doing solitary sitting in the mountains, so he sent an attendant to examine him. The attendant asked, "What did you realize at Baso's before you came to the mountain?" Taibai replied, "Once I asked Baso, 'What is Buddha?' He answered, 'The very mind is Buddha.' The instant I heard those words I suddenly attained a deep realization. After that, I came to the mountain."

The attendant said, "Recently Baso's teaching has changed."

"In what way?" asked Taibai.

"Nowadays Master Baso says, 'No mind, no Buddha.'"

Taibai said, "The great master Baso perplexes many Zen students. He may say 'No mind, no Buddha' if he wishes to, but for me it will be, 'The very mind is Buddha' until the end of the world."

The attendant returned and reported this to Baso, who commented, "The plum has ripened." The literal meaning of Taibai's name is Big Plum. Thus Baso's remark certified that Taibai's realization has ripened sufficiently. Incidentally, the koan "No Mind, No Buddha," is Case 33.

Shakyamuni Buddha's great enlightenment was simply the realization that "The whole universe is one and empty." The truth realized by all the past, present, and future Buddhas is identical to Shakyamuni's realization. In empty oneness there is no duality; it transcends all dualistic opposition. Just one at every point of time and space. This oneness is sometimes called "Mu," sometimes "the sound of one hand," sometimes "one's primal face before one's parents were born," or "the subtle Dharma," "the subtle mind of nirvana," "mind," "one mind," "Buddha," or "our essential nature," and so forth. All these names, however, are only symbols or labels for this empty oneness. Enlightenment is nothing other than grasping this oneness by living experience.

In the present koan, Mu or oneness appears under the word "mind." The whole universe is just this very mind. If this is so, then from morning until night, from waking until going to sleep, everything you see and hear and touch and feel and think is nothing but mind. Although it may move as greed, anger, or folly, or wanting to eat or love or hate, all these are no other than mind. The mountain is high, the river long. The leaves are green, and the flowers are red. Birds fly, wind blows, and rain falls. All these are just mind. What can there be outside of it?

Why is it that we cannot admit this? Because our dualistic concepts hinder us from realizing empty oneness naturally. Once you have grasped it, everything proceeds smoothly. There are no obstacles. You are able to live peacefully, and problems solve themselves naturally. We may even say problems evaporate by themselves. I suggest you look at the koan from this point of view. We must not forget, however, that this oneness can never be grasped by discursive thinking or by any scientific method. It can only be attained by enlightenment.

ON MUMON'S COMMENTARY

"If you grasp it on the spot, you wear Buddha's clothes, eat Buddha's food, speak Buddha's words, do Buddha's deeds; you are Buddha himself. Though this may be so, Taibai has, alas, misled not a few people into mistaking the mark on the balance for the weight itself. How can he realize that even the mere mention of the word 'Buddha' should make a man rinse his mouth for three days? If one is such a man, when he hears someone say, 'The very mind is Buddha,' he will cover his ears and run away."

Mumon says, "If you grasp Baso's meaning on the spot, you wear Buddha's clothes, eat Buddha's food, speak Buddha's words; you are Buddha himself." You may recall the first phrase of Hakuin Zenji's *Song of Zazen*, which says, "All living beings are intrinsically Buddha." But Buddha is merely the name given to the empty oneness which is our essential nature. It is the only one in the whole universe and with the whole universe. We cannot realize it because of our dualistic concepts.

When Baso says, "This very mind is Buddha," his meaning is, "One is all and all is one," as the third patriarch, Sōsan, says in his *Believing in Mind* (Shinjin-Mei). But here, too, if you become attached to Taibai's words, "The very mind is Buddha," you will go astray. Therefore Mumon warns us "Taibai has misled not a few people into mistaking the mark on the balance for the weight itself." The mark on the balance means a fixed concept or idea of the mind or the Buddha. Both are labels for oneness. Whatever label we put on it, if the label has meaning, then it cannot express oneness itself. Oneness transcends all names and labels or concepts. All these are merely pictures, not reality itself. When Mumon says "weight itself," he means "oneness itself," so the whole phrase means, as I keep telling you, that the concept is not the fact.

Mumon goes on to say, "How can he realize that even the mere mention of the word 'Buddha' should make a man rinse his mouth for three days?" If even a trace of a concept of Buddha arises in our consciousness, it defiles the purity of oneness. So a truly enlightened person will rinse out his mouth for three days to get rid of the impurity.

Mumon then says, "If one is such a man, when he hears someone say, 'The very mind is Buddha,' he will cover his ears and run away." "Such a man" means the man of true realization. He is the sort of man that hates to hear dirty words such as "mind," or "Buddha," or "essential nature," so he covers his ears and runs away.

ON THE VERSE

The blue sky, the bright day.
It is most detestable to hunt around;
If, furthermore, you ask, "What is Buddha?"
It is like shouting your innocence while holding the loot.

"The blue sky, the bright day." Everything is extremely clear, just like a blue sky that has no clouds. On such a bright day, everything is clear and perfectly distinct; there is no darkness, no shadow, no doubt. Everything is just as you see it, as you feel it, as you think it!

"It is most detestable to hunt around." There is no need anymore to search for the Buddha or to ask what the Dharma means.

"If, furthermore, you ask, 'What is Buddha?,' it is just like shouting your innocence while holding the loot." In the *Sutra of the Lotus Flower of the Wonderful Law*, we see Ennyadatta searching the town madly for his own head. You have your head and had it before you were born. You are using it freely and naturally and still you are searching for it. It is just as if you were shouting loudly, "I am innocent!" while you hold obvious proof of your thievery in your hand. Fool! But this is what we do every day of our lives.

Jōshū Sees Through
an Old Woman

31

THE CASE

A monk once asked an old woman, "What is the way to Taizan?" The old woman said, "Go straight on." After the monk had gone a few steps, she said, "This good, honest priest goes off that way, too."

Later a monk told Jōshū about this. Jōshū said, "Wait a bit. I will go and see through the old woman for you." The next day he went and asked the same question, and the old woman also made the same reply. On returning, Jōshū said to his disciples, "I have seen through the old woman of Taizan for you."

MUMON'S COMMENTARY

The old woman just sits in her tent and knows how to plan the strategy, but she still doesn't know how to capture the bandit. Old Jōshū was clever enough to steal into the camp and menace the fortress, but he hasn't the air of a magnanimous man. Pondering the matter, we must say they both had their faults. Tell me now, what insight did Jōshū get into the old woman?

THE VERSE

The question is the same,
The answer is the same, too.
Sand in the rice,
Thorns in the mud.

TEISHŌ ON THE CASE

This is the sixth time Jōshū has appeared in the *Gateless Gate,* so I am sure you all know him quite well by now. We will meet him once more in Case 37 and then twelve times in the *Blue Cliff Record* and five times in the *Book of Equanimity.* In any event, he is one of the greatest masters in the whole of Zen history.

Many times in Zen stories an old woman appears. You will remember the one who defeated Tokusan in Case 28. Here is another. Today's old woman is supposed to have lived in a small snack shop at the foot of Taizan.

Taizan, sometimes called Gotaizan or Seiryōzan, is a mountain in north China which has five peaks. As the sacred dwelling place of Bodhisattva Manjusri, it has been an especially holy mountain from the time of the Six Dynasties. Bodhisattva Manjusri is the symbol of the wisdom of enlightenment, the attainment of which is the most important task of the practicing Buddhist. According to monastic rules, a statue of Manjusri is to be placed in the center of the Zen hall. From ancient times Zen practitioners have made pilgrimages to this holy mountain where Manjusri is revered.

The road to Taizan is thought to have come to a fork at the spot near the old woman's shop. Whenever a monk stopped and asked her the way to Taizan, she would always answer, "Go straight on," and when the monk began to walk on as directed, she would say behind his back, "He looks like a good, honest monk, but he goes off the same way as everybody else." The tone of her voice would be a bit contemptuous.

You know that from the Zen point of view if a practitioner searches for Manjusri somewhere outside of himself, he is going the wrong way. He must search within himself. The monk's question has the ordinary meaning, "Which road shall I take to get to Taizan, left or right?" The old woman's answer seems to say, "If you want to get to Manjusri, just go straight on," which might be interpreted, "If you want to attain enlightenment, just go straight on, working on Mu!"

Since most of the monks did not understand the meaning behind the old woman's words, they would continue on their way according to her directions. In disappointment, the old woman would call from behind, "What an earnest fellow, but, alas, he goes off that way too."

The monk who appears in this koan was probably a disciple of Jōshū. He mentioned this incident and asked the master's opinion. Jōshū said,

"Wait a bit. I will go and see through this old woman for you." The next day he was off, asking the same question and getting the same answer. When he returned he said to his disciples, "I have seen through the old woman of Taizan," but he did not say how he had done it. Now this is the important point of the koan. What did Jōshū perceive in the old woman? I think you will see that there are three possibilities. The first is that Jōshū found her deeply enlightened, the second that he found her totally blind, and the third that he found her somewhat enlightened. To examine this and present an answer in a few pithy words is the point of this koan.

This is a rather difficult koan. Harada Sogaku Roshi once said that it took him seven or eight years before he was able to see it clearly. In contemplating enlightenment, we must be aware of two principles. One is that every enlightenment is always enlightenment but in a multiplicity of degrees of depth and clarity. The second is that even though there are degrees, true enlightenment is one and the same by nature. In Japanese we call it *dōchū iben* (difference in sameness) and *ichū dōben* (sameness in difference). These two principles are used in examining enlightenment. We must contemplate this koan from these two points of view. Jōshū, the great Zen master, was able to penetrate and discern the depth of the old woman's enlightenment. If you were Jōshū, how would you describe it? Try to show me with an epigram.

On the other hand, if we look at this koan from the highest, purely essential, point of view, it could be presented as follows:

A monk asked an old woman, "What is the way to Taizan?" Just this. The old woman said, "Go straight on." Just this. The old woman said, "This good, honest monk goes off that way, too." Just this. The next day Jōshū went and asked the same question, and the old woman gave the same answer. Just this.

Jōshū did not say anything about good or bad, but he saw through her all the same. Until that time, no one had been able to understand the old woman. For the first time, her heart and soul were penetrated by a true acquaintance.

ON MUMON'S COMMENTARY

"The old woman just sits in her tent and knows how to plan the strategy, but she still doesn't know how to capture the bandit. Old Jōshū was clever enough to steal into the camp and menace the fortress, but he hasn't the air of a magnanimous man. Pondering the matter, we must say they both had their faults. Tell me now, what insight did Jōshū get into the old woman?"

At first Mumon criticizes the old woman. He says she just sits in her tent and plans the campaign, but she doesn't know how to capture the enemy. Her attitude is always passive. She does not show any positive activity, such as plunging into the enemy's camp and capturing the general.

Mumon goes on to say, "Jōshū was clever enough to steal into the camp and menace the fortress, but he hasn't the air of a magnanimous man. Pondering the matter, we must say both had their faults." Mumon says that Jōshū's conduct is not that of a man of virtue, which means it is not the behavior of a great Zen master. He says that both of them are at fault. That may be true, but to revert to the two principles for examining enlightenment, is it sameness in difference or difference in sameness?

Now tell me, what was Jōshū's insight into the old woman?

ON THE VERSE

The question is the same,
The answer is the same, too.
Sand in the rice,
Thorns in the mud.

The monks usually asked, "Which way shall I take to Taizan?" As a rule, the woman replied, "Go straight on." Jōshū asked the same question, and the woman gave the same answer. The questions are the same. The answers are the same. But Jōshū's question has a barb in it, and a barb is like a grain of sand in rice. If you chew carelessly, you will injure your teeth. Or it's like the barb of a thorn in mud. If you step on it barefooted, you will hurt yourself. Jōshū's piercing eye gleamed the way Mumon described it in the verse of Case 11: "His eye is like a shooting star; his spirit is like lightning; the sword that kills, the sword that gives life."

A Non-Buddhist
Questions Buddha

32

THE CASE

A non-Buddhist in all earnestness asked the World-Honored One, "I do not ask about words, I do not ask about no-words." The World-Honored One just sat still. The non-Buddhist praised him, saying, "The World-Honored One in his great benevolence and great mercy has opened the clouds of my delusion and enabled me to enter the Way." Then, bowing, he took his leave. Ananda asked Buddha, "What did the non-Buddhist realize that made him praise you so much?" The World-Honored One replied, "He is just like a fine horse that runs even at the shadow of a whip."

MUMON'S COMMENTARY

Ananda is Buddha's disciple, but his realization is less than the non-Buddhist's. Now tell me, how far is the distance between the non-Buddhist and Buddha's disciple?

THE VERSE

Walking on the edge of a sword,
Running over a ridge of jagged ice;
Not using steps or ladders,
Jumping from the cliff with hands free.

TEISHŌ ON THE CASE

The three people appearing in this koan are the World-Honored One (a title of Buddha explained in Case 6), his cousin and favorite disciple, Ananda, whom we met in Case 22, and a non-Buddhist, who was probably a philosopher. This non-Buddhist said, "I do not ask about words, I do not ask about no-words. Please teach me the absolute reality that transcends both of these."

You will remember that in Case 8 I told you about the verse from the *Prajna Paramita Sutra:* "Shiki soku ze kū, kū soku ze shiki" (All phenomena are nothing but emptiness; emptiness is nothing but all phenomena). Now, when the non-Buddhist says "words" he means being, namely, phenomena, and by "no-words" he means nonbeing, that is to say emptiness. Both of these belong to the world of the senses or thought. They are not reality. So the non-Buddhist was really asking Shakyamuni to show him that which transcends the phenomenal world of being and nonbeing.

Shakyamuni Buddha, penetrating the non-Buddhist's state of mind, presented the whole of the absolute reality by just sitting. If you think of the essential world as the zero-infinite denominator of my fraction, you will understand that not only Shakyamuni's "just sitting," which has the denominator beneath it, but also your sitting, standing up, your laughing, crying, the flow of water, clouds moving about in the sky—everything in the world—is nothing other than absolute reality, the real fact which transcends the phenomenal world of dualistic opposition.

Zen and Zen masters have different ways of presenting this absolute reality. Whenever monks asked Master Ro for instruction, he would turn around and, without a word, face the wall. The priest Gutei would raise a finger, as we learned in Case 3. The priest Dachi (*da* means to beat and *chi* means the ground) used to beat the ground with a stick. All these actions are nothing other than the presentation of the whole of the essential world. They are also the perfect manifestation of our essential nature.

Here, in this koan, the manifestation is just sitting. We must not forget that the living example of Shakyamuni's sitting is nothing other than our own zazen. It is through zazen that we come to extinguish our consciousness and thereby attain satori and true peace of mind. At the same time, when we are sitting in zazen, no matter how we are doing it, whether just sitting in *shikantaza* or doing Mu or breath-counting, our essential nature manifests itself perfectly. There is no difference between Shakyamuni and us, and we are always in the Lotus Land.

The non-Buddhist came to realize all this in the flash of an instant! In profound gratitude he exclaimed in praise, "The World-Honored One in his great benevolence and great mercy has opened the clouds of my delusion and enabled me to enter the Way!"

Where did he enter? There is no entrance or gate! When you go from darkness into daylight, you will find that there is no within or without, no inside or outside. To realize this is what is meant by "to enter." In emptiness there is nothing to be seen, nothing to be attached to. Everybody and everything, all times and all places, are perfect manifestations of it. In his delusion, the non-Buddhist had gone astray, searching here and there for something called the absolute truth. When the clouds parted, he grasped it. He bowed profoundly, and took his leave.

Obviously, Ananda's eye was still unenlightened, and he had no idea of what transcends being and nonbeing. So after the non-Buddhist left, he asked Shakyamuni, "What did he realize that made him praise you so much?"

"He is just like a fine horse that runs even at the shadow of a whip!" was the reply.

This is a simile from the *Zōagonkyō Sutra*, or *Anguttara Nikāya*, where Buddha compares people to four kinds of horses. The first are those that start even at the shadow of a whip and perform the will of the horseman. They are like those who feel the impermanence of the world when they hear of the death of someone in another village. The second kind are those that start when their hair is touched by the whip. They are like those people who feel the impermanence of the world only when they hear of the death of someone they know in their own village. The third kind starts when its hide is touched by the whip. They are like those people who feel the impermanence of the world only when they are faced with a death in the family. And the fourth kind are those that start only when the whip reaches their bones! They are like those people who do not feel the impermanence of the world until personally faced with a serious illness.

These similes are meant to indicate the depth of each individual's causal relation to the Dharma and also the degree of aspiration on the part of the student. Those unconcerned with the Dharma of the Buddha are totally outside the four classes of horses. Shakyamuni was praising the non-Buddhist highly when he rated him with the first class. At the same time, he was also prodding and encouraging Ananda by presenting the essential reality itself.

ON MUMON'S COMMENTARY

"Ananda is Buddha's disciple, but his realization is less than the non-Buddhist's. Now tell me, how far is the distance between the non-Buddhist and Buddha's disciple?"

I think you know that from the essential point of view there is no difference between them. Neither is there any difference between the Buddha and us. From the phenomenal point of view, however, the distance is vast. Ananda was enlightened only after forty years of hard practice. The non-Buddhist attained realization the moment he looked at the Buddha sitting in silence. Why can't you become enlightened instantly as the non-Buddhist did? You must reflect on the shallowness of your Dharma relation and exert yourself to the utmost.

ON THE VERSE

Walking on the edge of a sword,
Running over a ridge of jagged ice;
Not using steps or ladders,
Jumping from the cliff with hands free.

Anyone who is walking on the edge of a sword or over a ridge of jagged ice cannot hesitate even for a moment or else he will slip and be injured. When someone grasps absolute reality, he experiences it in a second. If he hesitates on even a bit of a concept, his true life is lost. The non-Buddhist did not hesitate. He attained satori like a flash of lightning.

We cannot attain true realization by proceeding step by step, like going up a ladder. We must take a leap as if we were jumping into the air from a high cliff, with our hands attached to nothing!

No Mind, No Buddha

THE CASE

A monk asked Baso in all earnestness, "What is Buddha?" Baso replied, "No mind, no Buddha."

MUMON'S COMMENTARY

If you can see into what was said here, your study is at an end.

THE VERSE

If you meet a swordsman, you may present a sword;
You should not offer a poem unless you meet a poet.
When you speak to others, say only three-quarters of it;
You should never give the remaining part.

TEISHŌ ON THE CASE

This koan and Case 30 are companion koans. They are the preaching of Master Baso and, in their contrast, present the two sides of his teaching.

Today, as in the past, most people search for the truth outside of mind. This is a weakness and a sickness in ordinary people. We should know that as long as we look for truth or reality in the objective world, we will never attain true peace of mind.

In order to remedy this malady, Baso gave the following instruction, "The very mind is Buddha." Among the many people who had their third (enlightened) eye opened by these words, Taibai Hōjō is the most famous. In Case 30 I told you about his enlightenment and how he went into the mountains to deepen his practice. Now I would like to tell you a story about him during that time.

In olden times, Zen practitioners used to go about visiting Zen masters and having mondo; this was called *angya,* or pilgrimage. It was the custom to take along a staff. One day a monk from Baso's monastery was in the mountains hunting for a branch of a tree to serve as his staff for *angya* when he got lost. Eventually he came to a hut where he found an old man who he thought was a woodsman.

The monk asked, "How can I get out of this mountain?"

The old man replied, "Go on following the flow of water."

And, indeed, by following the stream the monk could get to the village, but the words of the old man were more than geographical directions. To "go on following the flow of water" is very valuable Zen instruction.

In the practice of Zen we must proceed every day, every moment, quite naturally according to the present situation. All our actions should be as ordinary as the flow of water. To go against the stream is not the way of Zen. When we meet a child, we must become a child. When we meet an old man, we must become an old man. When we are with a senior, we must pay him or her suitable respect. When we are with a junior, we must guide him or her with the utmost kindness. As I have said before, we must use the sword freely, now to kill, now to give life, according to the time, place, and circumstances. That is the meaning of the old man's words, "Go on following the flow of water."

When he returned to the monastery, the monk told Baso what had happened on the mountain.

Baso replied, "That old fellow might have been Taibai Hōjō. He opened his eye after hearing my words, 'The very mind is Buddha,' and afterwards hid himself. I've heard rumors that he is continuing the practice after realization alone in that mountain. Why don't you go see him again and examine him?"

At this point, the story I told you about in Case 30 begins, where the monk goes and finds Taibai and tells him that Baso's teaching, "The very mind is Buddha" has changed to "No mind, no Buddha." The unshaken old man's reply was, "The great Master Baso perplexes many Zen men. He may say, 'No mind, no Buddha' as he will, but for me it is, 'The very mind is Buddha' forever."

When Baso heard this, his cryptic remark was, "The plum has ripened!" Taibai means big plum, and the master was certifying Taibai's state of realization.

The most fundamental delusion ordinary people have is that they think the objective world which they can grasp with their senses is the only one that exists. They do not think that there is any other world. This is not true. In order to break this delusion and help people open their real eye, Baso taught, "The very mind is Buddha." With these words many people attained satori, but many other people were apt to form ideas about the mind or the Buddha.

Some people, for example, may think that the mind has a form of some kind, being heart-shaped or round, and so forth. Others may think it is something which separates from the body at death and flies away by itself like a cicada. Other people may take the superficial consciousness, the six senses, for the real mind. It was to help people get rid of these concepts that Baso preached, "No mind, no Buddha."

We should know that both mind and Buddha are concepts. However deeply we may search for our mind, we will never find it to have form, color, weight, or a place of abode. In a word, it is empty. When we feel joyful, it is very clear to us that the joy arises out of our mind, but of itself joy has no substance. We cannot show others what it looks like, for it too is empty. In the same way, all the activities of the mind are, in the end, totally void.

Do you remember the Verse in Case 12?

The reason those who learn the Way don't realize the truth
Is simply that they perceive the discriminating consciousness they've
*   had all along.*
It is the origin of endless life-and-death;
Fools take it for the essential self.

Sometimes Baso taught, "The very mind is Buddha" and at other times, "No mind, no Buddha." But these are not two different teachings; both point to our essential nature. When we see, that's it. When we hear, that's it. But when we say "mind," a concept is attached to it. In order to sweep away this concept, Baso taught, "No mind, no Buddha."

ON MUMON'S COMMENTARY

Mumon says, "If you can see what was said here, your study is at an end."
WHACK!

What is there? Nothing!

If you realize this, your study of Zen is over. If you realize Baso's inner world when you hear, "No mind, no Buddha," your Zen study is at its end. Of course, there is no end to the practice of Zen. This study of Zen means the practice you must carry on under a master, and that will some-day come to an end.

ON THE VERSE

If you meet a swordsman, you may present a sword;
You should not offer a poem unless you meet a poet.
When you speak to others, say only three-quarters of it;
You should never give the remaining part.

To give a sword to a man who is not interested in swords or the art of swordsmanship is sheer nonsense. Likewise, it is folly to offer poetry to a man who is not able to appreciate it. In the same way, it is foolish to speak about Zen to those who have no Zen experience, and when you do talk about Zen, you should not tell all. Save at least one-quarter to let the Zen students work on by themselves. If you are too kind to them, they will become spoiled and will never be able to attain true Zen experience.

Knowing Is Not
the Way

THE CASE

Nansen said, "Mind is not Buddha; knowing is not the Way."

MUMON'S COMMENTARY

It should be said of Nansen that he has grown old and knows no shame.
Just opening his stinking mouth he exposed the disgrace of his own household. There are very few, however, who are grateful for his kindness.

THE VERSE

When the sky clears, the sun appears;
When the rain falls, the earth is wet.
With all his heart, he has preached everything,
But I fear nobody can believe it.

TEISHŌ ON THE CASE

This is the fourth time Nansen appears in the *Gateless Gate;* he also figures in Cases 14, 19, and 27.

You will remember that when Nansen was asked by Jōshū in Case 19,
"What is the Way?" Nansen replied, "The ordinary mind is the Way."
Then in Case 27 when asked by a monk, "What is the truth that has not
been preached?" Nansen answered, "This is not mind; this is not Bud-

dha; this is not a thing." In the previous koan, Nansen's teacher, Baso, was asked by a monk, "What is Buddha?" and the reply was, "No mind, no Buddha." In this koan Nansen is saying, "The mind is not Buddha; knowing is not the Way."

All these koans belong to the same category. We find four important words—Buddha, mind, knowing, and Way. Though these four words are all different, each one points to the same fact, but as you know, words are merely names or labels which evoke concepts concerning the fact. They are not, and never can be, the fact itself. When Nansen says, "Mind is not Buddha; knowing is not the Way," he is trying to exterminate the delusive pictures in our brain which are attached to the fact.

From the essential point of view, when we say "Buddha," the whole universe is Buddha. Nothing remains outside of Buddha. When we say "mind," the whole universe is mind. Nothing remains outside of it. It is the same with "knowing" and "Way." From the Zen point of view, the words Buddha, mind, knowing, and Way are nothing other than Mu, the sound of one hand clapping, just sitting or counting breaths. Even though I say it this way, some dregs of conceptualization still remain. If I swept away all the sediment, how would I say it? Simply standing up itself, sitting down itself, crying itself, laughing itself, and so on.

As long as you understand the fact by thinking or intellectual reasoning, however, there is still room for delusive thoughts to arise. To eradicate them completely, we must kill our consciousness at least once and then come back to life again. Then for the first time we will realize clearly that not only Buddha, mind, knowing, Way, standing up, sitting down, crying, and laughing but also Tarō, Hanako, John, Mary, everybody, and everything are nothing but the great and wonderful independent light itself.

Nevertheless, some people, hearing that Nansen once said, "The very mind is Buddha," take their superficial consciousness as Buddha and the knowledge of realization as the Way. In order to remedy this at another time, Nansen said, "Mind is not Buddha; knowing is not the Way." If you grasp this Way conceptually, you are wrong. Nansen has no such thought in his mind. He is telling you just to sweep away all such conceptual thoughts and strip your consciousness naked.

It will not be easy to actualize and be able to express this state of mind. Nansen himself was able to preach as he does in this koan only after thirty or forty years of hard practice.

ON MUMON'S COMMENTARY

"It should be said of Nansen that he has grown old and knows no shame. Just opening his stinking mouth he exposed the disgrace of his own household. There are very few, however, who are grateful for his kindness."

Mumon's critical remarks are, as usual, abusive on the surface but praising at heart. We are not qualified to judge the saying of the Zen masters of the past until we have opened our own eye. But once we have attained true enlightenment, we can even criticize the words of Shakyamuni or Bodhidharma!

This does not mean that the one criticizing is higher in his degree of realization than the one criticized. In this case, we must acknowledge that Nansen would still be higher than Mumon in his state of realization.

Mumon says, "It should be said of Nansen that he has grown old and knows no shame. Just opening his stinking mouth he exposed the disgrace of his own household. There are very few, however, who are grateful for his kindness."

This means that Nansen's words, "Mind is not Buddha; knowing is not the Way," are too kind for his students. He is acting like a grandmother who uses endearing talk with her grandchildren. He should be ashamed of himself for spoiling the students. He opened his stinking mouth and disclosed the disgrace of the whole family of Buddhism. Nevertheless, there may be a few who can understand and be grateful for his kindness.

ON THE VERSE

When the sky clears, the sun appears;
When the rain falls, the earth is wet.
With all his heart, he has preached everything,
But I fear nobody can believe it.

It's all very natural and according to reason—like saying that my father is older than I, or that when a dog turns to the west, its tail points to the east. How can anything else be so?

When Dōgen Zenji returned to Japan from China, he said, "I, the priest in the mountain, did not stay at many monasteries. Only by chance did I meet my late teacher Tendō and become able to realize directly that the eyes are horizontal and the nose is vertical; thus I am unable to be deceived by others."

"I have returned to my native country with empty hands. There is not even a hair of Buddhism in me. Now I pass the time naturally; the sun rises in the east every morning, and every night the moon sets in the west. When the clouds clear, the outline of the mountains appear, and as the rain passes away, the surrounding mountains bend down. What is it, after all?"

And some time later, from out of his quietness came the words:

A leap year comes after three years,
The cock crows at about four.

Everything is perfect and complete as it is, always and everywhere. True Buddhism, or the satori of Zen, is as simple and as natural as that! The last two lines of Mumon's verse say:

With all his heart he has preached everything,
But I fear nobody can believe it.

WHACK! There! I have finished preaching everything that is in my heart. But I am afraid that only a few of you can realize this WHACK!

Seijo's Soul Is Separated

35

THE CASE

Goso asked a monk, "Seijo and her soul are separated; which one is the true Seijo?"

MUMON'S COMMENTARY

If you realize the true one in this, you will understand that getting out of one shell and entering another is just like a traveler staying at an inn; if you have not realized it, don't rush about wildly. When earth, water, fire, and wind are suddenly about to decompose, you will be like a crab which has fallen into boiling water and is struggling with its seven arms and eight legs. At that time, don't say I didn't warn you.

THE VERSE

The clouds and the moon are the same;
Valleys and mountains are different from each other.
All are blessed, ten thousand times blessed!
Is this one? Is this two?

TEISHŌ ON THE CASE

Goso is Zen master Hōen, who lived on Mount Goso. Literally, Goso means the fifth patriarch, but the Goso in this koan was not the fifth patriarch, Kōnin, who appeared in Case 23. Master Hōen entered the priesthood at the age of thirty-five and eventually became the Dharma successor of Master Haku'un Shutan. Master Engo, who wrote the opening instructions and both the short and long critical comments on each koan in the *Blue Cliff Record,* was his disciple. Hōen passed away in 1104 at the age of about eighty.

The story of Sei (*Seijo* literally means "the girl Sei") comes from an old Chinese legend of the T'ang period.

Once upon a time in the province of Kō there lived an old man named Chōkan. Chōkan loved his daughter Sei very much. She was very beautiful, and Chōkan used to tease her when she was still a child, saying that her beauty matched that of her cousin, the handsome Ōchū. Just about the time that the two cousins realized they were in love, Chōkan announced his choice of another man as husband for Sei. The young lovers were heartbroken. Ōchū left the town, setting off in a small boat. He had rowed a distance when he noticed someone running along the bank, waving to him. To his great joy he found that it was Sei who had followed him. They decided to travel to a far-off land and make a life together.

A few years later, when Sei had become the mother of two children, she realized for the first time how deep the parent's love is. Her conscience began to bother her about the way she had treated her beloved father. Her husband, Ōchū, who also regretted what they had done to Chōkan, suggested that they return to their homeland to ask for his forgiveness.

When they arrived in the province of Kō, Sei remained in the boat while Ōchū went to apologize to Chōkan and tell him what had happened. The old man listened incredulously. Finally he asked Ōchū whom he was talking about. The young husband replied, "Your daughter Sei."

"But Sei never left home!" the old man exclaimed. "Shortly after you went away she became ill and is still confined to bed. She hasn't uttered a word since you left."

"You must be mistaken," Ōchū replied. "Sei followed me, and we went together to a far-off country. We're married and have two children. She is in excellent health and wants to see you again and ask your forgiveness for running away and marrying without your permission. If you don't believe me, come down to the boat and see for yourself."

The old man was reluctant, so Ōchū went alone to bring Sei back to her father's house. In the meantime, Chōkan went into the bedroom to tell the sick Sei what had happened. Without a word, the invalid rose from her bed and rushed out to meet the approaching Sei, and the two became one.

Chōkan said to his daughter, "Ever since Ōchū left, you have been dumb and lifeless, as though your soul had fled."

Sei told him, "I didn't know I was home sick in bed. When I heard that Ōchū had left, I followed his boat as if in a dream."

That is the gist of the story. Goso took it up as teaching material and asked a monk, "There are two Seis; which is the true one?"

It is not necessary, of course, for the purpose of Zen study to think about whether the story is probable or not from the scientific point of view, or to decide which is the true Sei by psychiatric analysis. Goso is trying to make the monk realize the true one by passing through the perplexity of two Seis. As long as you are attached to the dualistic concept of two Seis, you cannot grasp the true one. Which is the true one? What is the true Sei? As you know, when you have truly become one with Mu, you realize what Mu is. When you have really become one with Sei, you will see the true Sei easily.

ON MUMON'S COMMENTARY

"If you realize the true one in this, you will understand that getting out of one shell and entering another is just like a traveler staying at an inn; if you have not realized it, don't rush about wildly. When earth, water, fire, and wind are suddenly about to decompose, you will be like a crab which has fallen into boiling water and is struggling with its seven arms and eight legs. At that time, don't say I didn't warn you."

Our life-and-death is like a man who emerges from one shell or husk and enters another. It is like a traveler who stays at a lodging house one night and leaves it the next morning. It is merely a superficial change; the essential nature does not change at all.

Mumon says, "If you have not realized it, don't rush about wildly." If you have not realized it, the best thing for you is to sit calmly on your cushion and continue to practice zazen. You should not rush about seeing a lot of Zen masters or visiting monastery after monastery looking for this religion or that philosophy. Such rushing around is useless for attaining self-realization and freeing ourselves from the sufferings of the delusive world. Without directly grasping the true one by experience we will never be able to solve our problem of life and death.

Mumon continues, "When earth, water, fire, and wind are suddenly about to decompose, you will be like a crab which has fallen into boiling water and is struggling with its seven arms and eight legs."

"When earth, fire, water, and wind are about to decompose" means when we are about to die. People of ancient India thought that all physical things, including our bodies, are composed of the four elements—earth, water, fire, and wind—and that after death our body dissolves into these four elements. If we have not been enlightened and are at the point of departing from this life, we will struggle in anguish at the horror of death, just as a crab that has fallen into boiling water kicks and flounders with all its arms and legs.

In his concluding sentence, Mumon tells us, "At that time you should not accuse me of not having taught it to you. It will be too late for sorrow. Buddhas and patriarchs are constantly giving you all kinds of instruction about it."

ON THE VERSE

The clouds and the moon are the same;
Valleys and mountains are different from each other.
All are blessed, ten thousand times blessed!
Is this one? Is this two?

"The clouds and the moon are the same" means that differentiation is nothing but equality. Though the clouds and the moon appear as separate things, they are nothing but the manifestation of one essential emptiness. Though the two Seis lived separately, they were two appearances of one essential nature. Sometimes we feel sad, sometimes happy. Sadness and happiness are not the same, but when we realize that each of them is totally void and has no substance, we will realize that the two are different manifestations of one empty essence.

The second phrase, "Valleys and mountains are different from each other," means that equality is nothing but differentiation. Though valleys and mountains are different manifestations of one essential emptiness, valleys are not mountains, and mountains are not valleys. They are completely different.

One Sei was lying in her father's home in a stupor. The other Sei was living with her husband in a far-distant land. Though their essential nature is one, being totally void, they were living separately, each retaining her own individuality. Both sadness and happiness come from the same origin, which is completely void; but when we feel sad there is no happiness at all, and when we feel happy, sadness is not to be seen.

"All are blessed, ten thousand times blessed" means everything is blessed as it is. Felicitations to all! What else is there to search for?

Meeting a Man Who Has Accomplished the Way

36

THE CASE

Goso said, "If you meet a man on the path who has accomplished the Way, do not greet him with words or silence. Tell me, how will you greet him?"

MUMON'S COMMENTARY

If you can answer this question fittingly, you are certainly to be congratulated. But if you cannot, you should look for it attentively, wherever you are.

THE VERSE

Meeting on the path a man who has accomplished the Way,
Do not greet him with words or silence.
I will punch you in the face;
If you want to realize, realize on the spot.

TEISHŌ ON THE CASE

Goso is the Zen master who appeared in the previous case. He once said, "If you meet a man on the path who has accomplished the Way, do not greet him with words or silence. Tell me, how will you greet him?"

"A man who has accomplished the Way" means a man who has attained perfect enlightenment, such as a great Zen master or a bodhisattva or a Buddha. When you encounter such a person on the street and say nothing to him, it is impolite. If you greet him with glib words, that too is impolite. Therefore Goso says not to greet him with words or silence. How will you greet him?

There are several koans which belong to this category. For example, in Case 20 of the *Mumonkan:* "Why does a man of great strength not lift up his leg?" Or in Cases 70, 71, and 72 of the *Blue Cliff Record:* "How will you speak with your mouth closed?" In olden days, this kind of koan seems to have been very popular.

The present koan is very short and simple, but without a clearly enlightened eye we cannot completely grasp the essence of the question. If you can penetrate this case, you will be able to penetrate all forty-eight koans of the *Gateless Gate* with no difficulty whatsoever.

You should greet a man who has accomplished the Way neither with consciousness nor with nonconsciousness. In order to greet him correctly, you must transcend consciousness and nonconsciousness, words and silence.

I think some of you are familiar with the koan "Yuima's not-two." [1] It is Case 48 of the *Book of Equanimity* and Case 84 of the *Blue Cliff Record.* The koan is a mondo between the Bodhisattva Manjusri and the great layman Yuima.

When Yuima was asked by Manjusri Bodhisattva, "What is your view about the Dharma gate of not-two?" Yuima was silent. His silence is not simply a lack of words. It has a profound meaning. An ancient Zen master was to say of it, "Yuima's silence sounds like a roar of thunder." Do you know what that means? Can you hear the roaring thunder of silence?

As long as words are merely words and silence merely silence, we cannot enter the gate of not-two. From morning till night, each of us is in the Dharma gate of not-two, or more accurately, each of us is always using the Dharma gate of not-two. To put it still another way, each of us is nothing but the Dharma gate of not-two itself. But, because we are attached to dualistic ideas and thoughts, we cannot acknowledge the fact.

As I tell you repeatedly, every koan should be contemplated from the essential point of view. What is the content of words from the essential point of view? What is the content of silence from the essential point of view?

If you realize this, the koan will not be difficult for you.

ON MUMON'S COMMENTARY

"If you can answer this question fittingly, you are certainly to be congratulated. But if you cannot, you should look for it attentively, wherever you are."

If you can answer the question, every koan will be self-evident to you. You will be able to penetrate them all, just as you can move about without restriction in the free air. If "it" is not self-evident, then you must search for "it" constantly and attentively.

What is "it"? For those who are working on Mu, "it" is Mu. For those who are doing "just sitting" (*shikantaza*), "it" is your own self.

ON THE VERSE

Meeting on the path a man who has accomplished the Way,
Do not greet him with words or silence.
I will punch you in the face;
If you want to realize, realize on the spot.

Mumon's first and second lines repeat the case of the koan. "I will punch you in the face." A sudden punch in the jaw! Ouch! That's it! Ouch! That's everything! If you still cannot realize this, go back to your cushion and continue your practice of Mu or *shikantaza* all the more vigorously!

NOTE

1. Yuima is the Japanese name for Vimalakirti, brilliant lay disciple of Shakyamuni Buddha.

The Oak Tree in the Garden

37

THE CASE

A monk asked Jōshū in all earnestness, "What is the meaning of the patriarch's coming from the West?" Jōshū said, "The oak tree there in the garden."

MUMON'S COMMENTARY

If you see through Jōshū's response clearly, there is no Shakyamuni in the past, no Maitreya in the future.

THE VERSE

Words do not express the fact,
Speech does not match the student;
Attached to words, one loses the reality,
Stagnating in phrases, one is deluded.

TEISHŌ ON THE CASE

The patriarch here means Bodhidharma. For details on his life, see Case 41. The question, "What is the meaning of the patriarch's coming from the West?" is found many times in Zen. Although the answers vary, the question always means: What is the great spirit of Zen or the essential truth of Buddha's Dharma, which Bodhidharma brought from India to China?

Jōshū answered, "The oak tree there in the garden." With this answer he presented the world of oneness, which is nothing but the whole universe. The oak tree in the garden does not simply mean the oak tree as an object. It does not belong to the objective world.

Recall for a moment the fraction I use as a teaching device. The oak tree is the numerator and zero-infinity is the denominator. Jōshū presents the fraction itself as a whole. Actually, it is not necessary to say either "the oak tree" or "in the garden." "O" is enough, or "k" or "t." Any sound is sufficient. Anything, at any time, is the perfect manifestation of Mu, or the primal face, or the essential nature. As a test, just say, "The oak tree there in the garden." What difference is there between that and Mu?

Any word or phrase at any place, at any time can bring you to realization if you are ready. I heard there was an old woman who, at her first sesshin under Harada Roshi, attained kensho on the spot when she heard the Roshi saying, "Teizen no hakujushi (The oak tree there in the garden)."

It is said that at Kannon Monastery, where Jōshū lived, there were a lot of oak trees. So it was very natural for Jōshū to present the world of oneness by using an oak tree. In the *Gateless Gate,* the case stops at this point, but in the *Sayings of Jōshū-roku* there is more to this mondo. A more complete version is:

A monk asked Jōshū in all earnestness, "What is the meaning of the patriarch's coming from the West?" Jōshū said, "The oak tree there in the garden." The monk said, "Master, you should not show us by means of the objective world." The monk was trying to examine Jōshū, who replied quite naturally, "I do not show you by means of the objective world." So the monk asked again, "What is the meaning of the patriarch's coming from the West?" Jōshū answered, "The oak tree there in the garden."

Jōshū had a disciple named Kakutetsu-shi. After the Master died, Hōgen, whom we met in Case 26, asked Kakutetsu-shi, "I hear your late master had a koan about an oak tree. Is that true?"

Kakutetsu-shi replied, "My late master did not have any such koan. You should not abuse him." As Jōshū's Dharma successor, Kakutetsu-shi had completely comprehended his teacher's inner world. This one phrase, "The oak-tree-there-in-the-garden," has tremendous power to liberate all human beings from their dualistic ideas and thoughts.

There is a well-known saying by National Teacher Kanzan: "The oak tree has the activity of a robber." What do you suppose that means? If you can come to the answer, you will see that Jōshū was the greatest thief in the world.

There is an interesting story about this koan. Shidō Bunan Zenji, the Dharma grandfather of Hakuin Zenji, was traveling along the Tōkaidō, the famous old road from Kyōto to Edo (present-day Tokyo). A robber was following him and put up at the same inn one night so that he could enter Shidō's room in the dark and steal his money. The thief slid back the door a little and peeked in. There in the middle of the room was a garden with an oak tree in it! The robber was bewildered and looked about with great curiosity. Suddenly he heard a loud voice shout, "Who's there!" At that very instant the tree changed into the master, seated in zazen.

The intruder apologized to Shidō for his misconduct and asked to be taught this wonderful technique that would change him into an oak tree. Shidō taught him how to do zazen and gave him a koan. He followed his master's instructions faithfully and finally, overcoming his wickedness, lived as an honest man for the rest of his days.

ON MUMON'S COMMENTARY

"If you see through Jōshū's response clearly, there is no Shakyamuni in the past, no Maitreya in the future."

This means that if you realize Jōshū's answer directly and deeply, you will find that you have nothing to do with even Shakyamuni or Maitreya Bodhisattva, that there is neither past nor future within you.

ON THE VERSE

Words do not express the fact,
Speech does not match the student;
Attached to words, one loses the reality,
Stagnating in phrases, one is deluded.

This verse is not Mumon's. It was composed by Master Tōzan Shusho, but Mumon made use of it here.

The first line means that however skillfully we may use words, they do not give us the fact itself. If you try to approach the essence by comprehending the meaning of words, you will never succeed. No matter how loudly you cry fire, you will never feel the heat. No matter how many times you say sugar, you will never taste the sweetness.

"Speech does not match the student" means that speech is not intended to fit the degree of practice of the student. The speech of a true Zen master always presents the essence of the Dharma, the universe of oneness. It is not intended to be in accord with the disciple's degree of progress. It is not expedient.

The third line of the verse, "Attached to words, one loses the reality," means that those who become attached to explanations and meanings will never be able to grasp the real life of the fact. As I have so often told you, however minutely and exquisitely it may be explained, the true fact is beyond any explanation.

Finally, "Stagnating in phrases, one is deluded" means that those who adhere to the meaning of phrases become bewildered and are led endlessly around the periphery of the essential fact itself.

A Cow Passes Through a Window

38

THE CASE

Goso said, "For example, it's just like a great cow passing through a latticed window. Her head, horns, and four legs have passed through. Why is it that her tail can't pass through?"

MUMON'S COMMENTARY

If in regard to this you are able to turn yourself upside down, attain one single eye, and utter a turning word, you will be able to repay the four obligations above and help the living beings of the three realms below. If you are still unable to do this, reflect again on the tail; then you will be able to grasp it for the first time.

THE VERSE

If it passes through, it will fall into a ditch;
If it turns back, it will be destroyed.
This tiny little tail—
What a strange and marvelous thing it is!

TEISHŌ ON THE CASE

This koan is one of the eight which Hakuin Zenji selected as the most difficult. With it, we must thoroughly scrub off the grime that clings to us.

After we have finished this purification, we will be able to become the true Dharma body itself. We know, of course, that this is nothing other than Mu or the primal face.

As to the people in the koan, I have already told you about Master Goso in Case 36. He also appeared in the previous koan. I would like to point out again that Goso does not mean fifth patriarch but is the name of Master Hōen.

What does the cow mean? There are many interpretations of just what kind of animal is being referred to—an ordinary cow, a buffalo, or a water buffalo. But that is beside the point. I think all of you can easily see that it is another name for our essential nature. So in this koan Mu is appearing in the guise of a cow.

What does the window mean? Literally, of course, it is the latticed window of the cow shed. But here it means the three realms, the three delusive worlds of sensuous desire, form, and no-form. Living creatures who are dwelling in these worlds have not yet realized their own essential nature, the world of oneness. They are bound by dualistic ideas and thoughts, such as subject and object, delusion and enlightenment, saints and ordinary beings, good and bad, right and wrong, and are unable to free themselves from these traps.

Now, what do you think the head, horns, and four legs mean? They are all the knowledge and experience we have acquired since birth. In other words, they are the concepts, philosophies, ethics, and even the theories of Zen, which cling *a posteriori* to our essential nature. "The head, horns, and four legs have passed through the window" means that all concepts and ideas and the like which were adhering to our true nature have been totally eliminated.

Now the cow has freed herself from the delusive realms. She has realized that every concept produced by thinking is totally void. She has realized the essential world which, in the example of my fraction, is the world of the denominator.

But Goso says that the tail cannot pass through. Why not? It's unreasonable that a small thing should not be able to pass through an opening when a big thing can. It's absurd! But according to our practical common sense, every koan contains an absurdity, more or less. "Why" is Master Hōen's favorite word. It is a characteristic of his Zen teaching. He uses it to push his disciples to the great doubt, and in resolving it they penetrate the essential world.

Why can the tiny tail not pass through the window? Because its existence still remains. After we have realized that all phenomenal things are empty, what remains as existence? There is simply standing up or sitting down, drinking, eating, writing, reading, laughing, crying, and so forth, or the fraction itself.

ON MUMON'S COMMENTARY

"If in regard to this you are able to turn yourself upside down, attain one single eye, and utter a turning word, you will be able to repay the four obligations above and help the living beings of the three realms below. If you are still unable to do this, reflect again on the tail; then you will be able to grasp it for the first time."

In order to grasp true realization, we must destroy and overturn the practical world, which is based on the dualistic opposition of subject and object. In Zen training this is called killing self-consciousness. When we have wiped it out, all of a sudden a great new life appears. Then, for the first time, we can recognize the world of empty oneness which cannot be seen by our two physical eyes. It can only be seen by the single mind's eye—the eye of satori.

"And utter a turning word." As I told you before, a turning word means a word or phrase that has the power to transform a person who is deluded into a man of enlightenment. However difficult the koans or problems we encounter may be, once the eye of satori opens perfectly for us, we will be able to solve them all naturally and utter the turning word spontaneously.

"You will be able to repay the four obligations above." In Buddhism it is said that there are four grave obligations we ought to repay: to our parents, to all living beings in the world, to our sovereign, and to the three treasures (Buddha, Dharma, and Sangha).

To repay these four obligations is our most important duty. It is because of them that we are able to live our lives in safety and peace and, having a right knowledge of the purpose of life, endeavor to actualize it. The most authentic way of repaying these four obligations is to realize our true self. Once we attain self-realization, this duty becomes very easy and natural.

"And help the living beings of the three realms below." As I said before, the three realms are the delusive worlds of sensuous desire, form, and no-form. The world of no-form is the formless world of spirit only. The living creatures in these three realms are all suffering from the endless cycle of causation. But once we realize our true self, we recognize that all creatures in these realms are living within our own self. Then a strong aspiration arises naturally from the depths of our heart to save them all, no matter what the cost.

Mumon ends his commentary by saying that if you have not yet come to this stage, you must continue to reflect on the cow's tail and do your best to grasp it.

ON THE VERSE

If it passes through, it will fall into a ditch;
If it turns back, it will be destroyed.
This tiny little tail—
What a strange and marvelous thing it is!

The first line, "If it passes through, it will fall into a ditch," means that when you sweep away all delusive thoughts and realize the empty-limitless denominator, you are likely to fall into the world of emptiness. It is quite difficult to get out of this ditch.

"If it turns back, it will be destroyed" means that if you become separated from the essential world and return to the ordinary delusive world, your true life will be destroyed.

"This tiny little tail—what a strange and marvelous thing it is!" What a mysterious thing our essential nature is! It is beyond all thought, beyond any description or explanation! And the only way to get hold of it is by direct experience.

Unmon and a Mistake in Speech

THE CASE

A monk once asked Unmon, "The radiance serenely illuminates the whole vast universe . . ." Before he could finish the first line, Unmon suddenly interrupted, "Aren't those the words of Chōsetsu Shūsai?" The monk replied, "Yes, they are." Unmon said, "You have slipped up in the words."

Afterwards, Zen Master Shishin brought the matter up and said, "Tell me, at what point did he slip?"

MUMON'S COMMENTARY

If, as regards this case, you have grasped Unmon's lofty and unapproachable activity and how the monk slipped up in his words, you are worthy to become a teacher of men and heavenly beings. If you are not yet clear about it, you have not even saved yourself.

THE VERSE

Angling in a swift stream,
Those greedy for bait will be caught;
If you open your mouth even a bit,
Your life will be lost.

TEISHŌ ON THE CASE

There are three names in this koan, Master Unmon, Chōsetsu Shūsai, and Master Shishin. You have met Unmon before in Cases 15, 16, and 21. If you want to read about his life again, please refer to Case 15. Shishin Goshin, a Zen master of the Ōryū branch of Rinzai, is the Dharma successor of Master Soshin. It was while he was under Soshin's guidance that he attained great enlightenment upon hearing the sound of the *kyōsaku*. He named himself Shishin, which means dead mind.

Now a word about Chōsetsu Shūsai, the author of the verse the monk began to quote. His family name is Chō. Setsu is his first name and literally means unskillful. Shūsai means an able student or a bright boy, but in ancient China it had a different meaning. It meant the man who has passed the government's examination for screening applicants to high official positions.

In the beginning Chōsetsu went to Master Zengetsu for guidance in Zen but was later persuaded by his teacher to go to Master Sekisō. He did this and was asked by his new teacher to give his name. Chōsetsu told him, "My family name is Chō and my given name is Setsu." Remember that *setsu* means unskillful. Sekisō said to him, "Though you may try to discover the substance of skillfulness, it can never be found. You say your name is Setsu. But where is unskillfulness?"

What Sekisō meant was, "Where is Setsu? Where is your substance? Where is your essential nature?" At this, Chōsetsu was suddenly enlightened. For the first time he realized a world where there is neither skillfulness nor unskillfulness. Setsu is nowhere. His whole substance is void. He expressed his enlightenment in the following verse:

> *The radiance serenely illuminates the whole vast universe,*
> *Saints, common mortals, and other living creatures—all dwell in one*
>   *house.*
> *When no thought arises, total oneness is completely manifested;*
> *If the six organs move even a little, it is covered with clouds.*
> *If you want to cut off delusive passions and thoughts, the sickness*
>   *increases all the more;*
> *If you want to go towards absolute reality, this too is wrong.*
> *In following the relations of the world there is no hindrance;*
> *Both nirvana and life-and-death are no more than empty flowers.*

To return to the koan, a monk wanted to ask Unmon a question by quoting from this verse. Before he could finish the first line, Unmon suddenly interrupted and said, "Aren't those the words of Chōsetsu Shūsai?"

The monk said, "Yes, they are."

Unmon said, "You have slipped up in the words."

Later Master Shishin took up this case and asked the assembly of his disciples, "Tell me, at what point did he slip up in the words?" You must give me the answer in the dokusan room. I'll give you a bit of a hint. This monk was asking for light when he was already in the light. It is just like a man hunting for his house when he is already in it. Or like the man who is living in his own house and, not knowing it, pays the rent.

When he quoted from Chōsetsu's verse, "The radiance serenely illuminates the whole vast universe . . ." the monk was thinking of these words as Chōsetsu's poem. He was, so to speak, looking for the radiance outside of himself. Without a moment's delay, Unmon gave a thrust saying, "Aren't those the words of Chōsetsu Shusai?" which means, "Isn't that a borrowed feather?"

The stupid monk answered, "Yes."

Unmon could only reply, "You have slipped up in the words."

We must all see our own radiance within ourselves. The flowers, the grass, the wall, the pillar, they are the radiance of the eye. The ticking of the clock, the barking of the dog, the hacking of a cough, these are the radiance of the ear. It's cold! It's hot! Ouch! It's itchy! These are the radiance of the body. To be glad, sad, full of love, or full of hate, all these are the radiance of the mind. Every radiance is nothing other than the radiance of our true self. How will you answer when you realize Unmon's question?

ON MUMON'S COMMENTARY

"If, as regards this case, you have grasped Unmon's lofty and unapproachable activity and how the monk slipped up in his words, you are worthy to become a teacher of men and heavenly beings. If you are not yet clear about it, you have not even saved yourself."

Unmon's way of guiding his disciples is lofty and unapproachable. He interrupted the monk's words before he could finish quoting the first line. I hope you will be able to appreciate the extremely high standard and inimitable skill of Unmon's way of teaching. His examination is very sharp and as quick as a flash of lightning. No one, not even Buddhas and patriarchs, can approach him.

ON THE VERSE

Angling in a swift stream,
Those greedy for bait will be caught;
If you open your mouth even a bit,
Your life will be lost.

"Angling in a swift stream" refers to Unmon's abrupt interruption. The monk was caught when he replied, "Yes." He is still not enlightened and is searching for the radiance outside of himself. That is being greedy for bait.

"If you open your mouth even a bit, your life will be lost" means that as long as you have any concepts about radiance and try to explain it intellectually, your essential life will be lost. The only way to avoid being caught by the angler in the swift stream is to attain enlightenment.

Kicking Over
the Water Jug

40

THE CASE

When Master Isan was under Hyakujō, he had the position of *tenzo*.
Hyakujō wanted to choose a master for Mount Taii. He called the head
monk and the rest of his disciples together to have them present their
views and said that the outstanding person should be sent. Then he
took a water jug, put it on the floor, and said, "You may not call this a
water jug. What will you call it?" The head monk said, "It cannot be
called a wooden sandal." Hyakujō then asked Isan. Isan immediately
kicked over the water jug and left. Hyakujō laughed and said, "First
monk, you have been defeated by Isan." So he ordered Isan to found the
new monastery.

MUMON'S COMMENTARY

Isan summoned up all his valor, but, alas, he could not jump out of Hyakujō's trap. Upon examination, he favors the heavy and not the light. But
why? Look! Though he removed his headband, he put on an iron yoke.

THE VERSE

Tossing away the bamboo buckets and ladles,
He makes a vigorous thrust and cuts off hindrances;

Hyakujō's heavy barrier cannot interrupt his rush,
Countless Buddhas come forth from his toes.

TEISHŌ ON THE CASE

Master Isan Reiyū entered the priesthood at an early age and at first stud-ied both Hinayana and Mahayana Buddhism. When he was twenty he turned to Zen and went to Hyakujō's monastery, pursuing his training there under the great master for more than twenty years. He died in 853 at the age of eighty-three.

The characteristics of Isan's Zen are his apt expression and an air of nobility. These came to be so highly appreciated that he is considered to be one of the greatest masters in Zen history. Together with his eminent disciple, Master Kyōzan, he is honored as the founder of the Igyō sect, one of the five branches of Chinese Zen Buddhism in the T'ang era. The name comes from the "I" of Isan and the "Kyō(=gyō)" of Kyōsan.

After he attained great enlightenment, Isan continued under Hyakujō and was made *tenzo*. This is one of the most important positions in the monastery; the person who is *tenzo* has charge of the monks' meals. Of course, the head monk is very important too. He is considered the model in the community and occupies the first seat. In this case, the head monk was the man who later became Master Karin.

There is an interesting story connected with this koan. Among Hyaku-jō's disciples was a layman by the name of Shiba Zuda. He was a veteran fortune-teller and based his predictions on such varied things as facial features, a site of land, or even the aspect of a house. One day, Shiba Zuda came to Hyakujō and said, "I have found a very nice place to build a monastery. If we open one there, many practitioners will congregate and Buddhism will flourish. The features of this mountain indicate that there is power to attract fifteen hundred monks."

Hyakujō said, "What if I went there myself?"

Shiba Zuda said, "No, not you. That mountain is rotund. You are thin. If you were there with your poor physique, only a thousand monks would come."

Hyakujō said, "Well then, why don't you look over my disciples to see whether or not there is anyone suitable."

First Hyakujō called the head monk. Shiba told him to give a cough and walk a few steps. The monk did as he was told and left the room. Shiba said, "He is hopeless."

Next Isan was called in. Shiba just gave him one quick glance and announced that he would certainly become a splendid master on that mountain.

That evening Hyakujō called Isan to his room and, after transmitting the Dharma to him, ordered that he open the new monastery. The name of the mountain on which it was to be built was Isan.

When the head monk heard of this decision, he protested that he was being discriminated against in favor of someone in the kitchen. A public examination became unavoidable. Hyakujō summoned the head monk and the *tenzo* in front of the assembled monks and said, "I will put a question to you. Whoever gives the better answer will be the one to go to the mountain."

Then he put a water jug before them and said, "You may not call this a water jug. What will you call it?" Hyakujō was testing the clarity of their enlightened eye.

As you know, from the essential point of view the water jug is void. Therefore, it is not wrong to call it anything you wish. In the language of my fraction, the water jug is the numerator; but we must never forget that the denominator is always there.

The head monk said, "It should not be called a wooden sandal."

You may realize by his answer that the monk's eye is a little enlightened. The degree of enlightenment, however, is still quite shallow. Perhaps he meant that the mountain is a mountain; the river, a river; and the water jug, a water jug. How can it be called anything else? This answer contains a certain degree of reasoning.

Then Hyakujō said to Isan, "*Tenzo*, what about you?"

Without saying a word, Isan kicked over the water jug with his foot and left. What does this mean? It means that in Isan's heart there is no enlightenment, no delusion, no Buddhism, no philosophy, no concepts, no thought. His departure is meant to say, "I'll have nothing to do with such a foolish matter. I'm busy in the kitchen!"

Essentially, there is not a thing at all in the whole universe. Where will the dust collect? I think you will be able to recognize the distance between the head monk and Isan. Perhaps Hyakujō smiled when he said, "Head Monk, you have been defeated by the *tenzo*." Isan was ordered to be the founder of the new monastery.

ON MUMON'S COMMENTARY

"Isan summoned up all his valor, but, alas, he could not jump out of Hyakujō's trap. Upon examination, he favors the heavy and not the light. But why? Look! Though he removed his headband, he put on an iron yoke."

Isan showed great spirit by kicking over the water jug in front of his master. This takes courage, but still he got caught in Hyakujō's trap.

"Upon examination, he favors the heavy and not the light." "Heavy" means the difficult work of establishing a new monastery and maintaining it. "The light" refers to the work in the kitchen.

"But why? Look! Though he removed his headband, he put on an iron yoke." Mumon is saying that Isan, having got rid of the light work as *tenzo* in the kitchen, where it is customary to wear a cloth tied around the head, takes on the opening of a new monastery. This is like putting a heavy iron yoke around your neck for the rest of your life. Mumon seems to be saying that Isan is rather foolish, but this is another example of the irony that Mumon is fond of. In reality, he is paying deep respect to Isan's great generous spirit.

I would like to tell you here what happened to Isan after Hyakujō ordered him to open the new monastery. Actually, he did not make any effort to do so immediately but built a small hut in the middle of the forest and sat alone. Of course, he made no effort to advertise.

For eight years no one came, so he decided to try some other place. As he was about to leave, a large tiger appeared and detained him by tugging at his sleeve. He was thus obliged to stay, and several days later three monks arrived. Then gradually the number of monks increased until eventually it reached the predicted fifteen hundred.

ON THE VERSE

Tossing away the bamboo buckets and ladles,
He makes a vigorous thrust and cuts off hindrances;
Hyakujō's heavy barrier cannot interrupt his rush,
Countless Buddhas come forth from his toes.

The bamboo baskets and ladles refer to the post of *tenzo*. He kicked over the water jug, openly and clearly cutting off all obstructions. No one can restrain him.

"You may not call this a water jug. What will you call it?" This is the heavy barrier which Hyakujō set up to examine Isan, but even that could not impede his rush.

"Countless Buddhas come forth from his toes" means kicking over the water jug is the perfect manifestation of Isan's Buddha nature. This remark seems to praise Isan highly, but if we listen carefully, we can also hear, "Isan, you are still young. Isn't there a milder, more subtle way?"

As I just said, when Isan followed his master's orders and opened a monastery, he did not begin by storing rice or planting vegetables or building a Zen hall. For eight years all he did was sit by himself. Some time later we see a monastery building and fifteen hundred monks. What does this teach us?

It teaches us simply and unmistakably that the content is more important than the container. What use is a gorgeous exterior if there is nothing inside? When the contents are valuable, a container will be forthcoming naturally.

In olden days, the content of the Buddha Dharma was so substantial that beautiful temples and monasteries came into being naturally as its container. Nowadays, the content of Buddha's Way has become doubtful, so maintaining the exterior is very difficult. It is indeed regrettable that today most Japanese temples and monasteries must exhibit their gardens and antiques in order to survive.

Bodhidharma Puts
the Mind to Rest

41

THE CASE

Bodhidharma sat facing the wall. The second patriarch, standing in the snow, cut off his arm and said, "Your disciple's mind is not yet at peace. I beg you, Master, give it rest." Bodhidharma said, "Bring your mind to me and I will put it to rest."

The patriarch said, "I have searched for the mind but have never been able to find it." Bodhidharma said, "I have finished putting it to rest for you."

MUMON'S COMMENTARY

The broken-toothed old barbarian came thousands of miles across the sea with an active spirit. It can rightly be said that he raised waves where there was no wind. In later life he obtained one disciple, but even he was crippled in his six senses. Ha! The fools do not even know four characters.

THE VERSE

Coming from the West and pointing directly to it—
All the trouble comes from the transmission;
The one who disturbs the monasteries
Is originally you.

TEISHŌ ON THE CASE

Bodhidharma, the twenty-eighth patriarch of Shakyamuni Buddha's Dharma, was Ceylonese. He is called the first patriarch of China because he was the first to transmit the Dharma there. Although the date of his reaching China is not agreed upon, it is commonly believed that he crossed the sea in 520. He is said to have passed away in 536.

Bodhidharma was the third son of the king of the country of Kōshi in southern India and in his childhood was called Bodaitara. One day the king's teacher, the Venerable Hannyatara, tested him by showing him a precious jewel. When he saw it, Bodaitara said, "This is merely a worldly treasure. However precious it may be, it is not the ultimate. The Dharma-treasure is supreme and nothing can compare with it."

When his father died, Bodaitara sat in samadhi for seven days, and the highest wisdom opened. After that his name was changed to Bodhidharma, which means, "All-Pervading Enlightened Mind." He remained a disciple of the Venerable Hannyatara for more than forty years. When the old master was dying, he said to Bodhidharma, "Sixty years after I die, you must go to China." This difficult and dangerous voyage was obediently undertaken. It took three years for Bodhidharma to reach the South China coast; it is said that he was 120 years old at that time.

In the beginning, Bodhidharma came in contact with Emperor Bu of the country of Ryō, but the emperor was not able to understand his instruction. Bodhidharma then crossed the Yangtze River and entered the country of Gi, where he went to Shōrinji Temple on Mount Sū. There he sat daily for nine years, facing the wall. It was at this time that Jinkō appeared.

Jinkō was the original name of the second patriarch in China, who became the great master Eka. From his childhood on, he was a very bright student of Confucianism, Taoism, and other Chinese philosophies. Later he also studied Mahayana and Hinayana Buddhism. Eventually he came to Bodhidharma as a disciple, and in the end he became his Dharma successor. He passed away in 593 and is believed to have been over 100 when he died.

It was on the evening of the ninth of December that Jinkō went to Bodhidharma. A heavy snow was falling, but Bodhidharma would not allow him to enter the room. Jinkō stood in the falling snow all night. By morning it had reached his knees. He wanted to know the absolute truth, even at the risk of his life. Seeing this, Bodhidharma had pity on him and asked, "What are you asking for, standing in the snow?"

In tears, Jinkō replied, "Your Reverence, please open the gate of mercy and save all beings." Notice he did not say "save me" but rather "save all beings." That is the great wish of all the bodhisattvas.

Bodhidharma replied, "The highest subtle way of Buddha cannot be attained without an immeasurably long training and almost unbearable effort. It can never be achieved by puny virtue, shallow wisdom, faint inspiration, or self-conceit." He did not turn around again.

Jinkō's yearning for the Way increased all the more. Taking out a small sword he had with him, he cut off his left arm to the elbow and presented it to Bodhidharma as a testimony of his desperate determination. At this point, and for the first time, Bodhidharma permitted him to enter the room. He was given the name Eka by his master. It is here that this case begins.

Jinkō said to Bodhidharma, "Your disciple's mind is not yet at peace. I beg you, Master, give it rest."

We are all searching for truth and peace of mind outside ourselves, which is like hunting for a man on an uninhabited island.

Bodhidharma said to Jinkō, "Bring your mind to me and I will put it to rest." What he meant was, "What is the mind? Where is it? Search for it and if you find it, bring it to me. Then I will give it rest."

Jinkō returned to his room and searched for his mind with all his heart but could not find it anywhere. Probably after several days had passed, he went again to the master's room and said, "I have searched with all my heart and soul, but I cannot find my mind."

Bodhidharma said, "Then I have already put it to rest for you."

Once you have found out that the island is uninhabited, your desire to search for a man there will end. When you stop desiring, your mind will come to rest. There will be no problems, no discontent, no frustrations, no uneasiness. You will be at peace, just as you are. When you have found that your whole being is empty, you will realize that there is nothing to search for. Then you will find that your mind is completely free from unrest and uneasiness. Is there any happiness other than this?

When Bodhidharma said, "I have finished putting your mind to rest," he meant: "What do you want besides that? You have found nothing that can be called mind. You have realized that what is called 'mind' is not substantial but empty. How can unrest emanate from a mind that is empty? Where can you find the substance of unrest? It is not to be found anywhere."

The case does not say anything about the consequence of this mondo, but we can well imagine that Eka attained great enlightenment at this point.

ON MUMON'S COMMENTARY

"The broken-toothed old barbarian came thousands of miles across the sea with an active spirit. It can rightly be said that he raised waves where there was no wind. In later life he obtained one disciple, but even he was crippled in his six senses. Ha! The fools do not even know four characters."

The broken-toothed old barbarian who came across the sea refers to Bodhidharma. While he was at Shōrinji Temple, two malicious priests, Kōzu Risshi and Bodai Rushi, envious of their famous master, tried eight times to poison him. Suspecting their wicked intention, Bodhidharma did not drink the potion but sampled it with his teeth, which immediately broke off. Therefore Mumon calls him a broken-toothed barbarian. On first hearing, it may sound a bit insulting, but after a while you will be able to hear friendly overtones.

"It can rightly be said that he raised waves where there was no wind." Here Mumon is speaking from the essential point of view, saying that Bodhidharma's coming to China is absolutely useless. Since people are all intrinsically Buddha, what more do they need? Bodhidharma has brought only trouble with him. It's like raising waves where there is no wind.

"In later life he obtained one disciple, but even he was crippled in his six senses." We know that Eka cut off his left arm. Mumon is telling us that Eka is deformed not only in his left arm but also in his six senses. What does this mean? When you attain deep enlightenment, you realize that both your whole being and the whole universe are empty. In fact, these two are intrinsically one. This is the "falling away of body and mind" you may have heard about. Mumon is saying that from the ordinary, common-sense point of view, such a person is deformed in his six senses. He has no eye to see with, no ear to hear with, no nose to smell with, and so on. But we must realize that when we see without the eye, that is true seeing. When we hear without the ear, that is true hearing. Only then will we be perfectly free from dualistic opposition.

"Ha! The fools do not even know four characters." "Ha!" (*Yi!*) is here, according to Harada Sogaku Roshi, loud contemptuous laughter. Calling Bodhidharma and Eka fools who cannot read the first four letters of the alphabet is another example of Mumon's irony. What he means is, both of you are fools who cannot read a-b-c-d. Bodhidharma, you are teaching Zen where there is nothing to teach. You have disabled your disciple in vain. Eka, why was it necessary for you to cut off your arm? How foolish! This may sound abusive towards the two patriarchs, but we must be aware of the underlying deep respect.

ON THE VERSE

Coming from the West and pointing directly to it—
All the trouble comes from the transmission;
The one who disturbs the monasteries
Is originally you.

Here is another example of Mumon's irony, and what he said in his commentary should shed light here. By this he means that Bodhidharma came all the way from India to China to enlighten people by pointing to their mind. "This is total nonsense!" Mumon is saying. "All living beings are intrinsically Buddha anyway. Because of all your teaching, monasteries have become noisy; all that zazen and all those koans and sesshins are most annoying. You are responsible for it all!"

A Woman Comes Out
of Samadhi

42

THE CASE

Once in the ancient days of the World-Honored One, Manjusri went to
the place where Buddhas were assembled and found that all the Buddhas were departing for their original dwelling places. Only a young
woman remained, sitting in samadhi close to Shakyamuni Buddha's
throne. Manjusri asked the Buddha, "Why can that woman be near the
Buddha's throne while I cannot?"

The Buddha said, "Just awaken her and raise her up out of samadhi
and ask her yourself."

Manjusri walked around the woman three times, snapped his fingers
once, took her up to the Brahman heaven, and exerted all his supernatural powers, but he could not bring her out of samadhi.

The World-Honored One said, "Even a hundred or a thousand Manjusris would not be able to bring her out of samadhi. Down below, past
twelve hundred million lands as innumerable as the sands of the Ganges,
is the Bodhisattva Mōmyō. He will be able to arouse her from her
samadhi."

Instantly the Bodhisattva Mōmyō emerged out of the earth and made
a bow to the World-Honored One, who then gave his command. The
Bodhisattva went before the woman and snapped his fingers once. At
this, the woman came out of samadhi.

MUMON'S COMMENTARY

Old Shakya plays a country drama on stage, but people of shallow realization cannot appreciate it. Just tell me: Manjusri is the teacher of the Seven Buddhas; why can't he bring the woman out of her samadhi while Mōmyō, who is a bodhisattva in the beginning stage, can? If you can grasp this completely, you will realize that surging delusive consciousness is nothing other than the greatest samadhi.

THE VERSE

One can awaken her, the other cannot;
Both have their own freedom.
A god-mask here and a devil-mask there;
Even in failure, an elegant performance.

TEISHŌ ON THE CASE

The story of this koan can be read in *The Sutra of the Collected Essentials of All Buddhas,* though here it is modified.

Long ago in the land of Tennō Tathagata, which is not in our galaxy, a conference was held, and many Buddhas gathered to attend the meeting. What was the agenda? No doubt it centered around the eternal problem that Buddhas and great bodhisattvas are always pondering: What shall we do to make all living beings attain the highest Way and accomplish the Buddha-body? For all Buddhas, of every time and place, there is no other aim to their works.

Because this conference was for Buddhas, bodhisattvas were not qualified to participate. Just as the conference finished, Bodhisattva Manjusri came to visit Shakyamuni Buddha, who was in attendance. All the Buddhas were leaving for their own Buddha-lands. Manjusri saw a young woman there, sitting in samadhi close to the Buddha's throne.

In ancient times in India it was believed that a woman was too sinful to accomplish Buddhahood. This thinking had a deep influence on the Japanese after Buddhism came to Japan. A strong bias against women was prevalent there for a long time, from the Heian era down to the end of the Tokugawa period. In accord with the tradition in those days, Manjusri was surprised to see a woman sitting in samadhi very close to Buddha's seat. He asked Shakyamuni, "How is it that a woman can get near Buddha's throne while I'm not permitted to?"

Shakyamuni Buddha said, "Wake the woman from her samadhi and ask her yourself."

So Manjusri walked around her three times, snapped his fingers, and practiced all his supernatural powers on her but was unable to bring her out of her deep samadhi. Seeing this, Shakyamuni Buddha said, "Even a hundred or a thousand Manjusris are unable to arouse this woman out of her samadhi. Down below, past twelve-hundred million countries as innumerable as the sands of the Ganges, is a bodhisattva called Mōmyō. He will be able to awake this woman from her profound absorption."

Thereupon Mōmyō emerged out of the earth and bowed to the World-Honored One, who gave him the order. Mōmyō went before the woman, snapped his fingers once, and brought the woman out of her samadhi.

The point of this koan, as Mumon points out in his commentary, is the question: Why is it that Manjusri, who is a bodhisattva of the highest degree, cannot bring the woman out of her samadhi, while Mōmyō, who is a bodhisattva of a lower degree, can do it easily?

Manjusri, a bodhisattva of the highest degree, is called the teacher of the Seven Buddhas. How is it that a bodhisattva can be the teacher of Buddhas? It is because he is a symbol of Prajña, the wisdom of the essential world (also called the world of complete emptiness or the world of absolute equality). This world is nothing other than what is realized in the enlightenment of all Buddhas. Thus Manjusri is called the teacher of Buddhas. Also, in Manjusri's world there is neither subject nor object, neither standing up nor sitting down, neither getting in nor getting out.

Mōmyō, on the other hand, is a bodhisattva of a lower degree who investigates the world of phenomena. He is the symbol of the world of absolute difference. In his world, we can freely stand up or sit down, get in or out, and so on.

Now, for those who have not yet opened the eye of self-realization, it will be difficult to catch the point of this koan. Therefore I will add a little explanation.

Everything in the world has two aspects, one essential and the other phenomenal. In the former, everything is empty. It has no form, no color, no weight, no height. From this aspect, therefore, everything is equal. In the latter, everything is the only thing in the whole universe having color, weight, and height. From this aspect all things are completely different. All this remains the same as far as living beings are concerned. We human beings have two aspects, one essential and one phenomenal. Absolute equality and absolute difference are two aspects of one being.

The most important point is that these two aspects are intrinsically one. For the sake of expediency, we explain them as two, but from the beginning they are one.

We may say, therefore, that everything has form and no form, everything has color and no color. In the same way, it is true that when we walk we do not take a step, and when we talk do not move our lips and tongue in the slightest!

I mentioned before that Manjusri is the symbol of the wisdom of the essential world and that Mōmyō, whose name literally means unenlightened, is the symbol of the world of differences. These clues are the key to solving the riddle of this koan.

ON MUMON'S COMMENTARY

"Old Shakya plays a country drama on stage, but people of shallow realization cannot appreciate it. Just tell me: Manjusri is the teacher of the Seven Buddhas; why can't he bring the woman out of her samadhi while Mōmyō, who is a bodhisattva in the beginning stage, can? If you can grasp this completely, you will realize that surging delusive consciousness is nothing other than the greatest samadhi."

Shakyamuni Buddha puts a country drama on stage. It is rather difficult to understand, and half-enlightened Zen people will find its meaning almost impossible to grasp.

Mumon says, "Now I will ask you a question. Manjusri is very wise. He is the teacher of the Seven Buddhas."

There are, of course, innumerable Buddhas from the beginningless past. From among them, present-day Buddhism worships seven in particular as its ancestors. The names and the order of the six preceding Shakyamuni Buddha are given in Case 22. Why is it that Manjusri, who is their teacher and the symbol of the wisdom of Buddha, cannot arouse the woman out of her samadhi?

As a bodhisattva, Mōmyō is just a beginner. In the complicated classification of the stages of a bodhisattva, he has attained only the first of fifty-two steps. He was able to bring this woman out of her samadhi very easily, however. Why? If you can grasp the "why" of this dilemma completely, you will find that even while you are in the midst of surging delusive thoughts, you are in the royal samadhi of enlightenment. While working in tumult, you are in the center of deep silence.

ON THE VERSE

One can awaken her, the other cannot;
Both have their own freedom.
A god-mask here and a devil-mask there;
Even in failure, an elegant performance.

Both Manjusri and Mōmyō have their respective freedoms. When Manjusri failed to awaken the woman, he was free not to awaken her. When Mōmyō succeeded in waking her, he was free to wake her. For a horse, it is freedom to gallop. For a snake, it is freedom to crawl, not gallop. But it is still freedom for a snake not to be able to gallop. Failure to gallop is an elegant performance for a snake. Take the example of a jet plane about to take off. A hundred thousand Manjusris might not be able to get it started, but a jet pilot could do so very easily.

Sometimes we are millionaires, sometimes paupers. Still, our essential nature does not change at all. We are always in the center of perfect freedom.

Shuzan's Shippei

THE CASE

Master Shuzan held up a *shippei* before his disciples and said, "You monks, if you call this a *shippei*, you are adhering to the fact. If you do not call this a *shippei*, you are opposing the fact. Tell me, you monks, what will you call it?"

MUMON'S COMMENTARY

If you call this a *shippei*, you are adhering to the fact. If you do not call this a *shippei*, you are opposing the fact. You should not use words. You should not use no-words. Speak at once! Speak at once!

THE VERSE

Holding up a shippei,
He issues the order to kill and to give life;
When adhering and opposing interweave,
Even Buddhas and patriarchs beg for their lives.

TEISHŌ ON THE CASE

Shuzan Shōnen Zenji was, in his youth, earnestly devoted to the *Lotus Sutra*. Later he became a disciple of Fuketsu Enshō Zenji, whom we met in Case 24. Shuzan attained deep enlightenment under Fuketsu and eventually became his Dharma successor. He was the fifth of Rinzai's descendants and passed away in 993 at the age of sixty-eight.

A *shippei* is a staff made of bamboo about half a meter in length and shaped like a small bow. A Zen master keeps it at his side in the zendo when he is guiding his disciples. It is one of the seven items that make up a Zen monk's equipment. The others are the *kesa*, a kind of surplice; the *koromo*, or robe; the sutras including records of the patriarchs' words; the *hossu*, a stick with a flexible, bushy end; the *shujō*, another kind of staff, somewhat longer than the others and used when walking out-of-doors; and the *nyoi*, a short wooden staff which has nowadays been replaced by the *kotsu*.

Once Shuzan held up a *shippei* before his disciples and said, "You monks, if you call this a *shippei*, you are adhering to the superficial fact (or negating its essence). If you do not call this a *shippei*, you are opposing the fact. Tell me, you monks, what will you call this?"

This koan is in the same category as Case 40, "Kicking Over the Water Jug." In that koan, as you will remember, Master Hyakujō took a water jug, stood it on the floor, and said to the assembled disciples, "You may not call this a water jug. What will you call it?" Isan immediately kicked over the jug and left the room. With this he passed the test and was appointed master of the new temple on Mount Taii. In the present koan, a *shippei* is presented instead of a water jug. What will you call it to pass the examination?

As I have so often told you, everything has two aspects, one phenomenal and the other essential. If you look at the *shippei* only from the phenomenal side and call it a *shippei*, you are adhering to the phenomenal viewpoint and ignoring the essential aspect. If you look at the *shippei* merely from the essential point of view—that is, from the aspect of complete emptiness—and do not call it a *shippei*, you are opposing the fact of its phenomenal side.

There is an old Zen story which is taken to be the source of this koan. When Zen Master Shō of Setsu Prefecture was a disciple of Master Shuzan, he was asked the same question, "If you call this a *shippei*, you are adhering to the fact. If you don't call this a *shippei*, you are opposing the fact. What will you call it?" Shō suddenly grabbed the *shippei* from Shuzan. Breaking it in two, he threw it on the ground and cried out, "What is this!" Shuzan shouted back, "You blind fool!" Instantly Shō awoke to great enlightenment.

Consider, for a moment, the fraction I often refer to. In this koan, the *shippei* is the numerator. If you call the staff a *shippei*, you are adhering to the numerator. The *shippei* does not know what its name is; it does not know that it is called a *shippei*. This word is merely a tag or a label given by man for the sake of convenience.

On the other hand, if you look at the *shippei* from the point of view of the denominator, you will not be able to call it by any name. That is because even though it contains infinite capabilities, it is absolutely empty. When you look at the *shippei* from its essential aspect and do not say anything, you are adhering to the denominator and opposing the numerator, the phenomenal fact.

In Zen, the most important point is whether the denominator, the essential world, the real nature, has been realized or not. Where there is no realization of this, there is no Zen. Denominator and numerator are used as expedients in explaining. Both are mere concepts of one side of the whole. In reality, there is neither denominator nor numerator, neither *shippei* nor non-*shippei*. What would you call it from the point of view of reality?

ON MUMON'S COMMENTARY

Mumon says, "If you call this a *shippei*, you are adhering to the fact. If you do not call this a *shippei*, you are opposing the fact. You should not use words. You should not use no-words. Speak at once! Speak at once!"

This commentary repeats Master Shuzan's words, and I have already given my interpretation of them. What will you call the staff? Tell me! Quickly!

ON THE VERSE

Holding up a shippei,
He issues the order to kill and to give life;
When adhering and opposing interweave,
Even Buddhas and patriarchs beg for their lives.

"To kill" means to take away the delusive concepts and thoughts which Zen students have. "To give life" means to bring these students to enlightenment. In handling the *shippei*, Master Shuzan freely kills the students and gives them life. We should appreciate his skill in guiding them.

"When adhering and opposing interweave, even Buddhas and patriarchs beg for their lives." This is high praise for Shuzan's ability as a Zen master. If you fiercely attack even Buddhas and patriarchs from both sides with, "Now you are adhering to the fact, now you are opposing the fact!" they will surrender and beg for their lives, crying, "Help! Help!"

Bashō's Shujō

THE CASE

Master Bashō said to the assembly, "If you have a *shujō*, I will give it to you. If you have no *shujō*, I will take it away from you."

MUMON'S COMMENTARY

Having it support us, we wade across a river that has no bridge. Having it accompany us, we return to the village on a moonless night. But if you call it a *shujō*, you will go to hell as swiftly as an arrow.

THE VERSE

The depths and shallows everywhere
Are all within his grip;
It supports the heavens and sustains the earth,
Everywhere it enhances the spirit of our sect.

TEISHŌ ON THE CASE

In the previous koan, I told you about the seven pieces of equipment that every Zen monk has. The *shujō*, or staff, which appears in this koan, is one of the most important. Some of these seven implements are supposed to signify parts of the Buddha's body. The *hossu*, for instance, which has a flexible, bushy end, represents the Buddha's white brow. The *shippei*, the bow-shaped bamboo staff that appeared in the previous koan, represents Buddha's arm. In this koan we have the *shujō*, a somewhat longer staff originally used when a monk was out walking. Besides serving as a kind of cane, it was useful to gauge the depth of rivers which had to be crossed, and it scattered insects which otherwise would have been stepped on and killed. The *shujō* represents Buddha's leg.

Zen Master Bashō Esei was a Korean who traveled around China in search of good Zen masters. Eventually he met Nantō Kōyū, a Dharma successor of Master Kyōzan. After Bashō became Kōyū's Dharma successor, he went to the mountain whose name he bears.

A very interesting mondo is recorded in Bashō's biography:

A monk asked, "What is the water of Bashō?"

The master answered, "Warm in winter, cool in summer."

The monk asked, "What is the sharpest sword?"

The master answered, "It proceeds three steps."

The monk said, "What is the use of it?"

The master answered, "It retreats three steps."

A detailed explanation of this mondo would take too much time here, but I hope it gives you some appreciation of Bashō's skill in responding to Zen questions.

The present koan seems a riddle indeed. Literally, it means, "If you have it, I'll give it to you; if you don't have it, I'll take it away from you." According to our everyday common sense, it is a contradiction in terms. Bashō is trying to confuse us and have us go beyond our perplexity to the great doubt at the very bottom of the question.

Let us look at this koan for a few minutes from two points of view, one deeper than the other. In Japanese we call them *shushō-hen* and *hombun-jō*. *Shushō-hen* means the ascending process of Zen practice. *Hombun-jō* can be translated as our essential nature. *Hombun* means our original self.

Now what does the koan mean when we look at it from the *shushō* point of view? In ordinary terms it could be stated as follows: Do you have the staff of enlightenment? If you say you have, I will beat you with a staff. Or you may say, "I have already thrown away enlightenment and have nothing within me." If that is so, I will deprive you of that nothingness. This view is not very deep.

When we consider the koan from the *hombun* or essential point of view, the staff stands for essential nature.

I would like to digress for a moment and point out to you how important the staff is in Zen. From very ancient times, many people have come to enlightenment through it. It is not surprising, therefore, to find that many koans have a staff as their main theme.

Besides two in the *Gateless Gate* (Cases 44 and 48), there are three in the *Blue Cliff Record*. Case 60 reads, "Unmon showed his staff to the assembly and said, 'This staff has become a dragon. It has swallowed the whole universe. The mountains, rivers, and great earth, where do they come from?'"

In Case 61 of the same book, the staff appears again. The koan reads: "Fuketsu gave instruction, saying, 'If one raises a speck of dust, the nation prospers. If one does not raise a speck of dust, the nation perishes.' At this, Setchō (the first compiler of the *Blue Cliff Record*) held up his staff and asked, 'Is there anyone who lives and dies with this?'" (He means: Is there anyone who can realize this staff completely?)

The *Blue Cliff Record* has another koan utilizing a staff. It reads as follows: "The hermit Rengehō took up his staff before the assembly and said, 'Why didn't the old patriarchs remain here after they reached it?' The monks were silent. He answered himself, 'Because it has no power to save people on the Way.' Then he said again, 'After all, what is it?' The monks were still silent, so he answered for them again, 'Carrying the staff at the back of my neck and taking no notice of what people think, I directly enter into the thousand, the ten thousand peaks.'"

In all these koans the staff should be taken as the essential world which is the zero-infinite. All these patriarchs took up the staff in order to make the disciples come to realize the essential world. When we look at the present koan from the deeper point of view, the staff is taken to express the essential world, which is nothing else but our own essential nature. From this point of view, the koan means, "If you think you have something called the essential nature, you are wrong. A concept like this is not the true realization. It is merely a picture, a representation of the essential nature. I will give you a beating with a staff."

Following this point of view, the second phrase, "To have no staff," means, "If you say you have no essential nature, because it is completely empty, then I must deprive you of that concept of emptiness." In this assertion, Master Bashō wants us to go beyond the concept of having and not-having, or being and not-being. In the essential world there is no such thing as dualistic opposition.

I was very interested to hear from one of the sisters in the zendo here that Christ uttered words that are almost identical: "To him who has, will more be given; and from him who has not, even what he has will be taken away." I wonder what Christ truly meant when he said that.

ON MUMON'S COMMENTARY

"Having it support us, we wade across a river that has no bridge. Having it accompany us, we return to the village on a moonless night. But if you call it a *shujō*, you will go to hell as swiftly as an arrow."

How free and helpful the staff is! This is natural, for the staff is as big as the whole universe. With it, not only can we safely cross a bridgeless river but also the river of delusions and the sea of life and death. The staff can become a dragon and swallow up the whole phenomenal world. But if you conceive even one little thought about the staff, the essential nature, you will fall to the ground of delusions as swiftly as an arrow.

ON THE VERSE

The depths and shallows everywhere
Are all within his grip;
It supports the heavens and sustains the earth,
Everywhere it enhances the spirit of our sect.

With this staff, Master Bashō can fathom with authority the depth or shallowness of Zen men everywhere. The moment he takes up the staff, the staff is nothing other than himself. He himself is not other than the whole universe. Thus he holds the whole universe within his power, enhancing the spirit of Zen school everywhere.

Who Is That One?

45

THE CASE

Master and Patriarch En of Tōzan said, "Even Shakyamuni and Maitreya are servants of that one. Just tell me, who is that one?"

MUMON'S COMMENTARY

If you clearly recognize that one, it will be just like meeting your father at the crossroads. It is not necessary to ask others whether it is he or not.

THE VERSE

Don't draw another's bow;
Don't ride another's horse;
Don't speak of another's faults;
Don't inquire into another's affairs.

TEISHŌ ON THE CASE

Master En of Tōzan is presumed to be Master Hōen of Goso, whom we have already met in Cases 35, 36, and 38.

This koan is very clear-cut and expresses the high spirit of Master Hōen. It urges us to be very confident in ourselves and to cultivate steadfastness of mind for, as we know, there are many people who lose the bright light of their essential nature and are content to be mean.

There is a famous story about this koan recorded in ancient Zen writings. When he was a disciple of Goso, Master Shōkaku was asked, "Who is that one?" He replied, "Kochōsan, Kokurishi." These two words are very popular names, like John and George in English or Tarō and Jirō in Japanese.

Goso told his disciple Engo (later the compiler of the *Blue Cliff Record*) about this reply. Engo said, "That answer seems to be right, but I wonder if his experience is true or not. You had better examine him once again." So the next day when Shōkaku came to him for *dokusan*, Master Goso asked the same question, "Even Shakyamuni and Maitreya are servants of that one. Tell me, who is that one?"

Kaku said, "I told you yesterday."

Goso said, "What did you say?"

Kaku said, "Kochōsan, Kokurishi."

Goso said, "Not right! Not right!"

Kaku said, "Why did you say 'right' yesterday?"

Goso said, "Yesterday it was right. Today it isn't right."

Upon hearing this, Shōkaku became deeply enlightened. Shōkaku's answer was the same as before, but why was it right yesterday and not right today? I am sure you know that the true fact is always in the present, not in the past or future. When one speaks of the fact in the past, it is not a living experience. Now just tell me, what answer would you give to Goso's question?

As Hakuin Zenji says in the beginning of his *Song of Zazen*, "All living beings are intrinsically Buddha." From the essential point of view, therefore, anyone is qualified to use either Shakyamuni or Maitreya or any other Buddha, bodhisattva, or patriarch as a servant. But mere intellectual understanding is of no use. We must grasp that fact directly by experience. This experience is called kensho.

ON MUMON'S COMMENTARY

"If you clearly recognize that one, it will be just like meeting your father at the crossroads. It is not necessary to ask others whether it is he or not."

Mumon's commentary is straightforward and easy to understand. Of course, if you meet your father on a crowded city street, you will know who he is. You won't need to ask someone else whether he is your father or not.

ON THE VERSE

Don't draw another's bow;
Don't ride another's horse;
Don't speak of another's faults;
Don't inquire into another's affairs.

In this verse the word "another" appears four times. This "another" is not the same as "that one," which we read about in the main case; even though the same Chinese character is used in both cases, the meaning is different.

"That one" in the main case is not used in the sense of "another" in the world of dualistic opposition. "That one" is the only One in the whole universe. Nothing remains outside of it. But the "another" in the verse is the "another" in the world of opposition, such as subject and object, oneself and others, and so on.

From the essential point of view, the whole universe is one, without any differentiation whatsoever. There is neither subject nor object. Subject and object are merely conceived ideas in which intrinsic oneness is separated into two. If there is no subject, there is no object; if there is no object, there is no subject. Therefore we can call the whole the subject or we can call it the object. Dōgen Zenji called it the "whole-I-self" or the "whole-other-self."

It is true to say, nevertheless, that we ordinary people think the opposition of subject and object is real. Actually, this is nothing but a delusion, and we should not be misled by delusions.

In order to make us realize the real truth of the essential world, the verse tells us:

Don't draw another's bow;
Don't ride another's horse;
Don't speak of another's faults;
Don't inquire into another's affairs.

As a matter of fact we cannot draw another's bow. We are always drawing our own bow. It is the same for the other three cases.

As I often tell you, the condition of our ordinary life is the world of opposition, such as subject and object, oneself and others. But such dualistic oppositions are not the real fact; they are, rather, conceptual images. So if we continue to proceed along the way of these conceptual delusions, we will certainly be confronted with hopeless situations. For example, just consider the opposition or confrontation between capital and labor or management and union. In spite of the fact that both parties live the same single life of enterprise, they are unable to acknowledge this essential fact, and both stick to their respective interests. If they continue to adhere to such a policy, what will be the outcome? This is a most serious problem in our present age. What transpires will have a grave influence on the fate of human beings far into the future.

One's self and others are intrinsically one. Some time ago, I read the following story, which is relative to this point:

A Zen master in deep samadhi visited heaven and hell after death. First he went to hell, where everyone was having dinner. They were all seated at long tables, facing one another. The tables were loaded with delicious food, but the chopsticks were over a meter in length, and try as they would, the people were unable to get the food into their mouths. There was a great commotion.

Next, the master went to one of the heavens (I think you know there are several heavens in Buddhism), and he found the people also seated around tables loaded with delicious food, just as in hell. Here, too, the chopsticks were exceedingly long, but everyone was using them very naturally, putting the food into the mouths of the people across the table! They were all enjoying the dinner, and the atmosphere was quiet and happy.

Dōgen Zenji says: "The beneficent deed renders kind service to all living beings, whether of high or low status. When we see a tortoise or an injured sparrow in trouble, we should simply do what we can to help them without expecting a reward. Foolish people may think that if we are kind to others first, it will involve loss to ourselves. That is not so. A beneficent deed is one single law. It rewards the giver and the receiver equally."

Stepping Forward From
the Top of a Pole

46

THE CASE

Master Sekisō said, "How will you step forward from the top of a hundred-foot pole?"

Another eminent master of old said, "Even though one who is sitting on the top of a hundred-foot pole has entered realization, it is not yet real. He must step forward from the top of the pole and manifest his whole body throughout the world in ten directions."

MUMON'S COMMENTARY

If you can step forward and turn your body around, there will be no place where you are called dishonorable. Even so, just tell me, how do you step forward from the top of the hundred-foot pole? Ahem!

THE VERSE

Making the eye on the forehead blind,
One clings to the mark on the scale;
Throwing away body and life,
One blind person leads many blind people.

TEISHŌ ON THE CASE

Sekisō Soen was an eminent Zen master of the Rinzai sect and a contemporary of Setchō, who composed the verses of the *Blue Cliff Record*. He was born in 986 and died in 1040 at the age of fifty-four. Though he did not live very long, Sekisō raised the spirit of the Rinzai sect to a high degree and left deep footprints in the history of Zen of that period in China.

What does "the top of a hundred-foot pole" mean? Figuratively, it is the stage of complete emptiness. When you attain self-realization, your eye will open first to the state of consciousness where there is absolutely nothing. That stage is called the "great death." It is a stage where there is no dualistic opposition such as subject and object, good and bad, saints and ordinary people and so on. There is neither one who sees nor anything seen. Zen usually expresses this stage with the words, "There is not a speck of cloud in the spacious sky."

Anyone who wants to attain the true Zen experience must pass through this stage once. If you remain there, however, you will be unable to attain true emancipation from deep attachment to this emptiness. This stage is often referred to as the pitfall of emptiness. It becomes a kind of Zen sickness.

When we attain kensho, we come to the top of the high pole where most of us are seized with this malady. It is said that even Shakyamuni succumbed to it for two or three weeks after his great enlightenment. The Zen master in this koan warns us not to linger at this point when he says, "Take a step forward from this stage and you will be able to manifest your whole body throughout the world in ten directions." That means that you must become completely free from all kinds of attachments.

Look at this stick, this *kotsu*. See, it is lying horizontally at first. This position represents our ordinary life. With the practice of zazen, working on Mu or counting our breath, one end of the stick will gradually come up, while the other is fixed at the original point. When the stick stands perfectly vertical, that is the state of complete emptiness. There you become completely one with Mu, and there is no concept or thought whatever in your mind. This is the great death. It is also the entrance to perfect enlightenment. This stage is void of mental activity. But you must not stop there. You must press on even harder. Then the top of the stick will move forward, and suddenly a whole new world will manifest itself! *This* is true enlightenment. Perhaps now you understand what this warning means.

"Another eminent master of old" in the case refers to Master Chōsa, who was Nansen's Dharma successor. He appears in Case 36 of the *Blue Cliff Record* and Case 79 of the *Book of Equanimity*. I would like to tell you about the latter koan because in it you can see the complete mondo between Chōsa and a monk, of which the present case is only a partial quotation. The koan goes as follows:

Chōsa had a monk ask Master E, "What about the time when you had not yet seen Nansen?" E sat still a while. The monk said, "What about after seeing him?" E said, "There wasn't anything special." The monk returned and told this to Chōsa. Chōsa said, "Even though one who sits on the top of a hundred-foot pole has entered realization, it is not yet real. He must step forward from the top of the pole. The world in ten directions is his whole body." The monk said, "How shall I step from the top of a hundred-foot pole? Chōsa said, "The mountains of the province of Rō, the waters of the province of Rei." The monk said, "I don't understand." Chōsa said, "Four seas and five lakes are all under the reign of the king." This is the mondo in its entirety as it appears in the *Book of Equanimity*.

In our present koan, the last phrase of the case reads: ". . . to manifest his whole body throughout the world in ten directions." This means you will realize that you are one and alone in and with the whole universe and that you should be able to do anything in an extremely free and positive way. That is the state of true enlightenment.

ON MUMON'S COMMENTARY

"If you can step forward and turn your body around, there will be no place where you are called dishonorable. Even so, just tell me, how do you step forward from the top of the hundred-foot pole? Ahem!"

To "turn your body around" means to move and act freely and positively at will. No matter where you may go, there will be no obstacle in your path. So you are estimable, even to the point of being called honorable.

But it is not easy to step forward from a hundred-foot pole! Just tell me, how would you do it? I think you know there is no way to find out other than to continue your practice of zazen.

The last word, "Ahem (*Sa*)!" expresses the sound of a hoarse voice. Here it means, "I have talked myself hoarse!" I have spoken too much.

ON THE VERSE

Making the eye on the forehead blind,
One clings to the mark on the scale;
Throwing away body and life,
One blind person leads many blind people.

The eye on the forehead means the enlightened eye. Though you have had kensho and attained the enlightened eye, if you stick to the world of emptiness, your enlightened eye will become blind again. Your whole being will be unable to move, as though your sight is clinging to a mark on the scale, taking it as definite and immovable.

"Throwing away body and life, one blind person leads many blind people" has various interpretations. In their ordinary sense, the words mean that if we are to step from complete emptiness into the broad, spacious world of lively and positive enlightenment, we must be determined to continue our practice for the rest of our lives. Otherwise it is just like the blind leading the blind; no one knows where he is going.

There is another somewhat deeper interpretation. The blind refers to a completely enlightened person. His essential nature does not see when he is seeing. His essential nature does not hear when he is hearing. In his essential nature, there is no one who is seeing and no object that is seen. So he is nothing but a blind person. From this point of view, the last two lines of the verse mean that when you devote yourself to post-kensho practice, your eye will open to the world of perfect enlightenment. Then, for the first time, you will become a true Zen person, adhering to nothing, neither the phenomenal world nor the essential world. For the first time, in the spirit of the Bodhisattva's Four Vows,[1] a benevolent aspiration to save others will well up from the depths of your heart. Such a person is truly qualified to be a Zen master and to lead and guide.

NOTE

1. One translation of these vows reads as follows: "Living beings are numberless, I vow to save them. Delusive passions are limitless, I vow to extinguish them. The Dharma gates are countless, I vow to master them. The Buddha's way is unsurpassed, I vow to attain it."

Tosotsu's Three Barriers

47

THE CASE

Master Tosotsu Etsu set up three barriers and asked his students:

"The purpose of making one's way through grasses and asking a master about the subtle truth is only to realize one's self-nature. Now, you venerable monks, where is the self-nature at this very moment?

"When you have attained your self-nature, you can free yourself from life-and-death. How will you free yourself from life-and-death when the light of your eyes is falling to the ground?

"When you have freed yourself from life-and-death, you know where to go. After your four elements have decomposed, where will you go?"

MUMON'S COMMENTARY

If you can say three turning words about these barriers, you will be the master wherever you may be, in close contact with the real essence in all situations. If you have not yet reached this stage, gulping down your food will fill you up quickly, while chewing well will make it more difficult to become hungry again.

THE VERSE

In one consciousness, we see the whole of eternity;
Eternity is nothing other than right now.

If you see through this one consciousness at this moment,
You see through the one who is seeing right now.

TEISHŌ ON THE CASE

Master Tosotsu Jūetsu (short form: Etsu) is a successor in the lineage of Rinzai. He entered the priesthood when he was a boy and studied both Hinayana and Mahayana Buddhism. Later he practiced Zen under many excellent Zen masters in different places. Eventually Tosotsu met Master Hōhō Kokubun and became his Dharma successor. He is the third descendant of Master Sekisō Soen, who appeared in Case 46. Tosotsu died in 1091 during the reign of Emperor Tessō of the Sung Dynasty.

This koan is known as the "Three Barriers of Tosotsu" and is one of the most famous and important of all koans. In Rinzai it is called, "koan in the sickroom," or "koan on the death bed." Although three barriers are mentioned, there is, after all, just one, and that is the barrier of kensho or self-realization.

Doubtlessly, kensho is the very core of Mahayana Zen. Without kensho, Zen lacks the religious power to save people in the truest sense of the word. Since ancient times, Zen people have called kensho "the Great Matter."

When we attain self-realization, for the first time we are able to surpass life-and-death and live in true peace of mind. To surpass life-and-death means to realize that in the essential nature there is neither birth nor death.

(1) The first barrier: What is the purpose of Zen devotees making pilgrimages here and there, making their way through grasses (walking along grassy roads) and visiting Zen masters for instruction? They do it solely in order to attain self-realization. Tell me, where is your self-nature at present?

The phrase "making their way through grasses" has two meanings. First, "grasses" means countless delusions. To attain kensho we must sweep away all delusive concepts and thoughts. Secondly, "making their way through grasses" means that Zen monks must travel around grassy places visiting good Zen masters. In Tosotsu's time, Zen masters usually lived in the forest or on a mountain, hence the reference to grasses.

In order to pass through Tosotsu's first barrier, you must grasp the essential nature by direct experience. It cannot be reached by reasoning or by logical thinking. In order to attain kensho, you must kill yourself.

That is to say, you should completely absorb yourself in the practice of Mu, or breath-counting, or *shikantaza* (just sitting), or sometimes in asking yourself, "What is Mind?" or whatever your practice is at the moment.

But you must remember that concentrating on an external object will never bring you to kensho. Your target has to be an interior, nonsubstantial (formless) one. When you become truly one with your target, your awareness of "I" will disappear, or either subject or object will totally vanish. This is the stage we call the "great death," but you should not stop there. Take one more step forward. Then suddenly the total void will break open and a brilliant new world will appear. This is true self-realization.

Bassui has a sermon on "Who Is It That Hears?" Let us consider what it says in this respect:

> At work, at rest, never stop trying to realize who it is that hears. Even though your questioning becomes almost unconscious, you won't find one who hears, and all your efforts will come to naught. Yet sounds can be heard, so question yourself to an even profounder level. At last, every vestige of self-awareness will disappear and you will feel like a cloudless sky. Within yourself you will find no "I," nor will you discover anyone who hears. This mind is like the void, yet it hasn't a single spot that can be called empty. This state is often mistaken for self-realization. But continue to ask yourself even more intensely, "Now, who is it that hears?" If you bore and bore into this question, oblivious to anything else, even this feeling of voidness will vanish, and you will be unaware of anything—total darkness will prevail. Keep asking with all your strength, "What is it that hears?" Only when you have completely exhausted the questioning will the question burst; you will feel like a man come back from the dead. This is true realization.[1]

Now can you tell me what your self-nature is? What is it? Just show me!

(2) The second barrier: When you have attained your self-nature, you can free yourself from life-and-death. How will you free yourself from life-and-death when your eyes are falling to the ground, which means when you are just at the point of death?

If you have realized your self-nature clearly, you will find that there is neither being born nor dying. Life-and-death are superficial changes in the phenomenal world. In the essential world, there is nothing to be called "life" or "death." Zero or nothingness, though it possesses invisible infinite qualities and possibilities, can neither be born nor perish. With realization, the problem of life-and-death is completely resolved and we can enjoy true peace of mind forever.

When you are at the very point of death, how will you free yourself from the horror and agony of death? Show me!

(3) The third barrier: When you have freed yourself from life-and-death, you know where to go. Where will you go after your body has decomposed into the four elements?

As for the four elements, we may simply think of them as meaning the physical body. Ancient Indian thought held that all matter consists of the four elements of earth, water, fire, and wind and that after death the physical body decomposes into these original elements.

The third barrier says that one who has freed himself from life-and-death will know where to go. Where is the place you are going to after death?

Ordinary people, even those who believe that there is a life after death, think or feel that there is some kind of border or distinction between life and death. But one who has most deeply realized the essential nature knows clearly that from the essential point of view there is not the slightest difference between them. Thus an ancient Zen master was able to say, "Within me, there is neither life nor death."

This koan is most important for checking whether one's self-realization is deep enough or not because most people who have attained a so-called realization are still apt to think that after death they simply become ashes or earth and that nothing will remain.

Now, please tell me where you will go after death!

ON MUMON'S COMMENTARY

"If you can say three turning words about these barriers, you will be the master wherever you may be, in close contact with the real essence in all situations. If you have not yet reached this stage, gulping down your food will fill you up quickly, while chewing well will make it more difficult to become hungry again."

Mumon's first sentence means that if you can say some words enabling you to pass through these barriers, you will be the master of both yourself and your circumstances, wherever you may be.

Mumon continues, "If you have not yet reached this stage, gulping down your food will fill you up quickly, while chewing well will make it more difficult to become hungry again." This means that if you are still not at that stage, you must keep on with your Zen practice most scrupulously and polish your realization. Zen practice is just like eating. If you gulp down your food quickly, you will soon feel full, but that fullness will not last long. You will be hungry again shortly. On the other hand, if you chew your food well, it will take longer to finish, but once filled, you are not likely to feel hungry again for a long time. As an ancient master has rightly said, "If you are once filled up, the hunger which lasted countless kalpas will be extinguished forever."

ON THE VERSE

In one consciousness, we see the whole of eternity;
Eternity is nothing other than right now.
If you see through this one consciousness at this moment,
You see through the one who is seeing right now.

Most people think that there is something called "time" outside themselves, which consists of past, present, and future. But where is the past? Can you show it to me? No. It has passed away. It exists nowhere but in our memory. Where is the future? Can you show it to me? No. It has not yet come. It exists nowhere but in our imagination. What really exists is nothing but the present. The moment you pronounce the first letter "p," however, it passes away into the void of the past. There is no way of catching the present.

Time can be divided into limitless short units and, finally, into almost no time at all. The tiny units that matter can be divided into are called particles, and they eventually come to be almost nothing. If you can realize this very instant as a particle of time, you will also realize that eternity does not exist anywhere except in one's consciousness, which itself is nothing but a particle of time.

"If you see through this one consciousness at this moment, you see through the one who is seeing right now." When you realize this moment, you realize your own self. This is called self-realization, or kensho. Everything is "right now." "Right now" is everything. Your essential nature is nothing other than "right now." "Right now" is not only eternity but the whole universe.

NOTE

1. Phillip Kapleau, *The Three Pillars of Zen* (Tokyo: John Weatherhill, 1965), p. 163.

Kempō's One Way

48

THE CASE

A monk asked Master Kempō in all earnestness, "In a sutra it says, 'Ten-direction Bhagavats, one Way to the gate of nirvana.' I wonder where the Way is." Kempō lifted up his stick, drew a line and said, "Here it is."

Later a monk asked Unmon to give instruction about this. Unmon held up his fan and said, "This fan jumps up to the heaven of the thirty-three devas and adheres to the nose of the deva Taishaku. When a carp in the eastern sea is struck with a stick, it rains torrents as though a tray of water is overturned."

MUMON'S COMMENTARY

One goes to the bottom of the deepest sea, heaving sand and raising dust. The other stands on the top of the highest mountain and causes white waves to billow up to the sky. On the one hand, they are gripping it tightly; on the other hand, they are letting it loose; so each of them extends a single hand and together they support the essential principle. It is just like two running boys colliding. In this world there will be no one who has realized the truth completely. Examining with the true eye, I find that neither of the old masters knows where the Way is.

THE VERSE

Before a step is taken, the goal is reached;
Before the tongue is moved, the speech is finished.
Though you may take the initiative, point by point,
You must know there is still the all-surpassing hole.

TEISHŌ ON THE CASE

Master Kempō was a disciple of Master Tōzan Ryōkai, one of the founders of the Sōtō sect. Except from a few very old chronicles where some of his teachings are recorded as sermons, we know little about him.

Once a monk asked Master Kempō, "A sutra says, 'Ten-direction Bhagavats, one Way to the gate of nirvana.' I wonder where the Way is." This phrase is found in the *Sūrangama Sutra*. Bhagavat is Sanskrit and has six meanings: freedom, prosperity, nobleness, name, auspice, and highness. Here we will take it to be another eulogizing name for Buddha. There are at least three interpretations concerning the phrase itself:

(1) Bhagavats in the ten directions have only one Way to nirvana, that is, all Buddhas in the whole universe have only one Way to get to nirvana.

(2) All things in the ten directions are none other than Buddhas. For all of them there is only one Way to nirvana.

(3) In the ten directions, everything is Buddha, everywhere is the one straight Way to nirvana.

From the Zen point of view, the second interpretation is deeper than the first, and the third is the deepest of all.

Nirvana is a Sanskrit word which has several meanings. From the standpoint of Mahayana Buddhism, it may mean eternal or absolute, calm joy or transmigration to extinction. This extinction does not mean individual extinction but the annihilation of all misery and entry into bliss. Nirvana is the highest state of enlightenment, the state of satori of Buddha, which is no other than the essential world.

Now, where is the Way to nirvana? Kempō drew a line and said, "Here it is."

Do you understand what Kempō meant? The Way is not only where Kempō drew the line but everywhere in all ten directions. When you stand up, it's there. When you sit down, it's there. When you feel hungry, it's there. When you are happy, it's there. No matter how long you search or where you may go to look for it, you will never find anything that can be called the Way. It is a roadless road.

Later a monk asked Unmon to explain what Kempō had said. Unmon held up his fan and said, "This fan jumps up to the heaven of the thirty-three devas and adheres to the nose of the deva Taishaku. When a carp in the eastern sea is hit with a stick, it rains torrents as if a tray of water has been overturned."

One of the heavens in the ancient Indian philosophy, the heaven of the thirty-three devas, is the second heaven in the realm of desire. The sovereign of that heaven is the deity Taishaku.

Unmon's answer will sound ridiculous to you if you have not yet attained realization. Just try to fathom what the carp and fan mean. If you have attained true self-realization, it will all be very clear to you, and you will meet and recognize Unmon face-to-face.

ON MUMON'S COMMENTARY

"One goes to the bottom of the deepest sea, heaving sand and raising dust. The other stands on the top of the highest mountain and causes white waves to billow up to the sky. On the one hand, they are gripping it tightly; on the other hand, they are letting it loose; so each of them extends a single hand and together they support the essential principle. It is just like two running boys colliding. In this world there will be no one who has realized the truth completely. Examining with the true eye, I find that neither of the old masters knows where the Way is."

As I so often tell you, everything in the world, including the world itself, has two sides. One is the essential side, where we do not recognize anything at all because it is totally empty. It is the world of Mu. When a Zen master wants to present this side, his activity is called "taking away" or "killing" or "pushing down" or "rolling up." The other side is phenomena; it is everything in the objective world. We can perceive this side with our six senses. When a Zen master wants to present it, his activity is "giving life" or "giving" or "releasing" or "unrolling."

Referring to Kempō, Mumon says, "One goes to the bottom of the deepest sea, heaving sand and raising dust." The bottom of the deepest sea means the state of consciousness where there is no movement or change; it is the essential world, the world of Mu. "Heaving sand and raising dust" refers to the movements of the phenomenal world. When Kempō draws the line and says "Here it is," he is presenting the phenomenal world while dwelling in the essential world.

Referring to Unmon, Mumon says, "The other stands on the top of the highest mountain and causes white waves to billow up to the sky." "The highest mountain" suggests the state of consciousness where there is neither subject nor object; the world of emptiness. To cause the white waves to billow up to the sky means the movements and actions in the phenomenal world. Therefore, both Kempō and Unmon are presenting the essential world and the phenomenal world simultaneously, and they are equally matched in their skill as Zen masters.

Mumon goes on to say, "On the one hand, they are gripping it tightly; on the other hand, they are letting it loose; so each of them extends a single hand and together they support the essential principle. It is just like two running boys colliding. In this world there will be no one who has realized the truth completely. Examining with the true eye, I find that neither of the old masters knows where the Way is." If they had known the Way truly, they would not have said as much as they did. They should know that the more they talk, the more they separate themselves from it. This is Mumon's kind admonition to all Zen masters in general.

ON THE VERSE

Before a step is taken, the goal is reached;
Before the tongue is moved, the speech is finished.
Though you may take the initiative, point by point,
You must know there is still the all-surpassing hole.

Everything is perfect and complete by itself from the very beginning. We are already in the very place we want to reach. When you want to enter the Way to the gate of nirvana, you are already on the very road. More accurately, you are already in nirvana. Everything is accomplished and always has been. What more is there to say?

Even though you may think you are taking the initiative all along the Way, without anyone being able to compete with you in degree of enlightenment, you must know there is still the all-surpassing hole. "The all-surpassing hole" refers to the all-surpassing state of perfect realization. In this highest of states, perfect enlightenment (the subjective) and the essential word (the objective) are totally one. The hole means the most crucial point, but it is nothing other than right here and now. Be on your guard not to conceive any ideas concerning it, or the hole will become a pitfall.

Mumon's Postscript

Adhering to the instructions by and accounts of the Buddhas and patriarchs, I have delivered my commentary like a judge who passes sentence on a criminal exactly according to his confession, without adding even one superfluous word. I have shown you my brain, taken off its lid and exposed the eyeballs. All of you should grasp IT directly and stop seeking IT from others.

A man of enlightenment will be able to grasp the ultimate point upon hearing only a small part of what I've presented. For him there is no gate to enter, no stairs to go up. He will pass through the barrier swinging his arms without asking the permission of the gatekeeper. Remember what Gensha[1] said: "No-gate is the gate to emancipation, no-consciousness is the consciousness of the devotee of the Way," and what Haku'un[2] said: "I know most clearly the Way. It is just this. Why can't it be passed through?"

These remarks of mine are just like smearing milk on red soil. If you pass through the gateless gate, you make a fool of Mumon. If you are unable to pass through the gateless gate, you are turning your back on yourself. It is rather easy to realize the so-called nirvana mind, but it is difficult to make clear the wisdom of discrimination.[3] If you realize the wisdom of discrimination, your land will become peaceful by itself.

The first year of Jōtei (*1228*),
Five days before the end of the summer sesshin.
Respectfully inscribed by Monk Mumon Ekai,
Eighth descendant of Yōgi.[4]

NOTES

1. Master Gensha Shibi (831–908 A.D.) was born in the province of Fuku, South China, during the reign of Emperor Bunsō of the T'ang dynasty. At the age of thirty, he became a monk. His master was Seppō, one of the most renowned Chinese Zen masters. It is said that when he was starting *angya* pilgrimage in search of excellent Zen teachers, he stumbled on a stone and injured his foot. At that moment he suddenly attained deep enlightenment. He returned at once to Seppō, and in response to Seppō's questioning, uttered the famous reply, "Bodhidharma did not come to the East Land (China), the second patriarch did not go to the West Heaven (India)." Eventually, Gensha succeeded to the Dharma of Seppō and helped him guide his disciples. In his later years, Gensha settled at Mount Gensha and passed away at the age of seventy-seven in 908 A.D.

2. Master Haku'un Shutan (1024–1073 A.D.) was a famous master of the Sung dynasty in the Yōgi line of the Rinzai sect. He died at age forty-eight during the reign of Emperor Shinsō of Sung.

3. The wisdom of discrimination is that wisdom which appears after enlightenment and discerns differentiation in the phenomenal world. The wisdom of discrimination is essential for the Zen master in guiding his disciples. He must discern the state of mind of his disciples, which differs in each individual.

4. Master Yōgi Hōe is the founder of the Yōgi School, one of the two schools of the Rinzai sect. The other is the Ōryū School. Masters Yōgi and Ōryū are both Dharma successors of Master Sekisō Soen. Master Yōgi died during the reign of Emperor Jinsō of Sung in 1049 A.D.

Mumon's Zen Warnings

MUMON'S ZEN WARNINGS

To obey the rules and regulations is to tie yourself without a rope. To act freely and without restraint is heresy and deviltry. To be aware of the mind, making it pure and quiet, is the false Zen of silent contemplation. To arbitrarily ignore causal relations is to fall into a deep pitfall. To abide in absolute awakening with no darkening is to wear chains with a yoke. Thinking of good and evil is being in heaven and hell. To have views about the Buddha and the Dharma is to be imprisoned inside two iron mountains. Becoming aware of consciousness at the instant it arises is toying with the soul. Practicing concentration in quiet sitting is an action of devils.

If you go forward, you will go astray from the essence. If you go back, you oppose the principle. If you neither go forward nor back, you are a dead man breathing. Tell me now, what will you do? Make the utmost effort to attain full realization in this life! Do not abide in misery forever.

Ōryū's Three Barriers

How does my hand compare with the Buddha's hand?
How does my leg compare with a donkey's leg?
All people have their own place of birth in karma.

Muryō Sōju's Verses on Ōryū's Three Barriers

How does my hand compare with the Buddha's hand?
  Groping for the pillow at my back, I could feel it.
  In spite of myself I burst out laughing.
  From the first, the whole body is the hand.
How does my leg compare with a donkey's leg?
  Before taking a step, I have already trodden the ground.
  Freely I pass over the four seas just as I wish.
  I ride topsy-turvy on Yōgi's three-legged donkey.
All people have their own place of birth in Karma.
  Everything penetrates to the world prior to consciousness.
  Nada broke his own bones and gave them back to his father.
  Did the Fifth Patriarch have to rely on a causal relation with a father?

"Buddha's hand," "the donkey's leg," and "the birth in Karma"—
these are not the Buddha, not the Way, not Zen. Do not wonder at the
steepness of the gateless gate. It has aroused the monks' animosity.

Mumon was recently at Zuiganji Temple. Sitting on the straw-rope
seat, he judged the words of Zen masters of old and new. He cut off the
thoughts of both sages and ordinary people. Many dragons in hiding
roared like thunder.

I invited Senior Monk Mumon to be the guest master. I thank him with
this rustic poem.

Late spring of the third year of Jōtei (1230 A.D.)
Written by Muryō Sōju

TEISHŌ ON ŌRYŪ'S THREE BARRIERS

The *Gateless Gate,* by Master Mumon, contains forty-eight cases. I have delivered my *teishō* on each of them. There remains one more case on which I must comment. It is a very important koan called "Ōryū's Three Barriers."

In the third year of Jōtei (1230), Master Muryō Sōju, who lived in Zuiganji Temple in the province of Mei, invited Master Mumon to deliver a *teishō* on the forty-eight cases for the monks. When Mumon finished the *teishō,* Sōju wrote verses on each of Ōryū's three barriers and presented them to Mumon as a token of his gratitude.

Ōryū's Three Barriers are:

1. How does my hand compare with the Buddha's hand?
2. How does my leg compare with a donkey's leg?
3. All people have their own place of birth in Karma.

The verses were added by Sōju to make their import understandable. They give Sōju's view concerning each of Ōryū's barriers.

Master Ōryū Enan of Ryūkō Prefecture is one of the greatest Zen masters of the Sung dynasty. He is the Dharma successor of Sekisō Soen and is famous as the founder of the Ōryū line of the Rinzai Sect.

In old China, Zen was divided into five sects, or Houses: the Rinzai, Sōtō, Unmon, Hōgen, and Igyō. The essential core of the teachings of all five sects was, of course, the same, because it was nothing but the Buddha's Way; but each had its own unique method of guidance.

During the Sung dynasty, the Rinzai Sect divided into two lines, the Ōryū and the Yōgi, both bearing the name of their founders.

Master Ōryū was born in the fifth year of the reign of Emperor Shinsō of the Sung dynasty in 1002 A.D. and died in 1069 at the age of sixty-seven. It was his custom to examine Zen students with these three koans, and according to tradition, very few passed even two of the three to Ōryū's satisfaction. Let us now consider Ōryū's Three Barriers.

1. How does my hand compare with the Buddha's hand?

By this question Ōyrū wants first to perplex our conceptual thinking and then to awaken us to the essential world, where there are no dualistic oppositions.

Sōju's verse says: "Groping for the pillow at my back, I could feel it. In spite of myself I burst out laughing."

Intrinsically, the whole body is the hand. There is a koan which confirms Sōju's saying. It is Case 89 of the *Blue Cliff Record*. The main case reads:

"Ungan asked Dōgo, 'What use does Bodhisattva Kanzeon of Great Mercy have for so many hands and eyes?' Dōgo said, 'It is like a man who searches for his pillow in the middle of the night with his hands groping in back of him.' Gan said, 'I understand.' Go said, 'How do you understand it?' Gan said, 'The entire body is hand and eye.' Go said, 'That is very well said, but you have said only eight-tenths.' Gan said, 'How would you say it, elder brother?' Go said, 'The whole body is hand and eye.'"

What difference is there between "the entire body" and "the whole body"? That is the point of the koan and belongs to koan study in the *dokusan* room, but some interpretation might be necessary.

Every one of us has two hands. When we are absorbed in doing something with both hands, we are not aware of two hands. My two hands are, in fact, living my life, which is not two. From life's point of view, there are not two hands. This is, of course, a form of conceptual thinking, but when Sōju touched the pillow at his back he suddenly realized his essential nature, which pervades the whole universe as life pervades the whole body. Struck with joy, he burst out laughing.

2. How does my leg compare with a donkey's leg?

Sōju's verse says: "Before taking a step, I have already trodden the ground. Freely I pass over the four seas just as I wish. I ride topsy-turvy on Yōgi's three-legged donkey."

In principle, the second koan is not different from the first, and the verse expresses Sōju's view of the essential world and the activities of the enlightened person.

"Before taking a step, I have already trodden the ground." When you are about to start out for a destination, the destination is where you are standing. The destination is nowhere other than the starting point itself. If you realize this, you can quite freely go anywhere in the world as you wish.

The verse of Case 48 of the *Mumonkan* says:

Before a step is taken, the goal is reached;
Before the tongue is moved, the speech is finished.
Though you may take the initiative, point by point,
You must know there is still the all-surpassing hole.

"I ride topsy-turvy on Yōgi's three-legged donkey."

This passage may seem rather strange. There is another Zen anecdote which touches on it. "A monk once asked Master Yōgi, 'What is Buddha?' 'A three-legged donkey goes by, clattering his hooves,' was his reply." "Three-legged" refers to the three bodies of Buddha, which are the Dharmakaya Buddha, the Sambhogakaya Buddha, and the Nirmanakaya Buddha, or you may think of it as Dharma Body, Essential Wisdom, and Emancipation. These three are eventually reduced to one, which is Emancipation.

The emancipated person rides on the donkey with emancipated legs, or we may say legless legs. To ride topsy-turvy on a donkey means to ride on a donkey with absolute freedom. The donkey stands for essential nature. So this passage means, "Empty man rides on emptiness with empty legs." This is no other than the acrobatics of emptiness, and we must know that, from the essential point of view, not only the activities of the enlightened person but all the activities of ordinary people are nothing but the acrobatics of emptiness.

3. "All people have their own place of birth in Karma."

When asked, "Where is your birthplace?" ordinary people answer with no hesitation, but a person who knows something about Zen will hesitate to answer immediately because he will think there should be some deep meaning to the question. In fact, however, the phenomenal world and the essential world are completely one from the beginning.

Sōju's verse says: "Nada broke his own bones and gave them back to his father. Did the Fifth Patriarch have to rely on a causal relation with a father?"

The ancient Chinese book *Gotōegen* tells that Prince Nada cut off his flesh and gave it back to his mother, broke his bones and gave them back to his father, and preached the Dharma for his parents. In the same book we are told that the fifth patriarch, Kōnin, was born of a virgin. In a previous life, he searched for the Way, planting pine trees. In old age, he met the fourth patriarch, Dōshin, and asked to become his disciple. Dōshin refused, giving the reason that the pine tree planter was too old. The fifth patriarch borrowed the body of a young woman and had himself born again in order to meet Master Dōshin again and become his disciple. In India, it was traditionally believed that our present life is the effect of the karmic causation of our past life, and that our parents serve only as a mediary condition, but this koan wants to lead us to the essential foundation of our life, which is beyond the phenomenal world. Thus Sōju says in his first passage, "Everything penetrates to the world prior to consciousness."

This means that everything in the phenomenal world has its ground in the essential world which transcends consciousness or phenomena. Everybody's birth has its ground in the essential world without being involved in the causal relation of parents. The present koan and Sōju's verse both exhort us to awaken to the essential world, namely our true self.

The last passage is Sōju's *teishō*. Sōju says: "Buddha's hand, the donkey's legs, and the birth in Karma—these are not the Buddha, not the Way, not Zen. Do not wonder at the steepness of the gateless gate. It has aroused the monks' animosity."

Not Buddha, not the Way, not Zen. What is it after all? To grasp it is not so easy. The way to the gateless gate is precipitous. Monks climbing up the way struggle, filled with animosity.

Mōkyō's Epilogue

MŌKYŌ'S EPILOGUE

Bodhidharma came from the West. His teaching did not rely on letters but pointed directly to the mind of man and advocated becoming Buddha by seeing into one's self-nature. To say "direct pointing," however, is already a meandering, and to add "becoming Buddha" is falling into senility. It is gateless from the beginning. Why is there the barrier or gate? His kindness is grandmotherly and spreads abusive voices. Muan (Mōkyō himself), by adding a superfluous word, wants to make a forty-ninth case. There might be some entanglement. Open your eyes widely and grasp it.

The summer of the fifth year of Shun'yū (1245 A.D.)
The second edition written by Mōkyō[1]

NOTE

1. Mōkyō (Muan) was a warrior who spent most of his life on the battlefield. It is recorded that he was deeply interested in Zen and had a profound knowledge of it, even calling himself "Layman Muan." "An" means "hermitage," so Muan designates himself (the master of) Mu hermitage. He passed away in September in 1246 A.D. during the reign of Emperor Risō of the Southern Sung dynasty. Judging from the date of this epilogue, he is believed to have written it the year before his death. The second edition of the *Mumonkan* must have been issued with this epilogue in 1245, when Master Mumon was sixty-three years of age.

Amban's Forty-ninth Case

THE CASE

Old Zen Master Mumon composed the forty-eight cases and judged the koans of venerable masters of ancient times. He is just like a fried bean-cake vendor who makes his buyers open their mouths and eat his cakes until they are unable either to swallow them down or vomit them up.

Even so, Amban[1] wants to bake yet another piece of cake in his red-hot oven to present to Mumon. I don't know where the old master will dig his teeth into it. If he can eat it in one bite, he will emit light and shake the earth. If not, it and the other forty-eight cases will all turn into hot sand. Speak at once! Speak at once!

A sutra says: "Stop it! Stop it! It should not be expounded. My Dharma is subtle and difficult to speculate on."

Amban says, "Where does the Dharma come from? On what basis does its subtlety lie? What is it when it is expounded? Why call only Bukan a chatterbox?[2] Shakyamuni himself was wordy. The old man raised phantoms and so entangled the descendants of hundreds and thousands of generations in creepers and vines that they are unable to stick their heads out.

Such amazing talks as these cases cannot be spooned, though we try to pick them up, or cooked enough, though we steam them in a boiling pot. There was an onlooker who asked in some confusion, "After all,

how will you decide?" Amban placed his ten fingernails together in sup-
plication and said, "Stop! Stop! It is not to be expounded. My Dharma
is subtle and difficult to speculate about." Then he suddenly drew a
small circle over the two characters for "difficult" and "speculate" and
showed it to the people. The five thousand scrolls of the Tripitaka[3] and
Vimalakirti's[4] gate of nonduality are all in it.

THE VERSE

If one says fire is light,
Do not respond, shake your head.
Only a thief recognizes a thief,
At one question he immediately nods.

> Early summer of the sixth year of Shun'yū (1246 A.D.)
> Written by Amban at a fishing villa by West Lake.

NOTES

1. His real name was Tei Seishi, Amban being his Zen (or literary) name. He
was a noted figure in politics as well as in the field of literature, and he died in
1251 in the Sung dynasty.

2. When Master Bukan was abbot at Kokuseiji Temple in Mount Tendai, Kanzan and Jittoku visited him in the kitchen. He greeted the two, saying, "Here
come Bodhisattvas Manjusri and Samantabhadra!" Upon this the two named him
"Bukan, the chatterbox."

3. See Note 2 to Case 25.

4. See note 1 to Case 36.

Introduction to the History of Zen Practice

Appendix 1

Since earliest times Buddhism has been a religion of human example, maintained and transmitted not by authoritarian dogma but by the practice and realization of generation after generation of students and adepts. The first Buddhist scriptures were records of the discourses of the Buddha Shakyamuni as he traveled and taught at hundreds of gatherings two and a half thousand years ago. Since then, because of the wide range of human potential and experience and the increasing complexity of societies, there has evolved a great variety of Buddhist texts, reflecting the ongoing accommodation of teaching and practice to the needs of the times.[1]

A thousand years after the passing of Shakyamuni, Buddhism had spread all over Asia, appearing in various forms, its teachings expressed through numerous languages and cultures. In China, after centuries of study and practical application of many forms of Buddhism, there evolved a way of Buddhism known as Ch'an (rendered "Zen" in Japanese), which produced many generations of illuminati and profoundly influenced the civilizations of East Asia.

In Zen particular emphasis was placed on the role of the human exemplar as the embodiment of the teachings. The reason for this was that the meaning of the teachings lies in their application and practice, and this practice could only be manifested through human effort. Timely and appropriate application of the teachings is the key ingredient without which they become a dead letter, or merely a record of past method. The lives of the adepts, the processes and results of their cultivation of Bud-

1. See Appendix 2: Writings and Zen Records Mentioned in the Introduction to the History of Zen Practice.

dhism, their words and silences, their doings and nondoings came to have great importance for Zen students in inspiring and directing their practice of Buddhism. Just as with the earlier forms of teaching, proper applications of Zen sayings became a critical issue in their use.

The history of Zen may be divided into several eras, which fade into each other and share in each other's characteristics yet nevertheless can be generally distinguished. Before the Zen patriarchs, adepts in China who followed the Buddhist scriptures in their methods were usually well-disciplined ascetics and often included incantation of scriptures and holy names in their practice as part of their concentration-contemplation techniques. There are a number of these people, including some renowned expositors of the classical Buddhist teachings, who are recognized as adepts in Zen histories, but except for the latter few, very little of the early meditators' own descriptions of their inner experiences has ever been revealed.

The era of Zen patriarchs, from the late fifth or early sixth century to the early eighth century, was one in which Zen emerged with other schools from the chaos of early Buddhist transmission in China, developing into a distinct way. During this period the teaching was mainly carried on by a few individual teachers; the way of Zen did not become widely known until the time of the fourth patriarch, in the first half of the seventh century. Under the influence of the fourth patriarch, Zen teachings circulated through China and entered Korea. The fourth, fifth, and sixth patriarchs of Zen were all nationally recognized; the sixth and last patriarch, originally an illiterate woodcutter from the remote south of China, became a most highly acclaimed and sought-after teacher whose words were later elevated to the status of scripture.

The next era of Zen history, from the late eighth century to the mid-tenth century, has sometimes been called the golden age of Zen. The inception of this era, the age of the latter patriarchs and the successors after them, coincided with the early T'ang dynasty, the golden age of Chinese civilization. While the T'ang dynasty declined, however, Zen Buddhism flourished and produced a legacy continuing for a thousand years. Numerous Zen transmission lines branching from the disciples of the fifth and sixth patriarchs developed and refined Zen methods, facing wider ranges of disciples as the practice of the other schools of Buddhism waned and increasing numbers of students entered the Zen orders. As the T'ang dynasty declined, more and more Confucians also took an interest in Zen, some going so far as to entirely forsake their civil careers for mendicancy. During this period Zen language began to evolve, with its special teaching devices, using media of expression congenial to the Chinese, such as aphorism, anecdote, and poetry.

While historians have called this the golden age of Zen, in the writings and sayings of the Zen teachers themselves it is referred to as a time of imitation and decadence in Buddhism. The further development of highly sophisticated teachings was necessitated by an increasing complexity and confusion in society and its individuals. The subsequent period of Zen, extending from about the tenth century through the thirteenth or fourteenth centuries, saw great elaboration on the work of the preceding era, concentrating especially on the stories, sayings, and formulae of the old masters. During this time there was a great flowering of Zen literature, which provided a more intimate glimpse of Zen life and the personalities of the great Zen teachers than ever before. There was also increased formalization and corruption in the Zen schools, prompting a growth of criticism and critical literature as well.

After the fourteenth century, with the decline in the number of competent teaching masters, there was a revived interest in scriptural studies among Zen students. Reintroduced to Zen during the preceding era was the practice of invocating the names of Buddha and reciting scriptures, which gained ever greater popularity among Zen students. Monastic life seems to have become increasingly ceremonialized, with the growing use of various incantation practices perhaps stimulated by the influx of Tantric Buddhism from Tibet and Mongolia into China during and following the thirteenth- and fourteenth-century Mongolian rule there.

In terms of pure Zen practice, emphasis in this latter era was placed first on a word or phrase used in deep meditation. This practice had been dominant since the mid-eleventh century, and the most popular words and phrases, taken as they were from records of sayings of the ancient Zen masters, were obviously in use much earlier. As time went on, the use of such words as "No" and "Who?" in meditation became a virtually universal practice among Zen students, and many masters realized their first awakening through this practice. After awakening, students were taught with complicated koans and often encouraged to read the scriptures and study the classical Buddhist teachings.

The practice of Zen devoted much time to sitting meditation. In pre-Zen meditation schools, practitioners customarily entered concentration for days at a time, carrying out contemplative practices according to methods imported from India. The Zen communities balanced meditation with the mundane tasks of everyday life, and instead of using systematic descriptions of meditation states and processes, employed the content of this everyday life as a medium.

The course of Zen discipleship was an individual as well as a group matter, and the teaching evolved from the relationship of teachers and students. Gradually the enlightenment stories, sayings and doings, dialogues, and other lore of the Zen illuminati came to be used as contemplation themes and aids to the direction of meditation and evaluation of spiritual experiences. These tales of the ancients, called koan, or "public cases," became an important part of Zen teaching and practice, their mysterious subtlety naturally withholding their truths until the appropriate state of mind and being is reached by the contemplator. It became a common Zen practice to "gaze at a saying," bringing everything into the light of the saying.

This was done according to a kind of order, according to the type of koan and the state of the meditator. Later this order and the koans assigned became more or less formalized.

Few generalizations can be made about the history of the koan and its use in Zen, since there was so much variation among individual teachers and students. The turn of the ninth century has often been singled out as a period of transition in Zen teaching from principle to action, particularly through the careers of two eminent teachers, Baso (Ma-tsu) (708–789), and his successor Hyakujō (Pai-chang) (720–814). Most of the record of Baso consists of tales of his interactions with disciples, and numerous stories were told of Hyakujō's encounters and dialogues with his fellow students under Baso and his own disciples later on. Hyakujō in particular frequently quoted the ancients to make his point and used old sayings as pointers for practice:

> Right now if your mind is like space, for the first time your study has some accomplishment. An eminent patriarch in India said, "The Himalaya is compared to great nirvana." The first patriarch in this country said, "Let your mind be like wood or stone." The third patriarch said, "Unmoving, forget objects." The sixth patriarch said, "Do not think of good or bad at all." My later teacher said, "Be like a man lost, unable to tell his whereabouts." Master Sōjō (Seng-chao) said, "Shut off knowledge, stop perception; solitary awareness is something obscure and unfathomable." Manjusri said, "Mind is like space, therefore respectful obeisance has nothing to look upon; the most profound scripture is neither heard nor accepted and upheld." Right now if you just don't see or hear anything existent or nonexistent at all, with your six sense faculties shut off, if you can study in this way, if you can "uphold

the scripture" in this way, then for the first time you have some accomplishment in practice. (Extensive Record of Hyakujō)

Hyakujō developed formulations for the application of Zen and the teachings, of which this direct approach to the space-like mind was a fundamental part. Hyakujō's great disciple Isan (Kuei-shan) also recommended this type of meditation for sudden awakening but wrote that those who were unable to attain abrupt transcendence by this method should carefully study the scriptures, indicating that the scriptures were never entirely abandoned in Zen teaching. Isan figures in many popular koan treated in the great koan collections, and several of his dialogues with his famous successor Kyōzan (Yang-shan) have been traditionally emphasized by Zen teachers over the centuries, illustrating important aspects of the teaching.

(Isan's) questions to Kyōzan about several encounters between Hyakujō's other great disciple Ōbaku (Huang-po) and his renowned successor Rinzai (Lin-chi) were recorded and added to the record of Rinzai, a major Zen classic; this is an early overt example of the use of anecdotes or sayings to bring out or test a student's insight. Several elements of evolving Zen lore—travel to various Zen centers, dialogue, use of poetic imagery and metaphors, and later assessment of events—can be seen exemplified in just such an excerpt from the famous Record of Rinzai:

> The Master went to Hōrin (Feng-lin). Hōrin asked, "I've something to ask; may I?" Rinzai said, "Why gouge out flesh and make a wound?" Hōrin said, "The moon on the ocean is clear, without shadows, but the wandering fish gets lost by itself alone." Rinzai said, "Since the moon on the ocean is shadowless, how can the wandering fish get lost?" Hōrin said, "Seeing the wind, you know waves are rising; gazing at the water, a crude sail wafts in the wind." Rinzai said, "The solitary disc shines alone, mountains and rivers are quiet; at the sound of my own laugh, heaven and earth are startled." Hōrin said, "You may illumine heaven and earth with your tongue, but try to say a single phrase appropriate to the situation." Rinzai said, "If you meet a swordsman on the road, show your sword; do not offer poetry to one who is not a poet." Hōrin then stopped. Rinzai chanted a verse:

> > The Great Way is beyond all similitude,
> > Whether you turn East or West,
> > Sparks cannot overtake it,
> > Lightning cannot reach it.

> Isan asked Kyōzan, "Since 'Sparks cannot overtake it and lightning cannot reach it,' what have the sages since time immemorial used to help people?" Kyōzan said, "What is your idea, Teacher?" Isan said, "There is only verbal

explanation, no real meaning at all." Kyōzan said, "I don't concur." Isan said, "What do you mean?" Kyōzan said, "Officially not even a needle can get in; privately, even a horse and carriage can go through."

Rinzai is known to have devised and used a number of formulations, including elaborations of Hyakujō's, which Rinzai illustrated in cryptic poetry. These formulae, expressing various aspects or stages of Zen experience, were thereafter used by teachers and disciples of Rinzai's lineage to question each other. Many verses of later Zen masters on the states represented by these formulae are recorded in Zen annals.

Tōzan (Tung-shan), a great contemporary of Rinzai, also devised several testing and teaching designs to bring out different levels of realization and practice. Tōzan was a spiritual descendant of Sekitō (Shih-t'ou), an outstanding contemporary of the aforementioned Baso. Sekitō (700–790) was one of the first teachers of the southern school of Zen to compose anything in writing, and he began the use of certain terms in the Zen idiom. Tōzan elaborated and refined the teachings of Sekitō and composed many mystic verses which were later widely studied.

Tōzan's formulae were analyzed, commented on, and newly versified by Sōzan (Ts'ao-shan), one of his distinguished disciples. Sōzan also devised his own formulations and was perhaps the first Zen teacher to classify koans systematically, which he did in the course of elucidating the teaching through Tōzan's or his own formulations.

While the teaching designs of these great masters were studied and appreciated in many teaching circles, they did not form a curriculum as such, for it was considered that literature and verbal expression were only an aid, and only one kind of aid at that, important though it may be in the sphere of its own function. A number of terms used by Isan, Kyōzan, Rinzai, Tōzan and (Sōzan) later became common to Zen expression, both in talking about experience and in assessing the inner significance of Zen stories; yet the Zen masters were well aware of the lulling effect of cliche, especially in conjunction with other forms of routine, and evolved a type of teaching which resembles what would be called "criticism" in a conventional field but which actually attacks the student's fixation on words. Certain "commentary" literature is also of this nature.

There are many scattered bits of evidence of the growing use of Zen stories and sayings among the teachers themselves in their dealings with their students. Unmon (Yün-men) (d. 949), a brilliant teacher of more than sixty enlightened disciples, used hundreds of koans in his teaching and created hundreds more of his own. For many of his own riddles Unmon also told his own answer and gave answers and alternatives for hundreds of ancient koans. Unmon did not want his words recorded, but his attendants used to jot down his amazing sayings and remarks on paper robes.

When he died, Unmon concluded his last admonitions, "If you don't understand, the Buddhas have a clear teaching—follow and practice it."

Hōgen (Fa-yen) (885–958), a descendant of Unmon's teacher Seppō (Hsüeh-feng), was the father of the last of the so-called five houses of Zen, which made a particularly great contribution to Korean as well as Chinese Buddhism, reviving both Zen and the scriptural teachings. Hōgen was fully aware of the significance of the koan in Zen study by that time, when he warned in his *Ten Guidelines for Zen Schools* against making personal judgments on sayings of the past and present without going through clarification and purification of the mind. He wrote:

> See how those worthies of former times traversed mountains and seas, not shrinking from death or life, for the sake of one or two sayings. When there was the slightest tinge of doubt, the matter had to be submitted to certain discernment; what they wanted was distinct clarity.

> First becoming standards of truth and falsehood, acting as eyes for intelligent beings, only after that did they raise the seal of the source on high and circulate the true teaching, bringing forth the rights and wrongs of former generations, bearing down on inconclusive cases.

> If, without undergoing purification and clarification, you make your own personal judgment of past and present, how is that different from insisting on performing a sword dance without having learned how to handle a sword, or foolishly counting on getting across a pit without having found out its size? Can you avoid cutting yourself or falling?

Hōgen also reiterated the traditional Zen warning against memorizing expressions without being capable of putting them into practice:

> A student of transcendent wisdom is not without a teacher's teaching, but once one has gotten the teacher's teaching, it is essential that the great function be manifested; only then will one have some personal experience. If one just sticks to his teacher's way and memorizes his expressions, it is not penetrating enlightenment at all, and is totally in the realm of intellectual knowledge. This is why an ancient said, "When one's view equals that of his teacher, he lessens the teacher's virtue by half; only when one's view surpasses his teacher is he able to bring out the teacher's teaching." The sixth patriarch said to elder Myō (Ming), "What I'm telling you is not secret; the

secret is in you." And Gantō (Yen-t'ou) said to Seppō, "Everything flows
forth from your own heart." Thus we know that words and speech, hitting
and shouting, do not come from a teacher's bequest; how could the marvelous function, free in all ways, demand another assent? (Ten Guidelines for
Zen Schools)

This admonition attacks the problem of cliche and blind adherence to
forms. Hōgen also stressed the need for correct understanding of the
scriptural teachings in order to practice and pass them on, and to avoid
adducing testimony wrongly from scriptures without mastering both the
Buddha's teaching and the Zen mind. Furthermore, Hōgen concludes
that since literal expression is part of the vehicle of the teaching, it is
therefore not a trivial matter or a leisurely pursuit. Hence, he recommended proper care for the manner of expression; as he says in regard to
words and composition, "The direction of the meaning is in the words, so
how could it be proper to compose them arbitrarily?"

The replies and remarks given by Unmon and Hōgen to koans were
usually very terse, much like those of the ancients they were quoting to
bring out certain points. Their treatment of koans shows something of
the special development of Zen teaching in which time does not exist, or
in which before and after exist only relative to the state of the individual
considering the issue:

A monk asked Seppō for some guidance. Seppō said, "What is it?" That
monk was greatly enlightened at these words. Unmon quoted this and said,
"What did Seppō say to him?"

Seppō said, "People sit by a basket of rice and starve to death, people die of
thirst by the side of a river."

Gensha (Hsüan-sha) said, "People sit inside a basket of rice starving to death,
die of thirst with their heads stuck in the water."

Unmon quoted them and said, "The whole body is rice—the whole body is
water." (Extensive Record of Unmon)

There were monks sitting in a row on the Hung-t'ang bridge in Fukien; an
official asked, "Are there any Buddhas here?"
Hōgen said in place of the monks, "Who are you?"

When Master Kyūhō (Chiu-feng) went into the city of Chianghsi, someone
asked him, "Entering the marketplace to teach, what do you use for eyes?"
Kyūhō said, "Sun and moon have never been out of order."

Hōgen said instead (of Kyūhō's answer), "Wait 'till you have eyes."
(Recorded Sayings of Hōgen)

The first teacher to versify koans extensively was Fun'yō (Fen-yang) (947–1024), an important figure in the early Sung dynasty revival of Rinzai style of Zen. Fun'yō studied with seventy other teachers from different lines of Zen and lectured and wrote extensively on Zen and Buddhist lore. The record of his works includes three collections of a hundred koans each. In one collection, Fun'yō added poetic summaries to each old case; for example:

Whenever Roso (Lu-tsu) saw a monk coming, he'd immediately face the wall.

When people come he faces the wall, sitting peacefully;
He doesn't talk of many things, or speak of same or different.
Kindly, he doesn't let you seek outside the mind,
Avoiding the use of "bright" and "dark" to fool the deaf and blind.
Autumn frost covers the ground, producing cold and warm;
Roso, in extending compassion, doesn't exert any effort.

Another collection consists of one hundred probing questions along with Fun'yō's answers. These are based on classical Buddhist and Zen themes, and according to Fun'yō were based on students' questions:

The earth has no partiality—why are high and low uneven?
Fun'yō: "It's obvious."

The gate of Dharma is wide and vast—why can't people of time enter?
Fun'yō: "Who are they?"

Before our eyes there is nothing—why then is it full to overflowing?
Fun'yō: "If you contend, there's not enough."

The third collection consists of one hundred old koan stories, with Fun'yō's substitute answers:

A monk asked Sanzan (Sha-shan), "What is the original body?"
Sanzan said, "Nothing resembles it."
Fun'yō said in Sanzan's place, "Why willingly be deceived?" (Recorded Sayings of Fun'yō)

The next outstanding figure in koan history after Fun'yō is the great master Setchō (Hsüeh-tou) (980–1058), a fourth-generation descendant of Unmon. Setchō made a collection of a hundred old stories with his own comments, and a collection of a hundred stories with his verse on each case, adding other remarks to a few as well. Setchō also commented on many more koans and wrote a great deal of poetry of all sorts besides, but he is especially known for the collection of one hundred koans with his verses. This work became a most popular Zen text, universally esteemed ever after.

By this time, bringing up and commenting or elaborating on old koans was a universal practice in the teachings of the Zen masters, though outside a number of more or less perennial koans, those used varied widely. The comments and conclusions of various teachers may show different perspectives or stages and often have no outward resemblance or apparent relation at all. One element of this development is, once again, the limited nature of even the most pregnant words; besides bringing out the many subtleties within the words of the ancients, the teachers of later generations also were obliged to bring up things unsaid at a given moment. This can be the source of much confusion in investigating Zen lore but also the source of much understanding. Often several layers of refinement would grow, as illustrated in the case of Seppō, his assistant Gensha, and his later disciple Unmon.

Sometimes koans were brought up before the assembly and questioned by students; sometimes they were brought up by the teacher, and students were questioned. The questioning might take place as a group or individually. Eventually much student-teacher contact either centered on koans or used them as a didactic device or medium of expression. Assessment of mental states and insights was often centered on the koans, as they were used as mirrors of the mind.

After Setchō, similar collections of old koans with appreciatory verses and prose comments were made by leading Zen teachers. Haku'un Shutan (Pai-yün Shou-tuan) (d. 1072), Tōsu Gisei (T'ou-tzu I-ch'ing) (d. 1083), Tanka Shijun (Tan-hsia Tzu-ch'un) (d. 1119), and Wanshi Shōgaku (Hung-chih Cheng-chüeh) (d. 1157) all composed collections of koans with verses. Engo (Yüan-wu) (d. 1135) made introductions, interlinear sayings, and discursive commentaries to each part of Setchō's now famous collection of one hundred koans with verse. This was published as the *Blue Cliff Record;* it became immediately popular and was always a most highly esteemed book. Engo also treated Setchō's *Cascade Collection* of a hundred koans with comments, producing the *Measuring Tap,* now a lesser-known work.

About a century later, the distinguished master Banshō (Wan-sung) dealt with the koan and verse collection made by Wanshi Shōgaku, who like Engo and Setchō had been a leading teacher of his time. The result of this effort was the *Book of Equanimity,* a work ranked with the *Blue*

Cliff Record, though more intricate and subtle. Banshō also lectured on Hung-chih's collection of a hundred koans with comments, producing the *Record of Further Inquiries.*

Banshō's distinguished successor Shōrin (T'sung-lin) took up the cases and verses in the collections of Tōsu and Tanka. It is also said that the introductions and interlinear sayings were added to the collection of Tōsu and Tanka, while the long commentaries are those of Shōrin. The koan texts completed by Shōrin, called the *Book of the Empty Valley* and *Book of the Vacant Hall*, are similar in form to the *Blue Cliff Record* but different in style; they are lesser known, however, perhaps because of the decline of interest in Zen study after the assertion of Mongolian rule over China in 1277. Shōrin was summoned to talk about Zen to Khubilai Khan, and for awhile the Khan liked Zen Buddhism, but eventually he came to prefer Tibetan Buddhism. Many attribute this to the attraction of shamanistic elements in Tibetan Buddhism, which would have been more congenial to the Mongols.

Throughout the twelfth century a number of Zen books of somewhat different composition also appeared, illustrating various aspects of Zen life, including koan use. Kakuhan's (Chüeh-fan's) famed *Book of the Forest* appeared in 1107, recounting and discussing Zen lore of all kinds past and present. Other books of contemporary Zen lore, stories of things seen and heard over years in the Zen communities, appeared between 1150 and 1200: *Recollected Conversations Lying in the Clouds*, *Book of the Fields of Silk Lake*, *Arsenal of Religion*, *Precious Lessons from the Zen Forests*, *Events from the Heyday of the Zen Communities.* Another type of literature to appear was the Zen letter, with the collected letters of Ōryū (Huang-lung) (d. 1069), Reigen (Ling-yüan) (d. 1117), Engo (Yüan-wu) (d. 1135), Daie (Ta-hui) (d. 1163) becoming popular in Zen circles.

In 1228, shortly after the publication of the *Book of Equanimity* and *Record of Further Inquiries*, the Zen teacher Mumon (Wu-men), in response to students' questioning, delivered a series of lectures on old koans, including both comments and verses on each case. Collected and published as the *Gateless Gate*, Mumon's work is free from the elaborate embellishment of earlier koan texts, being stark and simple by contrast. It was soon brought to Japan by a Japanese successor to Mumon and became perhaps the most popular classic koan text there, being highly esteemed for its value in actual practice.

The body of Zen lore that grew up through the eleventh and twelfth

centuries shows a growing consciousness of Zen history and evinces a renewed concern with formalization and vitiation of the inner dynamic. A
great twelfth-century master, Ban'an (Wan-an), as recorded in the anthology *Forest of Wisdom*, said,

> From the first Zen patriarch at Shao-lin the robe and Teaching were both
> transmitted; after six generations, the robe stopped and was not transmitted,
> and those in whom action and understanding corresponded were chosen to
> continue the "family work" over the generations; the path of the patriarchs
> became ever more refulgent, their descendents became more numerous.
>
> After the sixth patriarch, Sekitō and Baso were both true heirs, in accord
> with Prajñātāra's prophecy, "You need descendents to go on in your
> footsteps." The profound words and marvelous sayings of these two great
> men circulated throughout the land, and from time to time there were those
> who secretly accorded with them and personally realized them. Once there
> were many teachers' methods, students did not have one sole way open, as
> the original stream of Sōkei (Ts'ao-ch'i); the sixth patriarch branched out
> into five, square or round according to the vessel, the essence of the water
> being the same. Each had an excellent repute, and strived diligently to carry
> out his own responsibilities, casually to utter a word, giving a direction to
> include all the students. So communities sprouted up all over—it was not
> without reason.
>
> Hence, they would respond and expound back and forth to each other,
> exposing the subtleties and opening up the mysteries, sometimes putting
> down, sometimes upholding, in this way and that assisting the process of the
> teaching, their sayings flavorless, like simmering board-soup and cooking
> nail-rice, served to those who come later to chew on. This is called "bringing
> up the ancients." The verses (on the ancient cases) began with Fun'yō; then
> with Setchō the sound was widely broadcast, and he revealed the essential
> import, oceanic, boundless. Later authors ran after Setchō and imitated him,
> not considering the issue of enlightened virtue, but striving for vividness and
> novelty of literary expression, thereby causing later students of subsequent
> generations to be unable to see the ancients' message in its pristine purity and
> wholeness.
>
> I have traveled around to Zen communities and I have seen among my
> predecessors those who don't read anything but the sayings of the ancients
> and don't practice anything but the rules of Pai-chang. It isn't that they par-
> ticularly like ancient things, it's just that people of present times are not suffi-
> cient as models. I hope for people of comprehension and realization who will
> understand me beyond the words.

So great was the infatuation of Zen students with Engo's *Blue Cliff
Record* that Daie, one of his outstanding successors, destroyed the wood-
blocks of the book in the 1130s and dealt with the koans in a different

way. A thirteenth-century descendant of Engo and Daie explains this dramatic action and lauds the foresight of Daie:

> The Way that is specially transmitted outside of doctrine is utterly simple and quintessential. From the beginning there's no other discussion. Our predecessors carried it out without doubt, kept it without deviation.
>
> During the T'ien-hsi era of the Sung dynasty (1012–1022) Setchō using his eloquence and erudition, with beautiful ideas in kaleidoscopic display, seeking freshness and polishing his skill, followed Fun'yō's verses on the ancients, to catch and control the students of the time. The manner of the religion went through a change from this.
>
> During the Hsüan-ho era (1119–1125), Engo also set forth his own ideas, and from then it was known as the *Blue Cliff Record*. At that time, the complete masters of the age such as Neidōsha (Wayfarer Ning), Reigen (Lingyüan), Shishin (Ssu-hsin), and Bukkan (Fo-chien) could not contradict what he said, so new students of later generations prized his words and would recite them by day and learn them by night, calling this the ultimate study. None realized how they were wrong, and unfortunately the students' mental art deteriorated.
>
> In the beginning of the Shao-hsing era (1131–1163) Daie went into Min (Fukien) and saw the students were recalcitrant, galloping wildly over the days and months, getting so involved that it became an evil, so he broke up the woodblocks of the *Blue Cliff Record* and analyzed its explanations. Thus he came to get rid of illusions and rescue those who were floundering, wherefore he stripped away excess and set aside exaggeration, demolished the false and revealed the true, dealing with it in a special way. The monks began to realize their error, and didn't idolize it any more. So if it weren't for Daie's high illumination and distant vision, riding on the power of the vow of compassion to save the last age from its ills, the Zen communities would be in peril. (Precious Lessons from the Zen Forests)

Ban'an, who had been Daie's successor, also spoke out against stereotyped, rigid formalization of practices such as dialogue in the teaching hall, koan testing, and "entering the room," personal confrontation with the teaching master:

> When the ancients went up in the hall, first they brought up the essentials of the great teaching, and questioned the assembly; students would come forth and inquire further. Eventually it developed into the form of question-and-answer. People these days make up an unrhymed four line verse and call it "fishing words," one man pops out in front of the group, loudly recites a couplet of ancient poetry, calling this "an assault line." It's so vulgar and conventionalized, it's pitiful, lamentable.
>
> When the ancients held room-entering, they would first hang out the sign, and each individual, because of the importance of the matter of life and

death, would come bounding forth to settle their doubts and determine what
is so. We often see abbots in recent times making everybody come and pay
submission and respect, without question of whether they're old or ill. If
there is musk, it is naturally fragrant—what need is there to advertise it? By
this they wrongly create divisions, and guest and host are not at ease. Teaching abbots should think about this.

When venerated adepts famous for their practice come to a monastery,
when the abbot ascends the high seat he should defer respectfully, excusing
himself, bending from honor to humility, speak words to enhance respect,
then get down from the seat and together with the head monk and the whole
assembly, request [the visiting adept] to ascend the seat, asking to hear the
essentials of his way. I have often seen in recent times a competitiveness; [the
abbot] will bring up a public case of the ancients and have the [visiting adept]
decide it before the assembly—they call this testing him. Don't let this attitude sprout in your hearts. The sages of yore forgot feelings for the sake of
the truth, and all set up the way of teaching, responding, and calling to each
other, to cause the teaching to endure. How could they have permitted mental fluctuation to arouse these evil thoughts? Manners have deference as the
mainstay—we should ponder this deeply. (Precious Lessons from the Zen
Forests)

Daie himself had certainly not discarded koans in practice, and he
transmitted a great deal of ancient and contemporary Zen lore. He made
an anthology of Zen teachings and koans of ancient masters, and added
brief comments to many of them. This six-volume book, called *Treasury
of Eyes of True Teaching*, soon gained great popularity. His *Precious
Lessons from the Zen Forests*, an anthology of Zen writings and speeches
from the eleventh and twelfth centuries, bears largely on ethics and practical conduct. His letters, which were collected after his death, were included along with the thirty volumes of his sayings which were entered
into the Chinese Buddhist Canon shortly after Daie's death. These letters
give considerable attention to practical methods of experiential entry into
Zen enlightenment, especially concerning ways of lay practice in the
everyday life of the ordinary world. Later they became a popular classic,
Daie's best-known work.

Perhaps the most powerful and lasting influence of Daie (a teacher of
such stature that he was called a second coming of Rinzai himself) was
from his use of the koan and critical words or answers from the koan.
Daie especially emphasized generating an all-consuming doubt, using the
koan as a focal point. This he learned from Engo, who had told him after
an initial awakening that not to doubt words is a great disease. Daie espe-

cially singled out such famous koans as "Does a Dog Have Buddha-nature? No" for primary Zen work:

> Just take the deluded thinking mind, the discriminating judging mind, the mind which likes life and dislikes death, the mind of knowledge, opinion, and intellectual understanding, the mind which longs for quiet and detests commotion, and lay it all down at once: at this laying down, observe a saying—A monk asked Jōshū (Chao-Chou), "Does a dog have Buddha-nature?" Jōshū said, "No." This single word "No" is a weapon to destroy so much wrong knowledge and wrong consciousness. Don't understand it in terms of yes and no, existence and nonexistence; don't have a logical understanding, don't try to figure it out in your intellect, don't stick to "raising the eyebrows and blinking the eyes," don't make a living on words, don't drift into unconcern, don't take it to be in the raising of it, don't draw proofs from writings. Just bring it to mind time and time again, twenty-four hours a day, whether walking, standing, sitting or lying down, time and again raising it to awaken yourself: does a dog have Buddha-nature? No. Without departing from your daily activities try to do this.
>
> Just observe, 'A monk asked Jōshū if a dog has Buddha-nature or not. Jōshū said, no.' Please just take the mind engaged in idle thought, return it to the word "no," and try to think of that. Suddenly facing the point where thought can't reach, you find this one thought "no" breaks; this is right where you comprehend all time.
>
> A thousand doubts, ten thousand doubts, are just one doubt. If doubt is broken on a saying, then a thousand doubts, ten thousand doubts are broken at once. If the saying is not broken through, then for the time being keep on at it; if you give up the saying and then rouse doubts at different writings, rouse doubts at scriptural teachings, rouse doubts on the public cases of the ancients, rouse doubts in the mundane toll of your daily affairs, all of this is hindrance and bedevilment.
>
> Number One, don't take it at the bringing up, and also don't try to figure it out in thought; just set your mind to pondering the imponderable. The mind then has nowhere to go, and like a rat going into a horn, it is cut off.
>
> Also, when your mind is noisy, just bring up the saying that a dog has no Buddha-nature; the words of the Buddhas and Patriarchs, the sayings of the old masters in various places, have a thousand, ten thousand differences, but if you can pass through this word "no" you'll pass through them all at once, and don't have to ask others. If you only ask others about the words of the Buddhas, the words of the Patriarchs, the words of the masters everywhere, you'll never be enlightened. (Daie's Letters)

Daie's pointers of koan practice became standard guidelines, often quoted in later Zen handbooks. Mumon, author of the *Gateless Gate*, was a descendant of Engo, Daie's teacher, and experienced this type of

Zen practice under his teacher Gatsurin (Yüeh-lin). Mumon meditated on "No" for six years without gaining entry, finally giving up sleep, until he experienced an awakening. Later he also placed considerable emphasis on this kind of practice:

> A monk asked Jōshū, "Does a dog have Buddha-nature or not?" Jōshū said, "No." Very many are those who bring this up, and those who meditate on it are not few. This one word "no" is raised and dealt with alone: those who penetrate into this one word "no" and thus realize enlightenment are numerous as drops of rain; those who don't believe completely pass the time in vain. (Recorded Sayings of Mumon)

Mumon's teaching is characteristic of Rinzai-style Zen after Daie and he also emphasized the process of intense doubt which Engo and Daie had declared was so important:

> Penetrating Zen involves no particular cleverness: it's just a matter of rousing the mass of doubt throughout your body, day and night, never letting up. After a long time it becomes pure and ripe, and inside and outside become one; then you become one with space, then you become one with the mountains, rivers, and earth, then you become one with the four quarters, above and below. Haven't you heard it said "The whole earth is the student's self; the whole earth is the gate of liberation; the whole earth is one eye of a monk."
>
> When Chikugen (Chu-yüan) was in the congregation of Daie, he just contemplated the word "no" for forty days and was awakened. Daie then asked him to be the librarian. When he was contemplating the word, he was soaked by rain on the verandah but he didn't even notice; someone told him he was getting wet with rain and dragged him in, but he didn't pay any attention. Brethren, you should continue to work like this—if you do, there will be none who will get no result. (Recorded Sayings of Mumon)

The Zen way of bringing the clinging mind to an impasse and uprooting every nest of the self, traditionally represented in seemingly insolvable problems, is typical of Mumon's teaching, including that found in the *Gateless Gate*. In a talk which was later appended to the *Gateless Gate* as a guide to Zen meditation, Mumon said:

> If you follow regulations, keeping the rules, you tie yourself without rope, but if you act any which way without inhibition you're a heretical demon. If you keep your mind still and quiet, this is the false Zen of silent illumination, while if you let your mind go and forget circumstances, this is the deep pit of liberation. Clear alertness is wearing chains and stocks. Thinking of good and bad is hell and heaven. The view of Buddha, the view of Dharma, are two iron-enclosing mountains. Immediately becoming aware when thoughts arise

is playing with the mind; sitting still and cultivating concentration is the live-lihood of ghosts. Go forward and you miss the principle; retreat and you turn away from the source. Neither progressing nor retreating, you're a dead man with breath. So tell me, ultimately how do you practice? Work hard, be dili-gent; you must settle it in this life.

With no way to proceed, nowhere to take hold, nowhere to turn, what then? As Mumon himself put it, "Since there is no gate, how do you pass through?" To aid in this seemingly impossible task, Mumon designed this *Gateless Gate:*

The Great Way has no gate,
In myriad differences there is a road:
If you manage to pass this barrier,
You'll walk alone through the universe.

Thomas Cleary
Berkeley, California
Spring 1979

Writings and Zen Records Mentioned in the Introduction to the History of Zen Practice

Appendix 2

Note: The works that follow are listed in the order of their appearance in Appendix 1.

Extensive Record of Hyakujō (Pai-chang)
Hyakujō kōroku (Pai-chang kuang-lu)   百丈廣録

Record of Rinzai (Lin-chi)
Rinzairoku (Lin-chi lu)   臨濟録

Ten Guidelines for Zen Schools
Shūmon jukkiron (Tsung-men shih-kuei lun)   宗門十規論

Extensive Record of Unmon (Yün-men)
Unmon kōroku (Yün-men kuang-lu)   雲門廣録

Recorded Sayings of Hōgen Mon'eki (Fa-yen Wen-i)
Kinryō seiryōin Mon'eki Zenji goroku
Chin-ling Ch'ing-liang-yüan
Wen-i Ch'an-shih yü-lu   金陵清凉院文益禪師語録

Recorded Sayings of Fun'yō Mutoku (Fen-yang Wu-te)
Fun'yō Mutoku Zenji goroku
(Fen-yang Wu-te Ch'an-shih yü-lu)   汾陽無德禪師語録

Cascade Collection
Bakusenshū (Pao-ch'üan chi)   瀑泉集

100 Examples of Eulogies of the Ancients
Juko hyakusoku (Sung-ku pai-tse)   頌古百則

Measuring Tap
Gekisetsuroku (Chi-chieh lu)   擊節録

Blue Cliff Record
Hekiganroku (Pi-yen lu)   碧巖録

Book of Equanimity
Shōyōroku (Ts'ung-jung lu)   從容録

Record of Further Inquiries
Shin'ekiroku (Ch'ing-i lu)   請益録

Book of the Empty Valley
Kūkokushū (K'ung-ku chi)   空谷集

Book of the Vacant Hall
Kidōshū (Hsü-t'ang chi)   虛堂集

Book of the Forest
Rinkanroku (Lin-chien lu)   林間録

Recollected Conversations Lying in Clouds
Unga kidan (Yün-wo chi-t'an)   雲臥紀談

Book of the Fields of Silk Lake
Ragoyaroku (Lo-hu-yeh-lu)   羅湖野録

Precious Lessons from the Zen Forests
Zenrinhōkun (Ch'an-lin pao-hsün)   禪林寶訓

Events from the Heyday of the Zen Communities
Sōrin seiji (Ts'ung-lin sheng-shih)   叢林盛事

Letters of Ōryū E'nan (Huang-lung Hui-nan)
*Ōryū E'nan Zenji shosekishū (Huang-lung
Hui-nan Ch'an-shih shu-ch'ih-chi)*   黃龍慧南禪師書尺集

Letters of Reigen (Ling-yüan)
Reigen hitsugo (Ling-yüan pi-yü)   靈源筆語

Engo's Essentials of the Mind
Engo shin'yō (Yüan-wu hsin-yao)   圜悟心要

Letters of Daie (Ta-hui)
Daiesho (Ta-hui shu)   大慧書

Forest of Wisdom
Chirinshū (Chih-lin chi)　　　　　　　　智林集

Treasury of Eyes of True Teaching
Shōbōgenzō (Cheng-fa-yen-tsang)　　　　正法眼藏

Recorded Sayings of Mumon Ekai (Wu-men Hui-k'ai)
Mumon Ekai goroku (Wu-men Hui-k'ai yü-lu)　無門慧開語録

Gateless Gate
Mumonkan (Wu-men kuan)　　　　　　　無門關

Chapter on the Essential Purity of Detachment and Subtlety
Rimitaijōbon (Li-wei t'i-ching p'in)　　　　離微體净品

Treatise of the Jewel Treasury
Hōzōron (Pao-tsang lun)　　　　　　　　寶藏論

Personal Names, Place Names, and Writings (Japanese—Chinese)

Appendix 3

Japanese	Chinese	
Japanese	*Chinese*	
Amban	An-wan	晚庵
Ban'an	Wan-an	萬庵
Banshō	Wan-sung	萬松
Bashō Esei	Pa-chiao Hui-ch'ing	芭蕉慧清
Baso Dōitsu	Ma-tsu Tao-i	馬祖道一
Bokushū	Mu-chou	睦州
Bu	Wu	武
Bukan	Feng-kan	豊干
Bukkan	Fo-chien	佛鑒
Bukkō	Fo-kuang	佛光
Bunsō	Wen-tsung	文宗
Chō	Chang	張
Chōkan	Chang-chien	張鑒
Chōsa	Ch'ang-sha	長沙
Chōsetsu Shūsai	Chang-cho Hsiu-ts'ai	張拙秀才
Chūwa	Chung-ho	中和
Dachi	Ta-ti	打地
Daie	Ta-hui	大慧
Daiisan	Ta-kuei-shan	大潙山
Daizui	Ta-sui	大隋
Dōgo	Tao-wu	道吾
Dōshin	Tao-hsin	道信
E	Hui	慧
Echū	Hui-chung	慧忠

Eka	Hui-k'o	慧可
Ekai	Hui-k'ai	慧開
Engo	Yüan-wu	圓悟
Enō	Hui-neng	慧能
Esshū Kempō	Yüeh-chou Ch'ien-feng	越州乾峰
Fuketsu Enshō	Feng-hsüeh Yen-chao	風穴延沼
Fun'yō	Fen-yang	汾陽
Gantō Zenkatsu	Yen-t'ou Ch'üan-huo	岩頭全豁
Gatsurin Shikan	Yüeh-lin Shih-kuan	月林師觀
Gen	Yüan	元
Gensha Shibi	Hsüan-sha Shih-pei	玄沙師備
Gensō	Yüan-tsung	玄宗
Gettan Zenka	Yüeh-an Shan-kuo	月庵善果
Gi	Wei	魏
Gokoku-ninnō	Hu-kuo jen-wang	護國仁王
Goso Hōen	Wu-tsu Fa-yen	五祖法演
Gotaisan	Wu-t'ai-shan	五臺山
Gotō egen	*Wu-teng hui-yüan*	五燈會元
Gu	Yü	虞
Gutei	Chü-chih	俱胝
Hakka	Pai-chia	白家
Hakugaisan	Pai-yai-shan	白崖山
Haku'un Shutan	Pai-yün Shou-tuan	白雲守端
Hantan	Fan-tan	范丹
Hekiganroku	*Pi-yen lu*	碧岩録
Hōgen Mon'eki	Fa-yen Wen-i	法眼文益
Hōhō Kokubun	Pao-feng K'o-wen	寶峰克文
Hōji	Pao-t'zu	報慈
Hōrin	Feng-lin	鳳林
Hōshōji	Fa-hsing-ssu	法性寺
Hōzōron	*Pao-tsang lun*	寶藏論
Hyakujō Ekai	Pai-chang Huai-hai	百丈懷海
Igyō	Kuei-yang	潙仰
Insō	Yin-tsung	印宗
Isan Reiyū	Kuei-shan Ling-yu	潙山靈祐
Jii	Tz'u-i	慈懿
Jinkō	Shen-kuang	神光
Jinshū	Shen-hsiu	神秀
Jinsō	Jen-tsung	仁宗

Jissai	Shih-chi	實際
Jittoku	Shih-te	拾得
Jizō	Ti-tsang	地藏
Jō. *See* Sō Jō		
Jōshū Jūshin	Chao-chou Ts'ung-shen	趙州從諗
Jun'yū	Ch'un-yu	淳祐
Kakuhan	Chüeh-fan	覺範
Kakutetsu-shi	Chüeh-t'ieh-tsui	覺鉄嘴
Kan	Kuan	關
Kan'u	Kuan-yü	關羽
Kanzan	Han-shan	寒山
Kanzan	Kuan-shan	關山
Karin	Hua-lin	華林
Kasan	Hua-shan	華山
Kin	Chin	金
Kiun	Hsi-yün	希運
Kō	Huang	黃
Kōkanji	Hsiang-chien-ssu	香間寺
Kokuseiji	Kuo-ch'ing-ssu	國清寺
Kōnan	Chiang-nan	江南
Konan	Hu-nan	湖南
Kōnin Daiman	Hung-jen Ta-man	弘忍大満
Korei	Chü-ling	巨靈
Kōshinzan	Chiang-hsin-shan	江心山
Kōshū	Heng-chou	衡州
Kōshū	Kuang-chou	廣州
Kōsō	Hsiao-tsung	高宗
Kōsō	Kuang-tsung	光宗
Kōsō	Hsiao-tsung	孝宗
Kōtō	Kuang-tung	廣東
Kōtō Rishi	Kuang-t'ung Li-shih	光統律師
Kōu	Hsiang-yü	項羽
Kōyō Seijō	Hsing-yang Ch'ing-jang	興陽清讓
Kudoku-hōin'yūji	Kung-te pao-yin Yu-tz'u	功德報因佑慈
Kyōgen Chikan	Hsiang-yen Chih-hsien	香嚴智閑
Kyōsei	Ching-ch'ing	鏡清
Kyōzan Ejaku	Yang-shan Hui-chi	仰山慧寂
Kyūhō	Chiu-feng	九峰
Meishū	Ming-chou	明州

Mitsuan Kanketsu	Mi-an Hsien-chieh	密庵咸傑
Mō Kō	Meng Kung	孟珙
Muan	Wu-an	無庵
Mumon Ekai	Wu-men Hui-k'ai	無門慧開
Muryō Sōju	Wu-liang Tsung-shou	無量宗壽
Myō	Ming	明
Myōshin	Miao-hsin	妙心
Nan'in	Nan-yüan	南院
Nansen Fugan	Nan-ch'üan P'u-yüan	南泉普願
Nantō Kōyū	Nan-t'a Kuang-yung	南塔光涌
Nan'yō Echū	Nan-yang Hui-chung	南陽慧忠
Neidōsha	Ning tao-che	寧宗
Neisō	Ning-tsung	寧道者
Nō	Neng	能
Ōbaisan	Huang-mei-shan	黃梅山
Ōbaku Kiun	Huang-po Hsi-yün	黃檗希運
Ōchū	Wang-chou	王宙
Ō Rōshi	Wang-lao-shih	王老師
Ōryū E'nan	Huang-lung Hui-nan	黃龍慧南
Rakan Keishin	Lo-han Kuei-shen	羅漢桂深
Reigen	Ling-yüan	靈源
Reinan	Ling-nan	嶺南
Reishū	Li-chou	澧州
Reiun	Ling-yün	靈雲
Rengehō	Lien-hua-feng	蓮華峰
Rimitaijōbon	*Li-wei-t'i-ching-p'in*	離微體淨品
Rinzai Gigen	Lin-chi I-hsüan	臨濟義玄
Risō	Li-tsung	理宗
Ro	Lu	盧
Roso	Lu-tsu	魯祖
Ryō	Liang	梁
Ryūhō	Liu-pang	劉邦
Ryūshō	Lung-hsiang	龍翔
Ryūtan Sūshin	Lung-t'an Ch'ung-hsin	龍潭崇信
Sado	Ch'a-tu	查渡
San. *See* Sō San		
Sanzan	Sha-shan	杉山
Seigen	Ch'ing-yüan	青原
Seijo	Ch'ien-nü	倩女

Seijō	Ch'ing-jang	清讓
Seiryō	Ch'ing-liang	清涼
Seiryōzan	Ch'ing-liang-shan	清涼山
Seizazan	Ch'ing-tso-shan	青坐山
Seizei	Ch'ing-shui	清稅
Sekisō Soen	Shih-shuang Ch'u-yüan	石霜楚圓
Sekitō	Shih-t'ou	石頭
Sekkei	Shih-hsi	石溪
Sekkō	Che-chiang	浙江
Seppō Gison	Hsüeh-feng I-ts'un	雪峰義存
Setchō	Hsüeh-tou	雪竇
Shiba Zuda	Ssu-ma T'ou-t'o	司馬頭陀
Shinshū	Hsin-chou	新州
Shinsō	Shen-tsung	神宗
Shishin Goshin	Ssu-hsin Wu-hsin	死心悟新
Shō	Sheng	省
Shōgen Sūgaku	Sung-yüan Ch'ung-yüeh	松源崇岳
Shōkaku	Sheng-chüeh	聖覺
Shōjō	Shao-ting	紹定
Shoku	Shu	蜀
Shōrin	Ts'ung-lin	從倫
Shōrinji	Shao-lin-ssu	小林寺
Shōyōroku	*Ts'ung-jung lu*	從容録
Shūan Chinson	Hsi-an Ch'en-sun	習庵陳損
Shū kongō Ō	Chou chin-kang wang	周金剛王
Shuyōzan	Shou-yang-shan	首陽山
Shuzan Shōnen	Shou-shan Sheng-nien	首山省念
Sō San	Seng-ts'an	僧燦
Soshin	Tsu-hsin	祖心
Sō Jō	Seng-chao	僧肇
Sōtō	Ts'ao-tung	曹洞
Sōzan Honjaku	Ts'ao-shan Pen-chi	曹山本寂
Sui	Chui	騅
Sūzan	Sung-shan	嵩山
Taibai Hōjō	Ta-mei Fa-ch'ang	大梅法常
Taizan	T'ai-shan	臺山
Tangen Ōshin	Tan-yüan Ying-chen	耽源應真
Tanka Shijun	Tan-hsia Tzu-ch'un	丹霞子淳
Tendai	T'ien-t'ai	天臺

Tendō	T'ien-t'ung	天童
Tenryū	T'ien-lung	天龍
Tetsusō	Che-tsung	哲宗
Tōka	Tung-chia	東嘉
Tokusan Senkan	Te-shan Hsüan-chien	德山宣鑒
Tosotsu Jūetsu	Tou-shuai Ts'ung-yüeh	兜率從悦
Tōsu	Tang-tsu	檔子
Tōsu Gisei	T'ou-tzu I-ch'ing	投子義青
Tōzan Gohon	Tung-shan Wu-pen	洞山悟本
Tōzan Ryōkai	Tung-shan Liang-chieh	洞山良介
Tōzan Shusho	Tung-shan Shou-ch'u	洞山守初
Ungan	Yün-yen	雲岩
Unmon Bun'en	Yün-men Wen-yen	雲門文偃
Wakuan Shitai	Huo-an Shih-t'i	或庵師體
Wanshi Shōgaku	Hung-chih Cheng-chüeh	宏智正覺
Yakusan Igen	Yüeh-shan Wei-yen	藥山惟儼
Yōgi Hōe	Yang-ch'i Fang-hui	楊岐方會
Yōka Daishi	Yung-chia Ta-shih	永嘉大師
Yōken	Yeh-chien	葉縣
Zengetsu	Ch'an-yüeh	禪月
Zuigan Ju	Jui-yen-shou	瑞岩壽
Zuigan Shigen	Jui-yen Shih-yen	瑞岩師彦

Personal Names, Place Names, and Writings (Chinese—Japanese)

Appendix 4

Chinese	*Japanese*	
An-wan	Amban	晚月 安禪
Ch'an-yüeh	Zengetsu	
Chang	Chō	張
Chang-chien	Chōkan	張鑒
Chang-cho Hsiu-ts'ai	Chōsetsu Shūsai	張拙秀才
Ch'ang-sha	Chōsa	長沙
Chao-chou Ts'ung-shen	Jōshū Jūshin	趙州從諗
Che-tsung	Tetsusō	哲宗
Chiang-hsin-shan	Kōshinzan	江心山
Chiang-nan	Kōnan	江南
Ch'ien-nu	Seijo	倩女
Chin	Kin	金
Ching-ch'ing	Kyōsei	鏡清
Ch'ing-jang	Seijō	清讓
Ch'ing-liang	Seiryō	清涼
Ch'ing-liang-shan	Seiryōzan	清涼山
Ch'ing-shui	Seizei	清稅
Ching-tso-shan	Seizazan	青坐山
Ch'ing-yüan	Seigen	青原
Chiu-feng	Kyūhō	九峰
Chou chin-kang wang	Shū Kongō Ō	周金剛王
Chu-yüan	Chikugen	竹原
Chü-chih	Gutei	俱胝
Chü-ling	Korei	巨靈

Chüeh-fan	Kakuhan	覺範
Chui	Sui	騅
Ch'a-tu	Sado	查渡
Chüeh-t'ieh-tsui	Kakutetsu-shi	覺鉄嘴
Ch'un-yu	Jun'yū	淳佑
Chung-ho	Chūwa	中和
Fa-hsing-ssu	Hōshōji	法性寺
Fa-yen Wen-i	Hōgen Mon'eki	法眼文益
Fen-yang	Fun'yō	汾陽
Feng-hsüeh Yen-chao	Fuketsu Enshō	風穴延沼
Feng-lin	Hōrin	鳳林
Feng-kan	Bukan	豐干
Fo-chien	Bukkan	佛鑒
Fo-kuang	Bukkō	佛光
Han-shan	Kanzan	寒山
Heng-chou	Kōshū	衡州
Hsi-an Ch'en-sun	Shūan Chinson	習庵陳損
Hsi-yün	Kiun	希運
Hsiang-chien-ssu	Kōkanji	香間寺
Hsiang-yen Chih-hsien	Kyōgen Chikan	香嚴智閑
Hsiang-yü	Kōu	項羽
Hsiao-tsung	Kōsō	孝宗
Hsin-chou	Shinshū	新州
Hsing-yang Ch'ing-jang	Kōyō Seijō	興陽清讓
Hsüan-sha Shih-pei	Gensha Shibi	玄沙師備
Hsüeh-feng I-ts'un	Seppō Gison	雪峰義存
Hsüeh-tou	Setchō	雪竇
Hua-lin	Karin	華林
Hua-shan	Kasan	華山
Huang	Kō	黃
Huang-lung Hui-nan	Ōryū E'nan	黃龍慧南
Huang-mei-shan	Ōbaisan	黃梅山
Huang-po Hsi-yün	Ōbaku Kiun	黃檗希運
Hui	E	會
Hu-kuo jen-wang	Gokoku Niō	護國仁王
Hu-nan	Konan	湖南
Hui-chung	Echū	慧忠

Hui-k'ai	Ekai	慧開
Hui-k'o	Eka	慧可
Hui-neng	Enō	慧能
Hung-chih Cheng-chüeh	Wanshi Shōgaku	宏智正覺
Hung-jen Ta-man	Kōnin Daiman	弘忍大満
Huo-an Shih-t'i	Wakuan Shitai	或庵師體
Jen-tsung	Jinsō	仁宗
Jui-an-shou	Zuiganju	瑞岩壽
Jui-yen Shih-yen	Zuigan Shigen	瑞岩師彦
Kao-tsung	Kōsō	高宗
Kuan	Kan	關
Kuan-shan	Kanzan	關山
Kuan-tung	Kōtō	廣東
Kuang-chou	Kōshū	廣州
Kuang-tsung	Kōsō	光宗
Kuang-t'ung Li-shih	Kotō Risshi	光統律師
Kuang-yü	Kan'u	關羽
Kuei-shan Ling-yu	Isan Reiyū	潙山靈祐
Kuei-yang	Igyō	潙仰
Kuo-ch'ing-ssu	Kokuseiji	國清寺
Liang	Ryō	梁
Li-chou	Reishū	澧州
Li-tsung	Risō	理宗
Li-wei-t'i-ching-p'in	*Rimitaijōbon*	離微體淨品
Lien-hua-feng	Rengehō	蓮華峰
Lin-chi I-hsüan	Rinzai Gigen	臨濟義玄
Ling-nan	Reinan	嶺南
Ling-yüan	Reigen	靈源
Ling-yün	Reiun	靈雲
Liu pang	Ryūhō	劉邦
Lo-han Kui-shen	Rakan Keishin	羅漢桂深
Lu	Ro	盧
Lu-tsu	Roso	魯祖
Lung-hsing	Ryūshō	龍翔
Lung-t'an Ch'ung-hsin	Ryūtan Sūshin	籠潭崇信
Ma-tsu Tao-i	Baso Dōitsu	馬祖道一
Meng Kung	Mō Kō	孟珙

Mi-an Hsien-chieh	Mitsuan Kanketsu	密庵咸杰
Miao-hsin	Myōshin	妙心
Ming	Myō	明
Ming-chou	Meishū	明州
Mu-chou	Bokushū	睦州
Nan-ch'üan P'u-yüan	Nansen Fugan	南泉普願
Nan-t'a Kuang-yung	Nantō Kōyū	南塔光涌
Nan-yang Hui-chung	Nan'yō Echū	南陽慧忠
Nan-yüan	Nan'in	南院
Neng	Nō	能
Ning tao-che	Neidōsha	寧道者
Ning-tsung	Neisō	寧宗
Pa-chiao Hui-ch'ing	Bashō Esei	芭蕉慧清
Pai-chang Huai-hai	Hyakujō Ekai	百丈懷海
Pai-chia	Hakka	白家
Pai-yai-shan	Hakugaisan	白崖山
Pai-yün Shou-tuan	Haku'un Shutan	白雲守端
Pao-feng K'o-wen	Hōhō Kokubun	寶峰克文
Pao-ts'ang lun	*Hōzōron*	寶藏論
Pao-t'zu	Hōji	報慈
Pi-yen lu	*Hekiganroku*	碧岩録
Seng-chao	Sō Jō	僧肇
Seng-ts'an	Sō San	僧燦
Sha-shan	Sanzan	杉山
Shao-lin-ssu	Shōrinji	小林寺
Shao-ting	Shōjō	紹定
Shen-hsiu	Jinshū	神秀
Shen-kuang	Jinkō	神光
Shen-tsung	Shinsō	神宗
Sheng-chüeh	Shōkaku	聖覺
Shih-chi	Jissai	實際
Shih-hsi	Sekkei	石溪
Shih-shuang Ch'u-yüan	Sekisō Soen	石霜楚圓
Shih-te	Jittoku	拾得
Shih-t'ou	Sekitō	石頭
Shou-shan Sheng-nien	Shuzan Shōnen	首山省念
Shou-yang-shan	Shuyōzan	首陽山

Wan-sung	Banshō	萬松
Wang-chou	Ōchū	王宙
Wang-lao-shih	Ō Rōshi	王老師
Wei-ma	Yuima	維摩
Wen-tsung	Bunsō	文宗
Wu	Bu	武
Wu-an	Muan	無庵
Wu-liang Tsung-shou	Muryō Sōju	無量宗壽
Wu-men Hui-k'ai	Mumon Ekai	無門慧開
Wu-t'ai-shan	Gotaisan	五臺山
Wu-teng hui-yüan	Gotō Egen	五燈會元
Wu-tsu Fa-yen	Goso Hōen	五祖法演
Yang-ch'i Fang-hui	Yōgi Hōe	楊岐方會
Yang-shan Hui-chi	Kyōzan Ejaku	仰山慧寂
Yeh-chien	Yōken	葉縣
Yen-t'ou Ch'üan-huo	Gantō Zenkatsu	岩頭全豁
Yin-tsung	Insō	印宗
Yung-chia Ta-shih	Yōka Daishi	永嘉大師
Yü	Gu	虞
Yüan	Gen	元
Yüan-sung	Genso	玄宗
Yüan-wu	Engo	圓悟
Yüeh-an-shan-kuo	Gettan Zenka	月庵善果
Yüeh-chou Ch'ien-feng	Esshū Kempō	越州乾峰
Yüeh-lin Shih-kuan	Gatsurin Shikan	月林師觀
Yüeh-shan Wei-yen	Yakusan Igen	藥山惟儼
Yün-men Wen-yen	Unmon Bun'en	雲門文偃
Yün-yen	Ungan	雲岩

Lineage Charts

Appendix 5

Chart 1

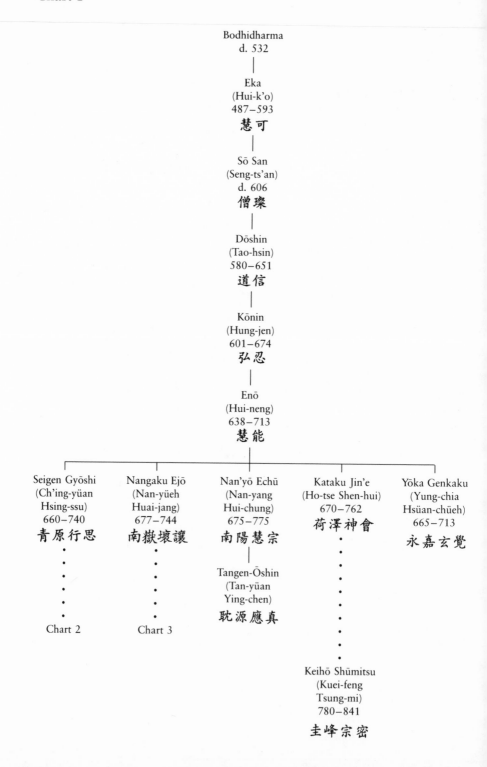

Bodhidharma
d. 532

Eka
(Hui-k'o)
487–593
慧可

Sō San
(Seng-ts'an)
d. 606
僧璨

Dōshin
(Tao-hsin)
580–651
道信

Kōnin
(Hung-jen)
601–674
弘忍

Enō
(Hui-neng)
638–713
慧能

Seigen Gyōshi
(Ch'ing-yüan
Hsing-ssu)
660–740
青原行思

Chart 2

Nangaku Ejō
(Nan-yüeh
Huai-jang)
677–744
南嶽壞讓

Chart 3

Nan'yō Echū
(Nan-yang
Hui-chung)
675–775
南陽慧宗

Tangen-Ōshin
(Tan-yüan
Ying-chen)
耽源應真

Kataku Jin'e
(Ho-tse Shen-hui)
670–762
荷澤神會

Keihō Shūmitsu
(Kuei-feng
Tsung-mi)
780–841

圭峰宗密

Yōka Genkaku
(Yung-chia
Hsüan-chüeh)
665–713
永嘉玄覺

Chart 2
Seigen Gyōshi's Line

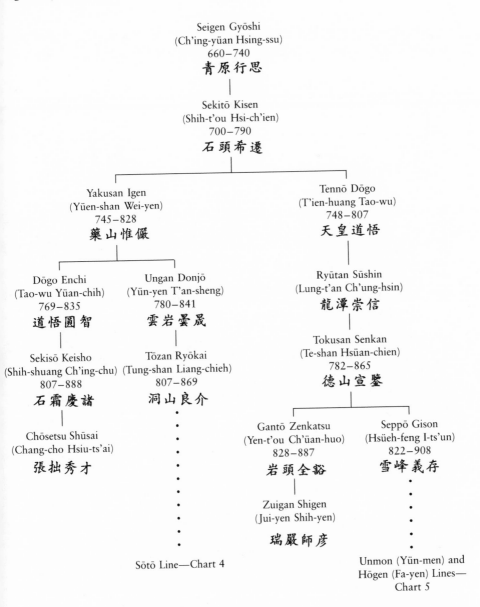

Seigen Gyōshi
(Ch'ing-yüan Hsing-ssu)
660–740
青原行思

Sekitō Kisen
(Shih-t'ou Hsi-ch'ien)
700–790
石頭希遷

Yakusan Igen
(Yüen-shan Wei-yen)
745–828
藥山惟儼

Tennō Dōgo
(T'ien-huang Tao-wu)
748–807
天皇道悟

Dōgo Enchi
(Tao-wu Yüan-chih)
769–835
道悟圓智

Ungan Donjō
(Yün-yen T'an-sheng)
780–841
雲巖曇晟

Ryūtan Sūshin
(Lung-t'an Ch'ung-hsin)
龍潭崇信

Sekisō Keisho
(Shih-shuang Ch'ing-chu)
807–888
石霜慶諸

Tōzan Ryōkai
(Tung-shan Liang-chieh)
807–869
洞山良介

Tokusan Senkan
(Te-shan Hsüan-chien)
782–865
德山宣鑒

Chōsetsu Shūsai
(Chang-cho Hsiu-ts'ai)
張拙秀才

Gantō Zenkatsu
(Yen-t'ou Ch'üan-huo)
828–887
巖頭全豁

Seppō Gison
(Hsüeh-feng I-ts'un)
822–908
雪峰義存

Zuigan Shigen
(Jui-yen Shih-yen)
瑞巖師彥

Sōtō Line—Chart 4

Unmon (Yün-men) and
Hōgen (Fa-yen) Lines—
Chart 5

Chart 3
Nangaku Ejō's Line

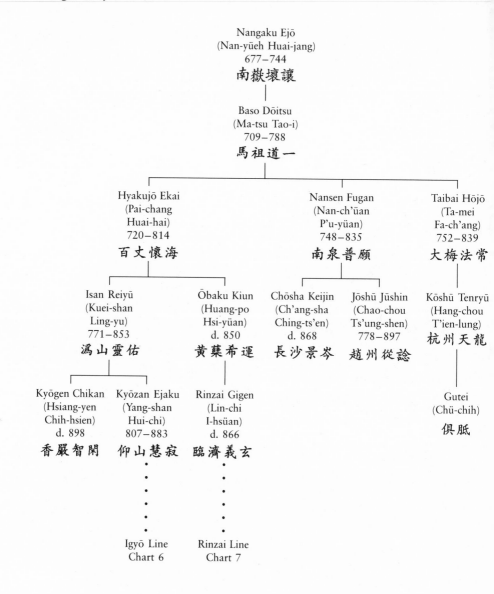

Nangaku Ejō
(Nan-yüeh Huai-jang)
677–744
南嶽壞讓

Baso Dōitsu
(Ma-tsu Tao-i)
709–788
馬祖道一

Hyakujō Ekai
(Pai-chang
Huai-hai)
720–814
百丈懷海

Nansen Fugan
(Nan-ch'üan
P'u-yüan)
748–835
南泉普願

Taibai Hōjō
(Ta-mei
Fa-ch'ang)
752–839
大梅法常

Isan Reiyū
(Kuei-shan
Ling-yu)
771–853
溈山靈佑

Ōbaku Kiun
(Huang-po
Hsi-yüan)
d. 850
黃蘗希運

Chōsha Keijin
(Ch'ang-sha
Ching-ts'en)
d. 868
長沙景岑

Jōshū Jūshin
(Chao-chou
Ts'ung-shen)
778–897
趙州從諗

Kōshū Tenryū
(Hang-chou
T'ien-lung)
杭州天龍

Kyōgen Chikan
(Hsiang-yen
Chih-hsien)
d. 898
香嚴智閑

Kyōzan Ejaku
(Yang-shan
Hui-chi)
807–883
仰山慧寂

Rinzai Gigen
(Lin-chi
I-hsüan)
d. 866
臨濟義玄

Gutei
(Chü-chih)
俱胝

Igyō Line
Chart 6

Rinzai Line
Chart 7

Chart 4
Sōtō Line

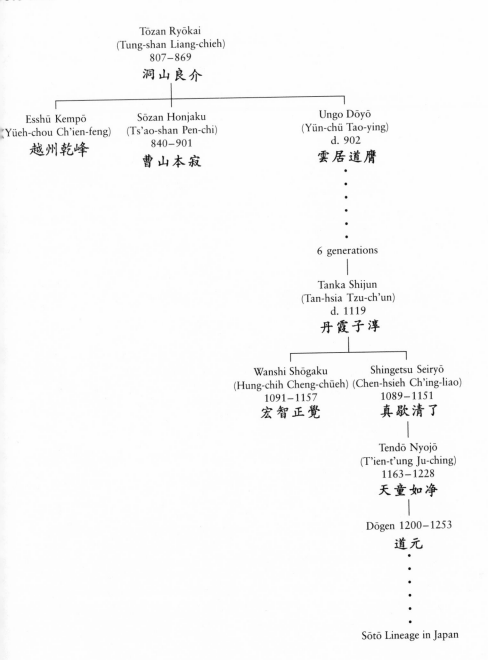

Tōzan Ryōkai
(Tung-shan Liang-chieh)
807–869
洞山良介

Esshū Kempō
(Yüeh-chou Ch'ien-feng)
越州乾峰

Sōzan Honjaku
(Ts'ao-shan Pen-chi)
840–901
曹山本寂

Ungo Dōyō
(Yün-chü Tao-ying)
d. 902
雲居道膺

6 generations

Tanka Shijun
(Tan-hsia Tzu-ch'un)
d. 1119
丹霞子淳

Wanshi Shōgaku
(Hung-chih Cheng-chüeh)
1091–1157
宏智正覺

Shingetsu Seiryō
(Chen-hsieh Ch'ing-liao)
1089–1151
真歇清了

Tendō Nyojō
(T'ien-t'ung Ju-ching)
1163–1228
天童如净

Dōgen 1200–1253
道元

Sōtō Lineage in Japan

Chart 5
Unmon and Hōgen Lines

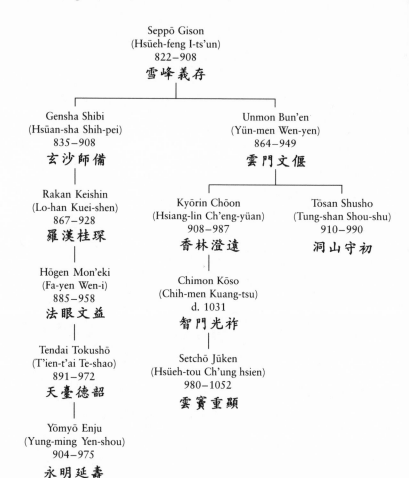

Seppō Gison
(Hsüeh-feng I-ts'un)
822–908
雪峰義存

Gensha Shibi
(Hsüan-sha Shih-pei)
835–908
玄沙師備

Rakan Keishin
(Lo-han Kuei-shen)
867–928
羅漢桂琛

Hōgen Mon'eki
(Fa-yen Wen-i)
885–958
法眼文益

Tendai Tokushō
(T'ien-t'ai Te-shao)
891–972
天臺德韶

Yōmyō Enju
(Yung-ming Yen-shou)
904–975
永明延壽

Unmon Bun'en
(Yün-men Wen-yen)
864–949
雲門文偃

Kyōrin Chōon
(Hsiang-lin Ch'eng-yüan)
908–987
香林澄遠

Chimon Kōso
(Chih-men Kuang-tsu)
d. 1031
智門光祚

Setchō Jūken
(Hsüeh-tou Ch'ung hsien)
980–1052
雲竇重顯

Tōsan Shusho
(Tung-shan Shou-shu)
910–990
洞山守初

Chart 6
Igyō Line

Isan Reiyū
(Kuei-shan Ling-yu)
771–853
潙山靈佑

Kyōzan Ejaku
(Yang-shan Hui-chi)
807–883
仰山慧寂

Kyōgen Chikan
(Hsiang-yen Chih-hsien)
d. 898
香嚴智閑

Nantō Kōyū
(Nan-t'a Kuang-yung)
850–938
南塔光涌

Bashō Esei
(Pa-chiao Hui-ch'ing)
芭蕉慧清

Kōyō Seijō
(Hsing-yang Ch'ing-jang)
興陽清讓

Chart 7
Rinzai Line

Rinzai Gigen
(Lin-chi I-hsüan)
d. 866
臨濟義玄

Kōke Zonshō
(Hsing-hua Ts'ung-chiang)
830–888
興化存獎

Nan'in Egyō
(Nan-yüan Hui-yung)
d. 930
南院慧顒

Fuketsu Enshō
(Feng-hsüeh Yen-chao)
896–973
風穴延沼

Shuzan Shōnen
(Shou-shan Sheng-nien)
926–993
首山省念

Fun'yō Zenshō
(Fen-yang Shan-chao)
947–1024
汾陽善昭

Sekisō Soen
(Shih-shuang Ch'u-yüan)
986–1039
石霜楚圓

Yōgi Hōe
(Yang-ch'i Fang-hui)
992–1049
楊岐方會

Rinzai-Yōgi Line

Ōryū E'nan
(Huang-lung Hui-nan)
1002–1069
黄龍慧南

Rinzai-Ōryū Line

Chart 8
Linzai-Yōgi Line

Yōgi Hōe
(Yang-ch'i Fang-hui)
992–1049
楊岐方會

Haku'un Shutan
(Pai-yün Shou-tuan)
1025–1072
白雲守端

Goso Hōen
(Wu-tsu Fa-yen)
1024?–1104
五祖法演

Kaifuku Dōnei
(K'ai-fu Tao-ning)
d. 1113
開福道寧

Engo Kokugon
(Yüan-wu K'o-ch'in)
1063–1135
圓悟克勤

Gettan Zenka
(Yüeh-an Shan-kuo)
1079–1152
月庵善果

Gokoku Keigen
(Hu-kuo Ching-yüan)
1094–1146
護國景元

Kukyū Jōryū
(Hu-ch'in Shao-lung)
1077–1136
虎丘紹隆

Daie Sōkō
(Ta-hui Tsung-kao)
1089–1163
大慧宗杲

Rōnō Sotō
(Lao-na Tsu-teng)
老衲祖燈

Wakuan Shitai
(Huo-an Shih-t'i)
1108–1179
或庵師體

Gatsurin Shikan
(Yüeh-lin Shih-kuan)
1143–1217
月林師觀

Shōgen Sūgaku
(Sung-yüan Ch'ung-yüeh)
1139–1209
松源崇岳

Mumon Ekai
(Wu-men Hui-k'ai)
1183–1260
無門慧開

Shinji Kakushin
(1207–1298)
心地覺心

Hakuin Ekaku
1685–1768
白隱慧鶴

Chart 9
Rinzai-Ōryū Line

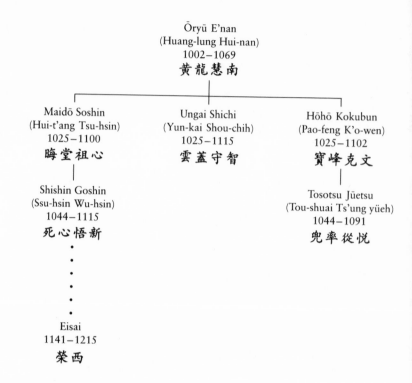

Ōryū E'nan
(Huang-lung Hui-nan)
1002–1069
黄龍慧南

Maidō Soshin
(Hui-t'ang Tsu-hsin)
1025–1100
晦堂祖心

Shishin Goshin
(Ssu-hsin Wu-hsin)
1044–1115
死心悟新

Ungai Shichi
(Yun-kai Shou-chih)
1025–1115
雲蓋守智

Hōhō Kokubun
(Pao-feng K'o-wen)
1025–1102
寶峰克文

Tosotsu Jūetsu
(Tou-shuai Ts'ung yüeh)
1044–1091
兜率從悦

Eisai
1141–1215
榮西

Chart 10

Historical Summary

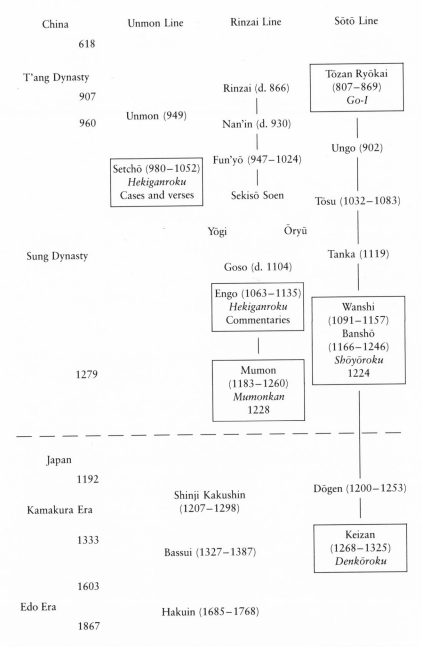

China	Unmon Line	Rinzai Line	Sōtō Line
618			
T'ang Dynasty		Rinzai (d. 866)	Tōzan Ryōkai (807–869) *Go-I*
907			
960	Unmon (949)	Nan'in (d. 930)	
		Fun'yō (947–1024)	Ungo (902)
	Setchō (980–1052) *Hekiganroku* Cases and verses	Sekisō Soen	Tōsu (1032–1083)
Sung Dynasty		Yōgi Ōryū	Tanka (1119)
		Goso (d. 1104)	
		Engo (1063–1135) *Hekiganroku* Commentaries	Wanshi (1091–1157) Banshō (1166–1246) *Shōyōroku* 1224
1279		Mumon (1183–1260) *Mumonkan* 1228	

Japan
1192

Kamakura Era
1333
1603

Edo Era
1867

	Shinji Kakushin (1207–1298)	Dōgen (1200–1253)
	Bassui (1327–1387)	Keizan (1268–1325) *Denkōroku*
	Hakuin (1685–1768)	

This table is based on a chart in *Barrera sin Puerta* (the Spanish edition of the *Gateless Gate;* Madrid, 1986) and is reproduced courtesy of Anna Maria Schlüter, the translator.